THE SOWING AND THE DAWNING

The Sowing and the Dawning

Termination, Dedication, and Transformation
in the Archaeological and Ethnographic
Record of Mesoamerica

EDITED BY

SHIRLEY BOTELER MOCK

UNIVERSITY OF NEW MEXICO PRESS
ALBUQUERQUE

© 1998 by the University of New Mexico Press
All rights reserved.
First Edition

LIBRARY OF CONGRESS CATALOGING-IN-PUBLICATION DATA

The sowing and the dawning: termination, dedication, and
transformation in the archaeological and ethnographic record
of Mesoamerica/edited by Shirley Boteler Mock—1st ed.
p. cm.
Includes bibliographical references and index.

ISBN 0–8263–1983–1 (cloth)

1. Mayas—Rites and ceremonies.
2. Mayas—Antiquities.
3. Votive offerings—Latin America—History.
4. Ceremonial objects—Latin America—History.
5. Dedication services—Latin America—History.
6. Ethnoarchaeology—Latin America.
7. Latin America—Antuquities.

I. Mock, Shirley Boteler, 1942–

F1435.3.R56S68 1998
972.81´016—dc21 98–23116
CIP

In Memoriam:

Frances Kathryn Hohman Meskill
Ph.D. Candidate
Department of Anthropology
University of Texas, Austin
July, 1997

"And here is the dawning and sowing of the sun, moon,
and stars. And Jaguar Quitze, Jaguar Night, Mahucutah,
and True Jaguar were overjoyed when they saw the day-
bringer. It came up first. It looked brilliant when it came
up, since it was ahead of the sun."
—The *Popol Vuh*, Tedlock 1985:165

and our mentor

Linda Schele, Ph.D.
John D. Murchinson Regents' Professor in Art
University of Texas, Austin
April, 1998

"And so it remained that they were respectful of their
father's heart, even though they left him at the Place of
Ballgame Sacrifice: 'You will be prayed to here,' his sons
told him, and his heart was comforted. 'You will be the
first resort and you will be the first to have your day kept
by those who will be born in the light, begotten in the light.
Your name will not be lost. So be it' they told their father
when they comforted his heart. 'We merely cleared the
road of your death, your loss, the pain, suffering that
were inflicted upon you.'"
—The *Popol Vuh*, Tedlock 1985: 159

Contents

v

THE SOWING AND THE DAWNING

CHAPTER ONE
Prelude

Shirley Boteler Mock
University of Texas, San Antonio
and the Institute of Texan Cultures at San Antonio

Broken systems live on in their debris, in parts, formerly coordinated, which have now become scattered over many levels and domains of the contemporary culture. Nevertheless, they retain traces of their former connectedness—indeed, by the intuitive genius of poets, who still hear in modern words the resonance of archaic structures. — Turner 1977:8

THE ARCHAEOLOGICAL RECORD BEQUEATHED TO US BY the ancient peoples of Mesoamerica, although often obscure and fragmentary, in reality provides a complex text with which to examine cultural processes often relegated to an epiphenomenal role. As a result of recent epigraphic breakthroughs and the development of more rigorous and precise field methodologies, Mesoamerican scholars have come to recognize that archaeological information reflects not only material conditions but also ideas and ideologies (e.g., Demarest and Conrad 1992; Freidel and Schele 1989; Freidel et al. 1993; Joyce 1991; McAnany 1995; Schele and Freidel 1990). Bolstered by the development of more contextual field methodologies and the collaboration of ethnographers and art historians, archaeologists have increasingly directed their efforts toward understanding the role of symbolic structures in cultural processes. The present volume is intended to help scholars working in Mesoamerica hear the resonance of 'archaic struc-tures' and to further engage them to seek new bridges to interpret and integrate the static material remains they recover.

This volume focuses on intriguing yet poorly understood material phenomena recovered by archaeologists—objects commonly referred to as ritual deposits, dedicatory or votive offerings, caches, or termination events. These offerings are only tantalizing pieces of the original contexts, which vary according to content, investment of energy, deposition, and intent. However, as David Freidel cogently observes in the final summary, they open the black box of ancient culture and invite us to peer in. Our insight into this black box of culture is filtered through the vagaries of the archaeological record, molded by the creative play of culture, and colored by the lens of the observable present.

It is difficult, for the purposes of study, to separate these occurrences from the bounded domain of ritual, since we seek to discover certain features of form, patterning, and redundancy as a mode of understanding. The attempt is facilitated by the fact that the Mesoamerican world view, both present and past, is unified by a few deep structural principles; this resilient body of shared understandings about the nature of the cosmos and humanity's role in it underlies the surface diversity. A wealth of scholarly research demonstrates the remarkable tenacity of these structural principles in Mesoamerica through time (e.g., Bricker 1981; Carlsen and Prechtel 1991; Freidel et al. 1993; Gossen 1974, 1986; Hill and Monaghan 1987; Hunt 1977; Reina and Hill 1978; Schele and Freidel 1990; Tedlock 1982; Vogt 1969, 1976), despite their transformations through human agency, ideology, or colonial expansionism.

The Mesoamerican cosmos was enlivened by an environment of dying, regenerating, transforming, often ambivalent animals, plants, and humans, embraced as paradigmatic sets for the mysteries of earth and life itself (Hunt 1977). In this volume, archaeological and ethnographic papers conjoin empirical data to extend these metaphoric and metonymic components woven of the same symbolic fabric. The Mesoamerican world view relates the natural forces of death and rebirth to cultural processes embedded in the landscape of the human body and its life cycles. Critical thresholds of human life—the accession or death of a ruler, a declaration of war, or the birth of a new year—are codified into a set of structural rules that mark and ritually reconcile ambiguities and social tensions. This process of humanization continues to resonate into the objects, houses, spaces, and sacred edifices that the people of Mesoamerica create, transform, and use. Names for different parts of the human body are replicated in names for the different parts of houses (as well as mountains, fields, and so forth). Vogt (1976:59) observes that the walls are the stomachs, the corners are the ears, the roof is the head, and the base is the feet. In the modern-day communities of Highland Chiapas, an infant receives a soul just as a new building or object is "ensouled" to inaugurate its passage into a new life. As the human body is broken down in the act of death, so the owner's "ensouled" material possessions are mutilated or ritually killed, ensuring closure and a final journey to the land of the dead (Vogt, this volume).

Authored by a diverse group of scholars, the path-breaking essays in this volume apply these concepts to principles structuring the deposition of dedicatory and termination offerings in the archaeological record, thereby emphasizing the expansiveness, perdurability, and recurrence of the underlying symbolic structures of death and rebirth. Because of historical processes, these archaic structures are also dynamic and incorporative, for they do not continue without some transformation or alteration (Hunt 1977; Sahlins 1981; Turner 1969, 1977). The task is to merge both the cosmological structure and the internal patternings or content. By examining the alter-

ations in content and deposition of these dedicatory and termination phenomena in prescribed cultural/historical patterns, we gain an evolutionary perspective that will help us understand these actions within the larger comparative framework of Mesoamerica. This in turn facilitates our efforts to make intelligent predictions about the archaeological record and thus to effect contextual recovery.

THE POETRY OF ARCHAIC STRUCTURES

An offering was placed in every Maya structure when it was dedicated or enlarged. These offerings vary considerably in richness, but one must remember that many of the finest offerings—feather ornaments, beautiful textiles, exquisitely carved pieces of wood—have turned to dust. Yet it is poor consolation when one finds some dust in a miserable pottery jar to remember that it may once have been objects of unexampled splendor. When, on another occasion I found in a cache the decapitated skull of some sacrificial victim between two pottery bowls, my disappointment, I am afraid, was too selfish to allow room for pity for the victim of long ago.

— J. Eric Thompson (1971:163)

J. Eric Thompson's observations reflect the infatuation of his times with exotic artifacts rather than the subtleties of archaeological context, an attitude undoubtedly influenced by the additional need to satisfy the esoteric interests of financial backers (Black 1990). Thompson (1971:130) was quick, however, to see the utility of studying contemporary Mesoamerican religious beliefs as an aid in interpreting material phenomena found in the archaeological record. Termination events, if even recognized in the archaeological record, remained a matter of curiosity, although Vaillant (1938:552) made an early attempt to understand them through the direct historical approach. He used the fifty-two-year-cycle event of the New Fire ceremony and embellishment of temples to interpret various piles of debris formed by ceremonial destruction at sites in the Valley of Mexico.

William R. Coe's (1959) treatment of caches and offerings in his monograph *Piedras Negras Archaeology: Artifacts, Caches, and Burials* represents the first scholarly attempt to synthesize and explain both termination and dedicatory practices. Clearly, as D. Chase (1988) has observed, most attention in early reports was directed toward listing the contents of the cache, rather than toward interpreting the find or recording its context (e.g., Smith 1950). In his ground-breaking volume, Coe (1959) argued that the nomenclature used by archaeologists to classify these material phenomena was not adequate to address Mesoamerican ordering principles. As the first archaeologist (Coe 1980:462) to contrast terminal offerings with hidden offerings or caches, he related the latter to the "construction itself—to a deity, a person, an event, a chronological cycle, or other purpose." In contrast, terminal offerings, whether whole or fragmentary, were superficially intruded on the surface of a structure to be buried.

These arbitrary distinctions become confusing once we become aware of the complexity and diversity of dedication and termination events, and their relation to mortuary processes in the archaeological record of Mesoamerica. Becker (1988:118) challenged us to deal with a very different conceptualization of these deposits. A classic example of this dilemma of terminology and interpretation is presented by Burial 160 at Tikal, Guatemala: As a source of power, the interment of human skeletal material can animate or "ensoul" the building, yet at the same time the physical act of cutting through the floor of the structure to enclose the burial offering is analogous to the ritual killing or defacement of the existing architectural structure (Becker 1988:122–23). Similarly, D. Chase (1988:93) observed that a cache of ceramic effigy stands and plates, placed in a structure at Santa Rita Corozal before its incorporation into a subsequent structure, might be called either a cache or a termination deposit.

Termination actions, although difficult to separate in all instances and often embedded in dedication events, generally include the defacement, mutilation, breaking, burning, or alteration of portable objects (such as pottery, jade, or stone tools), sculptures, stelae, or buildings. They may involve the alteration, destruction, or obliteration of specific parts; the moving of objects such as stelae or the scattering of their broken pieces; and even the razing and burial of a monumental structure before new construction. They may consist of defacing decorative masks or portraits on monumental structures, as seen at Tikal, to formally terminate their function (Becker 1988:123). Powerful objects from older structures might be moved and incorporated into new structures, as occurred with Stela 21 at Uaxactún (Ricketson and Ricketson 1937).

Perhaps the earliest evidence of the dedicatory and termination complex in Mesoamerica occurs at Olmec sites, such as La Venta and San Lorenzo in Tabasco, where archaeologists recovered elaborate interments of jade, stone sculptures, serpentine celts, and pottery layered in cinnabar and multicolored sands (Coe and Diehl 1980; Drucker et al. 1959:127–94; see also Reilly 1993). Contemporary with these events were the programs of ritualized destruction, burning, and redeposition of objects at sites such as Chalcatzingo in the Morelos Valley (Grove 1984:158–60). Altars were mutilated and buried along with other monuments, and much of the destruction focused on specific parts of portrait figures, such as the head, eyes, and hands. In some cases the destroyed portions were moved to be reassembled at another part of the site. Rather than attributing these actions to revolutions and iconoclasm, Grove (1984:159–60) contended that such deeds were performed to neutralize supernatural powers contained in the monuments and left uncontrolled by the ruler's death. Further, based on the data, he suggested that these actions, as metaphors of sacrifice, often occurred at period endings, such as the termination of a calendric period or ritual cycle.

Termination and dedication actions play a major role in the histories recorded at many Maya sites and are often associated with reestablishment or founding (Schele and Freidel 1990:428 [N. 21], 459 [N. 42]). According to Freidel and colleagues (1993:234), the Classic Maya described the act of dedication as "to make proper," "to bless," "to circumambulate," "to cense with smoke," "to deposit plates full of offerings," or "to set something in the ground." The Primary Standard Sequence, used on objects such as stelae, altars, seats, temples, and houses, functions as a dedicatory text recording the action of carving or writing. An Early Classic black cylinder cache vessel, with inscriptions on the lid identifying its function as a dedicatory vessel for the ruler and containing spondylous shell figurines, jade, textile, wood, and nine imitation stingray spines, was recovered under a stairway at Smoke Jaguar's palace structure at Tikal (Freidel et al. 1993:244; Harrison 1970, 1989; Schele and Freidel 1990:464). Freidel and Linda Schele (1989:236) suggested that the dedicatory occasion, possibly occurring over a period of several days, activated a "portal" or opening to the Otherworld, enabling a god or ancestral spirit to be materialized in ritual.

Dedicatory offerings often include items of value, such as raw or partially worked jade (e.g., Garber 1993; Kidder et al. 1946), jade beads, earflares (both whole and smashed; Garber 1983, 1993), or carved shell ornaments, in addition to bloodletters, incised eccentrics, and more mundane objects, such as shark's teeth and shells (Freidel et al. 1993:242). Undoubtedly, many of the objects were connected to shamanistic rituals (Schele and Freidel 1990:437 [N. 44]), incorporating or accruing power along with the structure and ruler. Sacred numbers in Maya cosmology, such as nine, also seemed to be a prominent feature in the deposition of offerings at sites such as Tikal and Uaxactún during the Late Classic (Coe 1980:466). At K'axob in Belize, three stones, symbolizing the three stones of creation, were interred within a Late Preclassic ceramic cache (Masson 1993:11). At Caracol, as at other Maya sites, censers were recovered in groups of twos (Chase 1988:94), an occurrence Chase related to the pairing of *katun* idols to mark the passage of twenty-year periods (see also Chase 1985a:119–21, 1985b).

Epigraphic (e.g., Coe 1973) and ethnohistorical evidence (e.g., Sahagún 1975; Tozzer 1941) also attests to a variety of portable and monumental objects that were the recipients of dedicatory offerings: buildings, benches, ceramic vessels, plazas, altars, stelae, and ball courts. The variety of forms, the context, and the placement of such dedicatory offerings encountered in the archaeological record show qualitative and quantitative changes relative to temporal or spatial association and/or sociopolitical motives or changes (e.g., Chase 1988; Coe 1980:466–67; Pendergast and Walker, this volume). Chase (1988:88) noted the variation in Early Classic caches at Santa Rita Corozal and Caracol, arguing that by Late Classic times there was a clear distinction between caches placed at Classic Maya monuments and those placed at structures, with a definite trend toward more standardized patterns of caching.

Dedicatory and termination offerings are often found at interstices on structures, such as stairways, axial centers, boundaries, openings such as doorways, or inside and outside corners. Evidence suggests that these sequenced events took place at liminal sites, places of transition, where contact with the Otherworld, and thus with power, was strongest. Many were carefully placed in horizontal or vertical patterns, such as cruciforms, to represent the Maya universe (Chase 1988:89–90; Masson 1993; McAnany 1995:85, 104–5), or along the axis of the sun's path (Joyce 1991:77). Both dedicatory and termination offerings are recovered by archaeologists in a variety of contexts: in construction fill, between layers of marl, on the surface of structures, or in stone-lined cists or chambers (e.g., Coe 1980; Nagao 1985:22). Ricketson and Ricketson (1937:139) differentiated between a cist and a cache at Uaxactún, defining the former as having clearer boundaries.

The Gift of Life

One common offering across time and space was the sacrificial victim, both animal and human, placed in the foundation of a new structure to bring it to life. Pohl (1981, 1983:62–63) associated caches of vertebrate remains, such as those of young deer, with the *cuch* ceremony illustrated on polychrome vessels and noted in the Dresden and Madrid Codices (Taube 1988). At K'axob a Preclassic plaza/patio cache of deer teeth and crania and the bones of frogs and fish was recovered in a cache of vessels stacked in two layers crosslike. Animal offerings recovered in a lip-to-lip cache placed on the central axis of a Late Preclassic structure at the site of Río Azul included dog, snake, and bird remains with a human skull fragment (Valdez 1992). A dog and a peccary skull were placed in a child mortuary offering at Cerros (Carr 1985). Bats and rats were recovered in a cist with an infant's skull at Uaxactún (Ricketson and Ricketson 1937:152). Landa reported boar, pigs, deer, and dog, in addition to human sacrifices, in Yucatan (Tozzer 1941:115, 143); in some cases these formed part of the annual New Year *Uayeb* ceremonies.

Mortuary practices as an integral part of the conceptual continuum of monumental dedication occur over a broad area, from the site of San José in northern Belize (Thompson 1939:219) to Nebaj in Guatemala (Smith and Kidder 1951:21–27) and Chichén Itzá in Yucatán (Ruppert 1952). Dedicatory offerings of infants in lidded urns, along with other materials, such as snails, obsidian blades, bird bones, copper rattles, and conch shells, were uncovered at a temple dedicated to Ehecatl-Quetzalcoatl at the Aztec site of Tlatelolco, near Tenochtitlán (Berrelleza 1991). Excavations at the Temples of the Sun and of the Feathered Serpent at the great urban center of Teotihuacán in central Mexico (Sugiyama 1989:104, 1993a:116, 1993b) uncovered some remarkable dedicatory offerings. Among these was a multiple burial of 200 sacrificed soldiers with rich offerings in the center of the Feathered Serpent Pyramid (see also Cowgill 1992). Saburo Sugiyama (1993b:117–20) interpreted the burial/dedication complex events as part of a calendric ceremony; the presence of worked and unworked shell, shell iconography, and Tlaloc vessels, and the location of the pyramid near a former river course suggest a relation to water.

Ceramic offering containers, both lidded and unlidded, begin with the Middle Preclassic period (1000–300 B.C.; see, e.g., Smith 1982:245 [Seibal]; Sharer and Sedat 1981

[El Porton]). They continue through the Late Preclassic and Classic periods (Garber 1986:118, 124; Hammond 1986; Hammond and Gerhardt 1991), and their popularity endures until the Late Postclassic (A.D. 1300–1530; D. Chase 1988). They may have served as a metaphor for *pibs,* "earth ovens," where like food the gods were transformed or conjured (Freidel et al. 1993:240, 245–46). Many of the containers were standard utility vessels, but others were a specialized part of the ceramic assemblage made specifically for the occasion (Chase 1988:84). Durán (1971:158–59) described a Tláloc renewal ceremony centered on the sacrifice of small children and noted that pottery, baskets, and other vessels were made specifically for the occasion. D. Chase (1988:87) noted the presence of Classic barrel-shaped cache vessels at Caracol, while Coe (1980:466, 1959) reported at Piedras Negras a specialized form of lidded cache vessel, its interior coated with lime, that was deposited in conjunction with altars in monumental structures. The cache contained a collection of flint, obsidian, jadeite and shell artifacts. Ball (1977:147, figs. 38–42, 44–45) described specialized Late Classic bird-shaped and anthropomorphic lidded effigy vessels from subfloor caches at Becan in Campeche, Mexico, as well as applique-spiked vessels and ladle censers.

During the Late Preclassic and Early Classic periods in the Maya Lowlands, one consistent dedicatory program was the placement of human skulls in large lip-to-lip, red-slipped ceramic vessels. This practice was especially prominent at the site of Uaxactún, where the offerings included other objects, such as shell, jade, obsidian, and stingray spines (Ricketson and Ricketson 1937:pls. 21, 23; Smith 1950:93). In one cache the skulls of both a child (with upper two or three cervical vertebrae present, indicating decapitation) and adults were found resting in two inverted lip-to-lip vessels (Smith 1950:90, 93). Similar caches containing human skulls were placed in buckets or pits dug below the floors of buildings and plazas at Tikal (Shook 1958). Other remains of possible sacrificial victims were also placed in ceramic vessels. Thompson (1971:167), for instance, described a cremated burial uncovered in what appeared to be a dedicatory cache between two inverted, rim-to-rim pottery vessels at San José, Belize. Certainly the practice of using human skeletal material was not limited to the Maya. Caso (1938) noted the inclusion of a cranium and vertebrae in a subfloor cache at Monte Alban in the valley of Oaxaca.

From the perspective of Santa Rita Corozal, D. Chase (1988; see also Coe 1980:468) clearly stressed the continuities in Classic and Postclassic caching patterns, with the exception of a focus on ceramic offerings in the Postclassic. By this time, emphasis fell less on the *pib* as a container than on the anthropomorphic ceramic figurines themselves as the conjuring medium for sacrificial offerings—in particular, incense figurines or effigy vessels that were often smashed on altars or floors upon completion of a *katun* event. The emphasis on full-figure forms and more standardized religious symbolism suggested to D. Chase (1988:98) public presentations intended to unite the Maya populace. Offerings were deposited at elite residential units during ritual circuits to reiterate the idea of boundaries and political unity (D. Chase 1986:356; see also Walker 1990).

With the development of a more contextual archaeology, we now know that dedication and termination actions were characterized also by subtle linkages in time and space. These rituals of transformation were extended and embellished by expression in multiple media, or paradigmatic sets, that incorporated music and dance performances, recitations, or war events and often occurred over several days or longer, coinciding with the solstice or alignments of certain planets. Dedication inscriptions indicate that these actions often took place at different times on various portions of a structure (Freidel and Schele 1989:236). Each individual ritual action qualified the meaning of those that preceded or followed it (Freidel et al. 1986). This transformational logic is graphically illustrated at the Maya site of Colha in northern Belize (see also Guderjan, this volume; Freidel et al., this volume; and Walker, this volume), where a spectacular Late Preclassic cache and subcache were recovered in the top of a small pyramidal structure covered by another structure (Potter 1994). The cache consisted of two large lip-to-lip ceramic vessels containing shell ornaments and beads, shark teeth, jade beads, and a large chert macroblade with blood residues. Stratigraphically below this was a "subcache": additional shattered jade bead fragments (fitted together, they formed a whole bead), a large macroblade core, and a single macroblade taken from the core. The blade in the overlying cache also fit the blade core and was determined to be the second blade struck from it. Potter (1994) interpreted this as a sequence of ritual events taking place before the deposition, including the striking of the first and second blades, interment of the core and first blade with smashed jade in the cache, use of the second blade in a blood ritual, and inclusion of other artifacts in the ceramic vessels (Potter 1994). The series of events points to a termination and dedicatory program occurring before construction of the incorporating structure.

Perhaps the best example of the subtle linkages of dedication-termination events in the archaeological record was uncovered at the Late Preclassic Maya site of Cerros, also in northern Belize (Garber 1983, 1986). The highly ritualized and sequential nature of this activity is documented in the placement of a marl pavement, associated with termination activities, and a lip-to-lip vessel cache, associated with dedication rituals, before the burial of Structure 5C-2nd and the completion of Structure 5C-1st encapsulating it (Freidel 1986a). Structure 5C-1st was "ensouled" by a dedicatory offering of a pottery bucket and plate lid on the central axis of the structure in conjunction with construction fill. Freidel and Schele (1989:239) argued that the objective was to span and link both the burial and the construction in an extended sequence of rituals. Other termination activities centered on the destruction of monumental Structure 5C-2nd include the sprinkling of marl; the scattering, burning, and breaking of jade ornaments; the defacing of the façades, masks, and earplug assemblages; and the redeposition of these and other broken objects elsewhere.

Freidel (1986b) proposed that later, realizing the futility of such efforts to revitalize the rulership at Cerros, the remaining Cerros inhabitants terminated the site with another purpose in mind. Closing their "portals" forever, they burned and ripped up sections of the giant masks, smashed ornaments of jade, and scattered large fragments of decorated ceramics into the marl in front of the western façade (Schele and Freidel 1990:127–128).

Similarly, a final termination event occurred at the site of Yaxuna in Yucatán during the Late Classic period, at a time of pronounced social change (see also Freidel et al., this volume). Smashed vessels and carbon were placed at liminal spots, such as a corner and doorways, of an important, range-type palace structure. Other termination actions included the smashing of water jars, the tearing down of the façade and roof, and the scattering of the veneer stones of the upper façade throughout the North Acropolis (Ardren et al. 1994:4): a sort of desanctification of the initial building and ensouling. As Ardren and colleagues (1994:1) reported, similar acts of destruction were recognized by Vaillant at Chichén Itzá in the 1930s. At Copan, lintels over doorways were noted to be the object of destruction during termination events, since their removal would cause a building to collapse

(Andrews 1991). Some termination actions were imposed by the owners of buildings to close their sacred portals, thus keeping them out of the hands of enemies.

In some cases, these sequential events can be extrapolated from earlier archaeological reports.

Smith (1950), for example, described a termination event in his report on a Bayal phase cache from a structure at Uaxactún, recovered below the surface of the upper front stairway and south of the center line. Containing fragments of vessels, incensarios, pottery masks, flanged incensarios, and painted plaster from a previous structure, the cache may have been intended to ensoul the new incorporative structure with the genealogical power of the old.

Sharer (1978:189) provided better insight into sequentially linked events from a Late Preclassic cache uncovered at the site of Chalchuapa on the southeast periphery of the Maya area. He interpreted the inclusion of ceramics, incensarios, obsidian blades, and offerings in the vessels as representing the first part of the construction dedication. Subsequent to this, offerings were placed on the ramp of the monumental structure. As a culminating act, all offerings were deliberately crushed and terminated by nine heavy stones, then buried by construction fill before a new ramp was built.

Scholars are just beginning to understand the extent of the cosmology of dedication and termination and to carefully weave these actions into the larger pan-Mesoamerican pattern. Among early attempts to interpret Aztec dedicatory events in the Basin of Mexico was the work of Eduard Seler (1960), the first anthropologist to interpret what at that time were referred to as votive caches. He drew analogies from ethnohistorical documents to support his interpretation of the symbolism of the interred objects; like Thompson, however, he concentrated on the more complete and elaborate offerings. Archaeologists have recovered a variety of such offerings at Aztec sites in the Basin of Mexico, such as Tlatelolco, Texcoco, Chapultepec, Tizapan, and Calixtlhuaca. At the site of Tula, Hidalgo, Acosta (1974:45) reported the discovery of monumental stone "atlantids," broken, fragmented, and buried in the fill of a trench running through a monumental structure. Matos (1982, 1984, 1987, 1988) examined the Templo Major dedicatory events as ideological representations of war and tribute, while Broda (1980), using sixteenth-century documents, interpreted the Templo Mayor as an "axis mundi and sacred mountain," a theme reiterated by Lopéz Luján in this volume.

At Xochicalco (Nagao 1985:20) in central Mexico, elaborate caches contained a variety of materials, such as jade and green stone ornaments, obsidian, shell, ceramic vessels, obsidian eccentrics, and onyx vessels symbolizing the political connections to the Maya Lowlands. Nagao (1985:2) examined changes in practices as deliberate attempts by the Aztec elite to support their hegemony. Caches and sacrificial offerings have been recovered at Cacaxtla in association with monumental structures, which Mendoza (n.d.) interpreted as manifestations of the Tlaloc-Venus war complex. Caso (1967:129ff) interpreted votive offerings as burials of the terminated or completed year before the New Fire ceremony (Nagao 1985:9).

At the great urban center of Teotihuacán, early Preclassic dedicatory offerings (c. 100 B.C.–A.D. 100) were simple compared to those of their Maya neighbors, usually containing only obsidian or pottery (Millon 1960; Millon and Bennyhoff 1961). Later Preclassic dedicatory offerings, however, included imported luxury items, reflecting the center's increasing political control over its region. Elaborate dedicatory offerings have been reported from the Temple of Quetzalcoatl in the Ciudadela (e.g., Rubin de la Borbolla 1947; Sugiyama 1991).

Destruction and Transformation

López Austín (1988:1:8) emphasized the importance of concepts about the human body in Mesoamerican cosmology, in which the human life cycle serves as a metaphor for continuous regeneration. Inextricably linked to this paradigm of a human-centered universe is the anthropomorphization of other animate and inanimate forms. Embedded in such an anthropocentric world view is the idea that all humans are personally linked to the cosmos, so that the cosmos and all things in it compose a "humanized realm" of interpersonal relationships (Douglas 1978:87).

In his classic study, Van Gennep (1972:23–24) argued that the sacrifices associated with the laying of house foundations, the construction of houses, and the changing of residence are analogous to human rites of passage marking death and rebirth. These rites of transition typically took place during crises in a person's life, such as birth, puberty, baptism, marriage, death, or investiture, and were followed by incorporation rites. In Mesoamerica this anthropomorphization is exemplified by the Divine Charter laid down by the Hero Twins of the *Popol Vuh* (Edmonson 1971; Tedlock 1982), who were born through the World Tree, and whose actions and death are perpetuated to re-create the world. Simultaneously, their human actions provide metaphoric referents for "the sowing and the dawning" of plants, the change of seasons, and the life cycles of the sun, moon, and planets. These transformation processes are called *Jaloj-K'exoj* by the contemporary Atitecos of Guatemala (Carlsen and Prechtel 1991:21–23). The root words *jal* and *k'ex* together form the conceptualization of a "concentric system of change within change, a single system of transformation and renewal" (Carlsen and Prechtel 1991:8). This regenerating concept, around which revolve rituals, myths, and beliefs, also permeates the epigraphy and the iconography displayed on the material phenomena of Mesoamerica (Carlson and Prechtel 1991:9).

For example, among the Aztec, the New Fire renovation rites, intertwined in the end of the Old Year and the beginning of the New Year, were a time of major changes, renovations, and alterations of the temples (Tozzer 1941:151). Within the context of a Mesoamerican cosmogony driven by the animistic forces of *Jaloj-K'exoj* and homologization of human body and house or edifice, other material phenomena were also involved in rites of separation, transition, and incorporation to ensure the well-being of society. These material manifestations of termination and dedication were animated and ensconced within the context of elaborate royal and communitywide calendric festivals and shamanistic rituals, and prefaced by purificatory rituals and taboos reestablishing the conditions of the First Creation as related in the *Popol Vuh*. The idea of ritual cleansing through the absorption of evil into a ritual object is common to Mesoamerican Indian cultures (Dow 1986:95). Landa (Tozzer 1941:151–52) described a New Year festival in connection with the *Uayeb,* or lost five-day rites of the Maya of Yucatan, a time of social disorder and chaos. After the festival was concluded, to celebrate the first day of Pop,

> They renewed on this day all the objects which they made use of, such as plates, vessels, stools, mats, and old clothes, and the stuffs with which they wrapped up their idols. They swept out their houses, and the sweepings and the old utensils they threw out on the waste heap outside the town; and no one, even he in need of it, touched it.

The *Cha Chac,* or rain-bringing ceremony, in Belize (Gann 1971:57–58; see also Redfield and Villa Rojas 1962:138 [Chan Kom, Yucatán]), performed in response to community needs, was an elaborate event lasting three days. Gann (1971:57–58) observed that all the objects used in the ceremony were new. "The huts and oven are made specially for the occasion; the gourd cups and bowls have never been used before; the pottery is new, and even the incense, corn husk cigarettes, and black native wax candles are specially prepared for the ceremony." Following the ritual, "everything ... including sheds, altar, and vessels was burnt, and very carefully reduced to ashes" (Gann 1971:57), plausibly to contain and destroy the absorbed evils of the community. Eyewitnesses described a nineteenth-century ceremony at Lazarero, Chiapas, in which "hundreds of figurines, painted bowls, and plates were smashed and buried with a human sacrifice to inaugurate a new epoch" (Morris 1987:31). Landa's *Relación de las cosas de Yucatán* contains descriptions of similar rituals, such as the renewal of wooden and clay idols, and the renovation and rebuilding of temples during the months of Chen and Yax, following which "they placed on the wall the memorial of their things, written in their characters" (Tozzer 1941:184).

We know that the Maya performed termination actions upon the occasion of a new construction to kill the old structure and contain its accumulated power, either as a final act or as a prelude. For instance, Krochock (1995:5) reports the intentional sealing off of the Hieroglyphic Jamba in the Mucado at Chichén Itzá as a final termination event. More difficult to understand is their deliberate placement of "problematic" materials, such as garbage, broken items, or rubbish, in or on certain parts of structures, since the Maya as a people were obsessed with purificatory rituals, such as purging, ritual enemas, sexual and food taboos, and cleansing (e.g., Tozzer 1941:152, 163, 323). Although these "problematic" materials we find in the archaeological record certainly had different permutations and meanings, we must consider that such formless or broken objects were symbols of beginning and growth as well as of decay (Douglas 1985). More than casual depositions of trash, they were intended to terminate contact with the powerful conduits to the Otherworld (Mock 1993).

The ancient Nahuas of Mexico expressed this concept as *tlazolli*, "something useless or used up," "something that has lost its original order or structure," such as broken sherds, dirt, excrement, charcoal, and bodily secretions. The transitive form of *tlazolli, izloa,* means "to abase oneself" (Burkhart 1989:88).

Within the context of an anthropomorphized world view, we might consider destructive actions on material objects, such as monumental buildings or ceramic pots, to be analogous to bodily mutilations, the ordeals inflicted on initiates to separate them from a previous way of life before incorporation into another permanent station (Turner 1969:169; Van Gennep 1972). In the termination process, the rules are reversed, and chaos and disorder are created within a "ritually framed license" (Goffman 1974)—in this case, the first sacrifice described in the *Popol Vuh*. These objects become *tlazolli* "divested of specific form and reduced to a condition that ... is without or beneath all accepted forms of status" (Turner 1969:170).

Obstruction of certain portions of a structure and destruction of some of the objects, or sacra, used in the termination and dedication actions may be explained by the perceived need to empty them of their power once that act is over. Each new phase requires new, "pure" sacra, such as "bodily ornamentation, costumes, or verbal rites" (Van Gennep 1972:60). Movement from disorder to order—whether the death or overthrow of a ruler, a new year, birth, or a change of status—requires a crossing of boundaries. Not only is danger controlled by rituals denoting separation from the old status and entry into the new, but also the harmful effects of changes and disturbances in a life cycle are reduced by reinforcing the normative structures of society (Douglas 1988:56, 98).

A New Beginning

As a process merging the binary oppositions of death and rebirth, the *Jaloj-K'exoj* concept is exemplified by Vogt (1969:369–74, 1976:18), who sees symbolic action as focused on the Tzotzil concept of *ch'ulel,* "inner soul." The life force of *ch'ulel* resides in all living things, as well as in material phenomena and sacred places (Freidel et al. 1993:123, 144–46; Vogt 1976:18–19; see also Vogt, this volume). Vogt (1976:19) has commented that "the most important interaction in the universe is not between persons, nor between persons and objects, but among the innate souls of persons and material objects." Just as the soul is "fixed" in a small child through baptism in Zinacantán, buildings are ensouled through dedicatory rituals performed during and after construction. These rituals include symbolic and blood sacrifices to ensure that the soul is settled in the structure (see Vogt, this volume; also Freidel et al. 1993:254).

The metaphoric relationship of house to human and the guiding *Jaloj-K'exoj* concept based on death and rebirth present another avenue of interpretation of at least some permutations of termination and dedication processes we recover in the archaeological record. Freidel and colleagues (1993; see also Vogt 1976:371–72) described a present-day K'iche'an (also Quiche) concept of *chanul* or *nawal*, "animal spirit companion" or "spiritual alter ego," a concept that has precedents in ancient Mayan ritual. Using the epigraphic data, they further described a royal rite of passage at Palenque in which the young second son of Pakal, the reigning king, became a replacement of K'an-Hok'-Chitam, his ancestor who died ninety-four years earlier. The ritual reincarnates the ancient king, K'an-Hok'-Chitam, placing his *ch'ulel*, "soul," in the young son of Pakal, who following the ritual is appropriately named K'an-Hok'-Chitam II.

The murals at the site of Bonampak in Chiapas depict a series of building dedication events that are coordinated with a rite of passage for the ruler's young son, who is presented to the invited dignitaries as the heir. The next event, consecrating the structure, takes place 236 days later, on the first appearance of Venus as evening star. Associated with this dedicatory event is bloodletting by the ruler, the sacrifice of captives, and war (Freidel et al. 1993:284). As Freidel, Schele, and Parker (1993:285) stated, these events "weave together the ensouling of the world, the activating of great human-made places, and the reproduction of political power in the dynasties."

Considering the metaphoric relationship of human and house within the Mesoamerican world view, it might be argued that the process of "replacement" or reincarnation described here is replicated in the architectural record in some contexts. In a similar rite of passage the souls, or *ch'ulel*, of deliberately terminated or killed buildings, like dead ancestral kings, are reincarnated through offerings into each new "descendant" building episode. Thus ancestral souls could be transferred not only between humans but also between classes of material phenomena associated with humans. In some cases, a new building was then placed on top of the old, ritually terminated, skeletal edifice and brought to life in an "ensouling" or animating event (Schele and Freidel 1990:428, N. 21), thereby being incorporated into society, like a newly baptized infant.

Some monuments thus have a layered genealogy, constantly increasing both qualitatively and quantitatively in the degree of ancestral *ch'ulel* with each destruction and creation event in a world structured by the guiding *Jaloj-K'exoj* concept (see also Freidel and Schele 1989; McAnany

1995:66). Each new building becomes the replacement of or substitute for the ancestor (e.g., Vogt 1976:373; Freidel et al. 1993:25, 181), while the old skeletal or terminated structures become the consumed offerings. Accordingly, monuments accrue power, just as the elite ruler accumulates power from sacrificial victims and shamanic contact with the ancestors of the Otherworld.

Ten of the essays in the volume were originally presented in April 1992 at the Society for American Archaeology meetings in Pittsburgh. Those papers focused on a variety of archaeological phenomena interpreted as termination and dedication events. The objective was to examine these events as deliberate programs of creation and destruction and to encourage further inquiry into their meaning among scholars of Mesoamerica. The present volume represents a more collaborative effort, including expanded versions of the original papers and additional invited papers from archaeologists, anthropologists, and art historians, with the goal of understanding the spatial and temporal extent and permutations of this behavioral complex in Mesoamerica. The comparative evidence will also contribute to the formulation of hypotheses related to behavioral processes, to be tested in future archaeological and ethnographic endeavors.

In chapter 2, Evon Vogt documents dedication and termination ceremonies among the Tzotzil Mayan–speaking Zinacantecos in Highland Chiapas. His essay reiterates the premise of this volume that ties to the ancient past are not severed, but are simply reinterpreted and transformed by descendants. Vogt's description of the *Hol chuk* house inauguration rites and the *Ch'ul kantela* completion rites illustrates the generative processes of sacrifice, reciprocity, and replacement intertwined with cosmology and the homology of human and divine action. Within such an anthropomorphized world view, rites of passage include the ensouling of houses through a symbolic feeding or sacrifice and ritual action to create and perpetuate social order and cosmology. Additionally, rituals accompanying human death—in particular, the destruction of objects possessing the soul of their owner—provide a transition between the Otherworld and rebirth of the soul into an honored ancestor.

Similar studies of contemporary belief systems and rituals in Mesoamerica continue to offer evidence of earlier ones rooted in the distant past. Using data from contemporary Tzeltal Maya in Chiapas as well as his fieldwork in Mexico, Brian Stross in chapter 3 focuses on the life cycle of death and rebirth and the social customs and traditions surrounding them as templates for the organization, justification, and format of dedication and termination events. Preferring the term *action* to the more narrowly defined *ritual* (see Monaghan, this volume), he explores their various components and permutations in the objects created by humans and their metaphoric relationship to rites of passage surrounding birth and death.

Parallels between ancient and contemporary termination and dedication actions are also the focus of R. Jon McGee in chapter 4, who discusses the contemporary Lacandon of southeastern Chiapas. Just as the ancient people of Mesoamerica animated their buildings through dedicatory programs, the modern-day Lacandon periodically animate or "ensoul" their god pots through propitiatory acts and prestations, including special prayers and offerings of anthropomorphic figures symbolizing human flesh and blood. Upon replacement with new ones, the old god pots are ceremonially killed and buried—a fact that can serve as a bridge to understanding dedication and termination actions in the archaeological record.

John Monaghan chooses a different route in chapter 5, noting the absence of dedication and termination actions among the Mixtec of Oaxaca. Rejecting the term *ritual* as too exclusive, he finds it more useful to embed these practices within the broader context of production. Using the metaphor of cooking, Monaghan encourages us to view Maya and Mixtec practices within a single framework of transformational relationships, creating a linkage between the material and the phenomenological, the natural and the cultural, and providing a contextuality based on human life forces.

Chapter 6, by David M. Pendergast, is based on his extensive archaeological fieldwork at the sites of Lamanai and Altun Ha in Belize. It illustrates the variety of dedicatory depositions and placement at these two Maya sites, which Pendergast attributes to different strategies pursued by the separate but neighboring polities. At the same time, he notes inconsistencies in presence or type of dedicatory events between antecedent and succeeding building modifications. He suggests that not all offerings were interred with dedicatory intentions; some were meant to amplify already existing power. "Empty" caches at Lamanai from the Preclassic to the Terminal Classic represent another missing piece in the cultural puzzle encountered by archaeologists working in Mesoamerica. Historical accounts suggest that many of these offerings consisted of animate or inanimate objects that would not have survived in the archaeological record.

In chapter 7 Sandra Noble Bardsley provides a new level of understanding of dedicatory events as a political strategy through cross-cultural comparisons. Focusing on stone benches as visual signs of authority at the Maya site of Copan, Honduras, she interprets dedicatory events as means of soliciting supernaturals to sanction human actions and examines changes in dedication patterns in relationship to shifts in political organization. Her essay illustrates the interrelationship between iconographical elements such as serpents, epigraphic inscriptions, stone monuments, and the evolutionary changes triggered by the implementation of new political strategies.

The ethnographic and archaeological chapters support the idea that many interments were by no means simple one-dimensional events, but rather multiple, sequentially integrated events (Freidel and Schele 1989:236). Following this idea of linkages, Debra Selsor Walker in chapter 8 discusses the ceramic subcomplex of Cerros, in particular, censer stacks (e.g., Freidel et al. 1993) associated with termination activities and their relationship to the monumental architecture. After analyzing deposits of halved vessels and whole vessels, and more subtle evidence, such as *saskab* layers and sherds recovered at Cerros, she hypothesizes that these events represent not only failed attempts to revive the ancient seat of power at Cerros but also later attempts to ritually close the portals to the Otherworld before abandonment of the community.

Similarly, in chapter 9 Thomas H. Guderjan discusses a series of complex events leading to, surrounding, and following the deposition of a major series of caches at a central building in the main plaza of an Early Classic structure at the site of Blue Creek in northwestern Belize. In the sequence of events the builders first constructed a large stone-lined shaft; within and outside it were placed a series of elaborate cache offerings, including broken sherds, one thousand worked jades, chert, shell, food residues, and evidence of human sacrifice. The cache was capped by a massive limestone bannerstone. Contending that the community was ruled by an independent royal lineage, Guderjan argues that the termination event was a turning point in the history of the Blue Creek settlement, marking a complete restructuring of political and civic affairs.

In chapter 10 Boteler Mock describes the interment of thirty mutilated and defleshed human skulls in a pit at Colha, Belize, during the Late to Terminal Classic decline of the site. Using comparative iconographical, ethnohistorical, and archaeological data of Mesoamerica to contextualize the event, she argues that the ignoble treatment of the skulls was a termination of the sacred power of the Colha elite through a symbolic defacement and desouling. This dénouement event, analogous to the destruction of monumental portraiture at sites such as Cerros and Copan, was literally a reenactment of events described in the *Popol Vuh.*

Termination and dedication actions were not exclusively performed by the Maya elite; they were mirrored, though somewhat differently, in nonelite households. In chapter 11 James F. Garber, W. David Driver, Lauren A. Sullivan, and David M. Glassman focus on a ritual complex of more modest offerings recovered in a nonelite house mound at Blackman Eddy, Belize, dating from the Early to Late Classic period. Not only do the layering, placement, and content of these ritual offerings over time emphasize death and regeneration as the critical thresholds of human life, but they also show the resiliency of these symbolic underpinnings despite the social context.

The importance of precise recording of architectural stratigraphy and the subtlety of termination-dedication events are shown in the description by David A. Freidel, Charles K. Suhler, and Rafael Cobos Palma of archaeological deposits at the site of Yaxuna in northern Yucatan. The authors of chapter 12 use carefully recorded data to support their hypothesis that the site of Yaxuna underwent a major defeat in war and systematic termination of ritual structures and major residences during the Early Classic period. Their fieldwork points to new directions for archaeologists to follow in correlating the ritual in the material record with sociopolitical events.

The remaining chapters extend the archaeological evidence for dedication and termination actions to other areas of prehispanic Mesoamerica (Sugiyama 1995). Spectacular evidence of the pan-Mesoamerican termination and dedication complex comes from the site of Teotihuacan in the form of the mass burial of two hundred sacrificial victims in front of the façades, at the four corners, and inside the Feathered Serpent Pyramid. In chapter 13 Saburo Sugiyama further pursues his consummate investigations, discussing the complex destruction and construction history of the Feathered Serpent Pyramid as institutionally organized actions at various times in the city's history. Termination actions included burning, painting, plastering over and/or mutilation of specific portions of monumental sculptures while they were still in place, and destruction of different construction episodes of the

pyramidal structure. He also argues that various episodes of looting human burials inside and outside the pyramid were part of this desecration program.

Termination and dedication actions also involve the appropriation of powerful objects from structures (or other objects) and their incorporation into new structures as a form of ensoulment. Such a program of dedicatory offerings or caches has been recovered at the Zapatec center of Monte Alban in Oaxaca. In chapter 14 Marilyn Masson and Heather Orr argue that the elite rulers of Monte Alban appropriated sacrificial victims and their *nahuales* in strategies of renewal and dedication commemorating significant life passages, calendrical events, and triumphs on the battlefield. Carved monuments depicting sacrificed captives were rededicated in secondary and tertiary contexts, and were thus reactivated as sources of power and denoters of sacred areas. Integral to this practice of building dedication at Monte Alban was the iconography of rulers in feline transformation, symbolizing military and shamanic prowess.

Chapter 15, Leonardo López Luján's essay on the Aztec Temple Major at Tenochtitlán, shows what can be discerned in the archaeological record through a study of contextual relationships. López Luján views each ritual offering as a precisely placed sign or symbol that when combined with others, constitutes a decipherable code. Using locational principles, López Luján interprets the rituals as a reenactment of the cosmogonic acts of the gods. An additional element of the re-creation was the interment of decapitated individuals as dedicatory offerings during the twenty-day period of Xipe Totec, coinciding with the spring equinox.

Finally, in chapter 16 David Freidel reiterates his commitment to contextual recovery and attempts to comprehend these episodes of destruction, regeneration, and transformation in the archaeological record through a careful interweaving of the archival, ethnographic, and epigraphic evidence. Termination and dedication were dual components of a Mesoamerican paradigm of regeneration and reproduction conjoined by the *Jaloj-K'exoj* concept. Despite the vagaries of history and the creative play of culture, the paradigmatic, transformative principle of "sowing and dawning" remains deeply embedded among the people of Mesoamerica today, whether we choose to call it ritual, production, or something else entirely. Freidel's insightful summary moves us to remain sensitive to the poetry of these archaic layers of meaning and intent, to these treasures of the spirit.

References Cited

Acosta, Jorge R.
1974   *La Pirámide de el Corral de Tula, Hidalgo.* In
        Proyecto Tula (la parte), coordinated by
        Eduardo Matos Montezuma. Mexico City:
        Departmento de Monumentos INAH
        Prehispanico.

Andrews, E. Wyllys
1991   "The Growth of a Royal Residential Complex
        at Copan, Honduras: The 10L-2 Group in the
        Late Classic Period." Paper presented at the
        47th ICA Conference, New Orleans.

Ardren, Tracy, David Johnstone, Sharon Bennett,
Charles Suhler, and David Freidel
1994   The Seltz Foundation Yaxuna Project, Final
        Report of the 1993 Field Season, Department
        of Anthropology, Southern Methodist Uni-
        versity: Dallas, Texas.

Ball, Joseph W.
1977   *The Archaeological Ceramics of Becan,
        Campeche, Mexico.* New Orleans: Middle Amer-
        ican Research Institute, Tulane University.

Becker, Marshall J.
1988   "Caches as Burials, Burials as Caches: The
        Meaning of Ritual Deposits among the Clas-
        sic Period Lowland Maya." In *Recent Studies
        in Pre-Columbian Archaeology,* edited by
        Nicholas J. Saunders and Olivier de
        Montmollin, 117–34. Oxford: BAR.

Berrelleza, Juan Alberto Román
1991   "A Study of Skeletal Material from Tlatel-
        olco." In *To Change Place: Aztec Ceremonial
        Landscapes,* edited by David Carrasco, 9–19.
        Boulder: University Press of Colorado.

Black, Stephen L.
1990   "Field Methods and Methodologies in Low-
        land Maya Archaeology." Ph.D. diss., Harvard
        University.

Bricker, Victoria R.
1981   *The Indian Christ, the Indian King: The His-
        torical Substrate of Maya Myth and Ritual.*
        Austin: University of Texas Press.

Broda de Casas, Johanna
1980   *The Great Temple of Tenochtitlan: Center and
        Periphery in the Aztec World.* Berkeley: Uni-
        versity of California Press.

Burkhart, Louise M.
1989   *The Slippery Earth: Nahua-Christian Moral
        Dialogue in Sixteenth-century Mexico.* Tucson:
        University of Arizona Press.

Carlsen, R. S., and M. Prechtel
1991   "The Flowering of the Dead: An Interpretation
        of Highland Maya Culture." *Man* n.s. 25(1).

Carr, H. S.
1985   "Subsistence and Ceremony: Faunal Utiliza-
        tion in a Late Preclassic Community at
        Cerros, Belize." In *Prehistoric Lowland Maya
        Environment and Subsistence Economy,* edited
        by Mary Pohl, 115–32. Papers of the Peabody
        Museum of Archaeology and Ethnology 77.
        Cambridge: Harvard University.

Caso, Alfonso
1938   *Exploraciones en Oaxaca: Quinto y Sexta
        Temporadas 1936–1937.* Instituto Panameri-
        cano de Geografia e Historia 34. Mexico City.

Chase, Diane Z.
1985a   "Ganned But Not Forgotten: Late Postclassic
        Archaeology and Ritual at Santa Rita
        Corozal, Belize." In *The Lowland Maya
        Postclassic,* edited by Arlen F. Chase and Pru-
        dence M. Rice, 104–25. Austin: University of
        Texas Press.
1985b   "Between Earth and Sky: Idols, Images, and
        Postclassic Cosmology." In *Fifth Palenque
        Round Table 1983,* edited by Merle G. Robert-
        son and V. M. Fields, 7:223–33. San Francisco:
        Pre-Columbian Art Research Institute.
1986   "Social and Political Organization in the
        Land of Milk and Honey: Correlating the
        Archaeology and Ethnohistory of the Post-
        classic Lowland Maya." In *Late Lowland Maya
        Civilization: Classic to Postclassic,* edited by
        Jeremy A. Sablorff and E. Wyllys Andrews V,
        347–78. Albuquerque: School of American
        Research and University of New Mexico
        Press.
1988   "Caches and Censerwares: Meaning from
        Maya Pottery." In *A Pot for All Reasons:
        Ceramic Ecology Revisited,* edited by Charles
        C. Kolb and Louana M. Lackey, 81–114. Spe-
        cial Publications of Ceramica de Cultura
        Maya et al. Philadelphia: Laboratory of An-
        thropology, Temple University.

Coe, Michael D.
1973   *The Maya Scribe and His World.* New York:
        The Grolier Club.

Coe, Michael, and Richard Diehl
1980   *In the Land of the Olmec.* 2 vols. Austin: Uni-
        versity of Texas Press.

Coe, William R.
1959   *Piedras Negras Archaeology: Artifacts, Caches,
        and Burials.* Philadelphia: University of Penn-
        sylvania Museum.

1980 [1965]. "Caches and Offertory Practices of the Maya Lowlands." In *Handbook of Middle American Indians, Volume 2: Archaeology of Southern Mesoamerica, Part 1,* edited by G. R. Willey, 462–68. Austin: University of Texas Press.

Cowgill, George L.
1992 "Toward a Political History of Teotihuacan." In *Ideology and Pre-Columbian Civilizations,* edited by A. Demarest and G. Conrad, 87–114. Santa Fe, N.M.: School of American Research.

Demarest, Arthur, and Geoffrey Conrad
1992 *Religion and Empire: The Dynamics of Aztec and Inca Expansionism.* Cambridge: Cambridge University Press.

Douglas, Mary
1978 *Cultural Bias.* London: Royal Anthropological Institute.
1985 *Purity and Danger: An Analysis of the Concepts of Pollution and Taboo.* London: Ark Paperbacks.

Dow, James
1986 *The Shaman's Touch: Otomi Indian Symbolic Healing.* Salt Lake City: University of Utah Press.

Drucker, Philip, Robert F. Heizer, and Robert J. Squier
1959 *Excavations at La Venta, Tabasco, 1955.* Washington, D.C.: U.S. Government Printing Office.

Durán, F. Diego
1971 *Book of the Gods and Rites and the Ancient Calendar.* Translated and edited by F. Horcasitas and D. Heyden, with foreword by M. Leon-Portilla. Norman: University of Oklahoma Press.

Edmonson, Munroe S.
1971 *The Book of Counsel: The Popol Vuh of the Quiche Maya of Guatemala.* Middle American Research Institute Publication 35. New Orleans: Tulane University.

Freidel, David A.
1986a "Introduction." In *Archaeology at Cerros, Belize, Central America, Volume 1: An Interim Report,* edited by R. A. Robinson and D. A. Freidel, xiii–xxiii. Dallas: Southern Methodist University Press.
1986b "The Monumental Architecture." In *Archaeology at Cerros, Belize, Central America, Volume 1: An Interim Report,* edited by R. A. Robinson and D. A. Freidel, 1–22. Dallas: Southern Methodist University Press.

Freidel, David A., M. Masucci, S. Jaeger, and R. Robertson
1986 "The Bearer, the Burden, and the Burnt: The Stacking Principle in the Iconography of the Late Preclassic Maya Lowlands." In *Sixth Palenque Round Table, 1986,* edited by Merle G. Robertson, 8:175–83. Norman: University of Oklahoma Press.

Freidel, David A., and Linda Schele
1989 "Dead Kings and Living Temples: Dedication and Termination Rituals among the Ancient Maya." In *Word and Image in Maya Culture: Explorations in Language, Writing, and Representation,* edited by W. F. Hanks and D. S. Rice, 233–243. Salt Lake City: University of Utah Press.

Freidel, David A., Linda Schele, and Joy Parker
1993 *Maya Cosmos: Three Thousand Years on the Shaman's Path.* New York: William Morrow.

Gann, Thomas
1971 *In an Unknown Land.* Freeport, N.Y.: Books for Libraries Press.

Garber, James F.
1983 "Patterns of Jade Consumption and Disposal at Cerros, in Northern Belize." *American Antiquity* 48(4):800–7.
1986 "The Artifacts." In *Archaeology at Cerros, Belize, Central America, Volume 1: An Interim Report,* edited by R. A. Robinson and D. A. Freidel, 1–22. Dallas: Southern Methodist University Press.
1993 "The Cultural Context of Jade Artifacts from the Maya Site of Cerros." In *Precolumbian Jade: New Geological and Cultural Interpretations,* edited by Frederick W. Lange, 166–72. Salt Lake City: University of Utah Press.

Goffman, Erving
1974 *Frame Analysis: An Essay on the Organization of Experience.* Cambridge: Harvard University Press.

Gossen Gary H.
1974 *Chamulas in the World of the Sun: Time and Space in a Maya Oral Tradition.* Cambridge: Cambridge University Press.
1986 "Mesoamerican Ideas as a Foundation for Regional Synthesis." In *Symbol and Meaning beyond the Closed Community: Essays in Mesoamerican Ideas,* edited by Gary H. Gossen, 1–8. Albany, N.Y.: Institute for Mesoamerican Studies, University of Albany.

Grove, David
1984 *Chalcatzingo, Excavations on the Olmec Frontier.* New York: Thames and Hudson.

Hammond, Norman A.
1986   "The Emergence of Maya Civilization." *Scientific American* 255(2):106–15.

Hammond, Norman, and Juliette C. Gerhardt
1991   "Offertory Practices: Caches." In *Cuello: An Early Maya Community in Belize,* edited by Norman Hammond, 225–31. Cambridge: Cambridge University Press.

Hill, R. M., II and John Monaghan
1987   *Continuities in Highland Maya Social Organization: Ethnohistory in Sacapulas, Guatemala.* Philadelphia: University of Pennsylvania Press.

Hunt, Eva
1977   *The Transformation of the Hummingbird: Cultural Roots of a Zinacantecan Mythical Poem.* Ithaca, N.Y.: Cornell University Press.

Joyce, Rosemary A.
1991   *Cerro Palenque: Power and Identity on the Maya Periphery.* Austin: University of Texas Press.

Kidder, Alfred V., Jesse D. Jennings, and Edwin M. Shook.
1946   *Excavations at Kaminaljuyu, Guatemala.* Washington, D.C.: Carnegie Institution of Washington.

Krochock, Ruth
1995   "Cross-Correlation of Epigraphic and Archaeological Data at Chichen Itza." Paper presented at the 60th Annual Meeting of the Society for American Archaeology.

López Austín, A.
1988   *The Human Body and Ideology: Concepts of the Ancient Nahuas,* translated by T. O. de Montellano and B. O. de Montellano. Vol. 1. Salt Lake City: University of Utah Press.

Masson, Marilyn
1993   "K'axob Caches and Community Integration: Preclassic Manifestations of a Pervasive Maya Pattern." Paper presented at the 58th Annual Meeting of the Society for American Archaeology, St. Louis.

Matos Moctezuma, Eduardo
1982   *El Templo Mayor: Excavaciones y Estudios.* Mexico City: Instituto Nacional de Antropología Historia.
1984   "The Templo Mayor of Tenochtitlan." In *Ritual Human Sacrifice in Mesoamerica,* edited by Elizabeth H. Boone, 133–64. Washington, D.C.: Dumbarton Oaks.
1987   "Symbolism of the Templo Mayor." In *The Aztec Templo Mayor,* edited by Elizabeth Boone, 185–210. Washington, D.C.: Dumbarton Oaks.

1988   *Vida y muerte en el Templo Mayor.* Mexico City: Editorial Océano.

McAnany, Patricia A.
1995   *Living with the Ancestors: Kinship and Kingship in Ancient Maya Society.* Austin: University of Texas Press.

Mendoza, Ruben G.
N.d.   "Tlaloc-Venus War Cult Caches of the Central Highland Oloman: Blood Sacrifice and the Rites of Symbolic Annihilation." Unpublished paper.

Millon, Rene
1960   "The Beginnings of Teotihuacán." *American Antiquity* 26(1):1–10.

Millon, Rene, and James Bennyhoff
1961   "A Long Architectural Sequence at Teotihuacán." *American Antiquity* 26(4):516–23.

Mock, Shirley Boteler
1993   "Ritual Passages: Dedication and Termination Events in the Archaeological Record of Mesoamerica." Paper presented at the 92nd Annual Meeting of the American Anthropological Association, Washington, D.C.

Morris, Walter F.
1987   *Living Maya.* New York: Harry N. Abrams.

Nagao, D.
1985   *Mexica Buried Offerings: A Historical and Contextual Analysis.* BAR International Series 235. Oxford.

Pohl, Mary D.
1981   "Ritual Continuity and Transformation in Mesoamerica: Reconstructing the Ancient Maya Cuch Ritual." *American Antiquity* 46(3):513–29.
1983   "Maya Ritual Faunas: Vertebrate Remains from Burials, Caches, Caves, and Cenotes in the Maya Lowlands." In *Civilization in the Ancient Americas: Essays in Honor of Gordon R. Willey,* edited by Richard M. Levanthal and Alan L. Kolata, 55–103. Albuquerque: University of New Mexico Press, and Cambridge: Peabody Museum of Archaeology and Ethnology, Harvard.

Potter, Daniel
1994   "Strat 55, Operation 2012, and Comments on Lowland Maya Blood Ritual." In *Continuing Archeology at Colha, Belize,* edited by Thomas R. Hester, Harry J. Shafer, and Jack D. Eaton, 31–38. Studies in Archeology 16. Austin: Texas Archeological Research Laboratory, University of Texas.

Redfield, Robert, and Alfonso Villa Rojas
1967   *Chan Kom: A Maya Village.* Chicago: University of Chicago Press.

Reilly, Kent
1993   "La Venta and the Olmec: The Function of Sacred Geography in the Formative Period Ceremonial Complex." Ph.D. diss., University of Texas at Austin.

Reina, Ruben E., and Robert M. Hill II
1978   *The Traditional Pottery of Guatemala.* Austin: University of Texas Press.

Ricketson, Oliver G., and Edith B. Ricketson
1937   *Uaxactun, Guatemala: Group E 1926–1931.* Carnegie Institution of Washington Publication 477. Washington, D.C.: Carnegie Institution.

Rubin de la Borbolla, D. F.
1947   "Teotihuacán: Ofrendas de los Templos de Quetzalcoatl." *Anales del Instituto Nacional de Antropologia e Historia* 6(2):61–72.

Ruppert, Karl
1952   *Chichen Itza, Architectural Notes and Plans.* Carnegie Institution of Washington Publication 595. Washington, D.C.: Carnegie Institution.

Sahagún, Bernardino de
1975   *General History of the Things of New Spain: Florentine Codex.* 2nd edition, revised. Santa Fe, N.M.: School of American Research.

Sahlins, Marshall
1981.   *Historical Metaphors and Mythical Realities: Structure in the Early History of the Sandwich Islands Kingdom.* Association for Social Anthropology in Oceania Special Publications 1. Ann Arbor: University of Michigan Press.

Schele, L., and D. Freidel
1990   *A Forest of Kings: The Untold Story of the Ancient Maya.* New York: William Morrow.

Seler, Eduard
1960   *Gesammelte Abhandlungen zur Amerikanischen Sprach(-) und Altertumskunde,* 5 vols. Graz: Akademische Druck und Verlangstalt.

Sharer, Robert
1978   "Special Deposits." In *The Prehistory of Chalchuapa, El Salvador, Volume 1,* edited by Robert J. Sharer, 180–94. Philadelphia: University of Pennsylvania Press.

Sharer, Robert, and David Sedat
1981   *Archaeological Investigations in the Northern Maya Highlands, Guatemala: Interaction and the Development of Maya Civilization.* Philadelphia: University of Pennsylvania Museum.

Shook, Edwin M.
1958   *Tikal Reports.* Philadelphia: University of Pennsylvania Press.

Smith, A. Ledyard
1950   *Uaxactun, Guatemala: Excavations of 1931–37.* Carnegie Institution of Washington Publication 588. Washington, D.C.: Carnegie Institution.
1955   *Archaeological Reconnaissance in Central Guatemala.* Carnegie Institution of Washington Publication 594. Washington, D.C.: Carnegie Institution of Washington.
1972   *Excavations at Altar de Sacrificios: Architecture, Settlement, Burials, and Caches.* Peabody Museum of Archaeology and Ethnology Papers 62(2). Cambridge, Mass.: Harvard University.
1982   *Excavations at Seibal: Major Architecture and Caches.* Memoirs of the Peabody Museum of Archaeology and Ethnology 15(1). Cambridge, Mass.: Harvard University.

Smith, A. Ledyard, and Alfred V. Kidder
1951   *Excavations at Nebaj, Guatemala.* Carnegie Institution of Washington Publication 594. Washington, D.C.: Carnegie Institution.

Sugiyama, Saburo
1989   "Burials Dedicated to the Old Temple of Quetzalcoatl at Teotihuacan, Mexico." *American Antiquity* 54:85–106.
1991   "A Brief Summary of the Central Burials inside the Feathered Serpent Pyramid at Teotihuacan and Implications." Paper presented at the 56th Annual Meeting of the Society for American Archaeology, New Orleans.
1993a   "Rulership, Warfare, and Human Sacrifice at the Ciudadela: An Iconographic Study of Feathered Serpent Representations." In *Art, Ideology, and the City of Teotihuacan,* edited by Janet C. Berlo, 205–30. Washington, D.C.: Dumbarton Oaks.
1993b   "Worldview Materialized in Teotihuacan, Mexico." *Latin American Antiquity* 4(2): 103–29.

Taube, Karl A.
1988   "A Study of Classic Maya Scaffold Sacrifice." In *Maya Iconography,* edited by Elizabeth P. Benson and Gillett G. Griffin, 331–51. Princeton, N.J.: Princeton University Press.

Tedlock, Barbara
1982   *Time and the Highland Maya.* Albuquerque: University of New Mexico Press.

Tedlock, Dennis

1985   *Popol Vuh: The Definitive Edition of the Mayan Book of the Dawn of Life and the Glories of Gods and Kings.* New York: Simon and Schuster.

Thompson, J. Eric S.

1939   *Excavations at San Jose, British Honduras.* Carnegie Institution of Washington Publication 506. Washington, D.C.: Carnegie Institution.

1971 [1963] *Maya Archaeologist.* Norman: University of Oklahoma Press.

Tozzer, Alfred M.

1941   *Landa's Relacion de las cosas de Yucatán.* Translated by Alfred M. Tozzer. Papers of the Peabody Museum of American Archaeology and Ethnology 18. Cambridge, Mass.: Harvard University.

Turner, Victor W.

1969   *The Ritual Process: Structure and Anti-Structure.* Chicago: Aldine Publishing.

1977   "Introduction." In *The Transformation of the Hummingbird: Cultural Roots of a Zinacantecan Mythical Poem,* 25–32. Ithaca, N.Y.: Cornell University Press.

Vaillant, George C.

1938   "A Correlation of Archaeological and Historical Sequences in the Valley of Mexico." *American Anthropologist* n.s. 40:535–573.

Valdez, Fred, Jr.

1992   "Late Preclassic Architecture and Ritual at Rio Azul, Peten, Guatemala." Paper presented at the 57th Annual Meeting of the Society for American Archaeology, New Orleans.

Van Gennep, A.

1972   *The Rites of Passage.* Translated by M. B. Vizedom and G. L. Caffee. Chicago: University of Chicago Press.

Vogt, E. Z.

1969   *Zinacantán: A Maya Community in the Highlands of Chiapas.* Cambridge, Mass.: Belknap Press of Harvard University.

1976   *Tortillas for the Gods: A Symbolic Analysis of Zinacanteco Rituals.* Cambridge, Mass.: Harvard University Press.

PART ONE
Ethnographic Evidence from Mesoamerica

CHAPTER TWO

Zinacanteco Dedication and Termination Rituals

Evon Z. Vogt
Harvard University

I N THE HIGHLANDS OF CHIAPAS IN SOUTHEASTERN Mexico, the Tzotzil-Mayan-speaking Zinacantecos (now some 25,000 in population) perform dedication and termination rituals containing elements that have come down to them from Classic Maya times. As elsewhere in Mesoamerica, where almost all the Native American people were converted to Catholicism by the conquering Spaniards in the sixteenth century, these Zinacanteco rituals incorporate features from colonial Spanish and, more recently, Mexican culture. But thirty-five years of intensive ethnographic field research conducted by the Harvard Chiapas Project, which I initiated in 1957, has enabled scholars to sort out some of these pre-Columbian and post-Conquest features and to describe ritual patterns that appear to stem from pre-Columbian Mayan ceremonial life (see, for example, Bricker 1989). In this essay I will briefly describe some of the dedication and termination rituals currently practiced in Zinacantán and suggest some implications of these ceremonies for the understanding of ancient Mayan ritual and cosmology.

HOUSE DEDICATION RITUALS

When a new thatched-roof, wattle-and-daub house (or a more modern tile-roofed adobe house) is constructed,

two rites are performed: *hol chuk*, "binding the head of the roof," which takes place when the walls are completed and the roof rafters are in place; and *ch'ul kantela*, "holy candle," performed as soon as possible after the completion of the new house (Vogt 1969, 1990, 1993, 1994).

The building of a thatched-roof house in Zinacantán is a complex process that has been described in detail by Warfield (1966) and Vogt (1969, 1993). In the process of construction many materials, conceived as belonging to *yahval balamil* (the "Owner of the Earth" or Earth Lord), are used: earth, mud, saplings, trees cut into wall posts and rafters, dried pine needles (to mix with the mud for the walls), vines for lashing, tall grass for thatching the roof. It is crucially necessary to compensate the Earth Lord for these materials taken from his domain. This payment is provided in the house dedication ceremonies, which also serve to supply a *ch'ulel*, "inner soul," to the house, making it a part of living Zinacanteco society. Further, the ceremonies make an important statement as to how the house symbolizes social order and provides a small-scale model of the universe.

The *hol chuk* rite is performed when the walls are completed and the rafters are in place. This simple ritual does not require a shaman; the workers who are constructing the house direct and perform it. They first suspend a long rope from the peak of the house. The end of the rope marks the

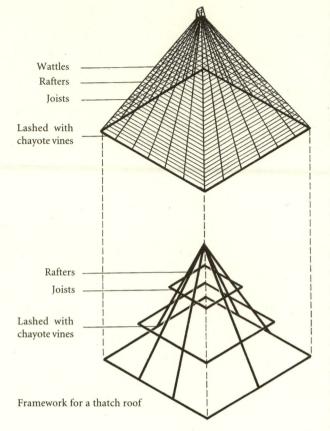

Wattles
Rafters
Joists

Lashed with
chayote vines

Rafters
Joists

Lashed with
chayote vines

Framework for a thatch roof

Fig. 2.1.   Framework for a thatch roof.

center of the floor, and a hole about 30 cm deep is dug at this point. Then four black chickens (one for each *chikin na,* "corner of the house") are tied to the end of the rope by their feet in such a way that their heads are concealed in the center hole. The chickens' heads are cut off and buried in this hole; women later cook the chickens for a ceremonial meal, following which the feathers, bones, and scraps are added to the center hole as an offering to the Earth Lord.

Two of the men then climb up onto the framework of the roof and "feed" it chicken broth and sugarcane liquor (called Pox in Tzotzil) by pouring both liquids on the four corners of the joints on each of the three levels (see below) and on the peak of the roof where the rafters come together (fig. 2.1). The rite culminates with the workers eating the chickens and drinking cane liquor, which is considered "the dew of the gods" (Vogt 1993:52). The seating order at these ceremonial meals is always the same: the table is oriented with its head (where the ancestral gods are believed to sit) toward the rising sun and its foot toward the setting sun. The participants are seated in small chairs at the sides and foot of the table in a strict rank-order: The senior man sits at the southeast corner, the next senior across from him. The third man sits to the left of the most senior man, and so on (fig. 2.2). This rank-order arrangement is a compromise between two basic principles: that the highest ranking man sits closest to the rising sun, and that higher ranking men have junior men seated on their left (Vogt 1990:128, 1993:4).

The second rite, *ch'ul kantela,* is performed as soon as possible after the completion of a new house. A shaman is engaged to perform this ceremony, which not only offers further compensation for the Earth Lord but also summons the ancestral gods to provide the house with an

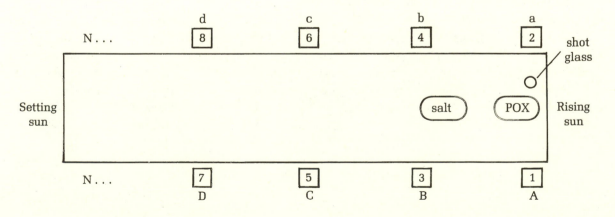

Fig. 2.2.   Rank-order of participants at a ritual meal.

innate soul. It is significant that a shaman is called *h'ilol,* literally "seer" in Tzotzil, for he or she has the power to "see" into the mountains and thereby to "see" and to communicate directly with the ancestral gods who dwell in the mountains surrounding the Zinacanteco hamlets and ceremonial center.

The participants in this second rite include the house owner and his immediate family, as well as his father and brothers and their wives and children, in this patrilineal, patrilocal social system of the Zinacantecos.

The ritual begins with the "planting" of the *krus ta ti'na,* "cross at the edge of the house" or "house door," in the patio just outside the new house. It is placed parallel to the two doorless sides of the house and is usually oriented so that prayers to this shrine will be offered in the direction of the rising sun. Three stakes are driven into the ground, and the shaman lashes the wooden cross to the center one because the cross (which is to be used as a channel of communication with the ancestral gods) must not touch the domain of the Earth Lord, which begins at ground level (Vogt 1993:44).

While musicians (violinist, harpist, guitarist, seated in that rank-order) play, three pine tree tops are tied to the cross, and bundles of red geraniums are attached to the pine. Fresh pine needles are spread in front, and white wax candles are lighted as copal incense burns in a censer and the shaman kneels and prays. As the white wax candles burn down, the ancestral gods are believed to be eating them as tortillas; the smoking incense provides cigarettes for them.

The shaman continues the ritual inside the new house, which has a fresh carpet of pine needles covering the floor. He first prays over the candles lying on the ritual table, which has been set just to the east of the center of the house. An assistant of the shaman then hangs a rope from the peak of the house, the end of which again marks the center of the floor, where a hole is dug, making certain that the remnants of the previously sacrificed chickens remain in the cavity.

A number of black roosters and hens corresponding to the number and sex of the family members are hung by their feet at the end of the rope. With the exception of one black rooster saved for later burial in the center hole, their heads are cut off and the blood is allowed to drain into the hole. The bodies of the chickens are scalded with hot water, plucked, and prepared for eating; their heads and feathers are buried with the blood as another offering to the Earth Lord.

The shaman then censes the remaining black rooster, kills it by pulling the neck, and pours a shot of liquor and a handful of earth over it. He then buries the entire bird in the center "grave," head toward rising sun—the burial position for unbaptized children. After the earth is tamped in on top, in the same manner used when a human body is buried in a cemetery, a small wooden cross about 30 cm high is planted at the east end of the grave and decorated with pine tips and red geraniums (Vogt 1993:52).

Each person present then comes forward to "meet" the white wax candles on the ritual table. The house owner, holding a bundle of pine tips, prays to the gods in traditional couplets:

In the sacred name of the holy God,
    Jesus Christ.
Take heed, holy torches,
    Take heed, holy candles,
    Take heed, holy alms.
Take heed, my Father,
    Take heed, my Lord!
Thou art ready,
    Thou art set.
Take heed, my Father,
    Take heed, my Lord!
They go to stand erect,
    They go to stand firm.
At the thresholds [i.e., the shrines at foot and summit of sacred mountains],
    At the altars,
Of the holy Fathers,
    The holy Mothers,
Is there still holy pardon,
    Is there still divine forgiveness? ...

So I beg holy pardon,
    So I beg divine forgiveness,
With my spouse,
    With my companion,
With my two gifts,
    With my two travails [i.e., children of house owner] ...

Favor my back,
    Favor my side,
It is only a little I want,
    It is only a bit I wish,
Like some of my Fathers,
    Like some of my Mothers,

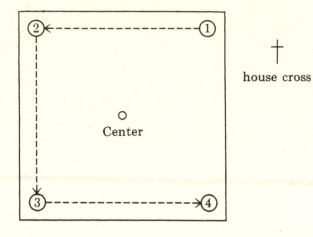

house cross

Center

Fig. 2.3. Counterclockwise procession to the four inside corners of the new house.

center, they sprinkle chicken broth and liquor on the corners and middle joints of the beams and on the lower ends of the six rafters.

After lighting white wax and tallow candles in the center of the house, the shaman washes the heads, arms, and hands of all persons who will live there. The family members bathe in water that usually contains three sacred plants: *tsis 'uch,* a wild laurel tree (*litsea glaucescens* HBK); *'aha-te'es,* a wild myrtle tree (*Gaultheria odorata* Willd.); and *vishobtakil,* one of several varieties of *pepperomia* that grows on the lower branches of oak and other trees in the evergreen cloud forest of Chiapas. They put on freshly washed and censed clothing. Then the entire ceremonial group sits down for a ritual meal of tortillas and chicken (Vogt 1993:54).

Following the meal, the shaman prepares the candles and flowers for a pilgrimage to the mountain shrines. As the procession leaves the house, its owner chants (in part) to those remaining there:

> God,
>   My Lord,
> See here, my Father,
>   See here, my Lord,
> May I pass before Thy glorious face,
>   May I pass before Thy glorious eyes ...
>
> I shall step,
>   I shall walk,
> To the four thresholds,
>   To the four altars,
> Of the Holy Fathers,
>   Of the Holy Mothers.
>
> For this, my lowly mouth departs,
>   For this my humble lips depart,
> For this, my holy chunk of incense,
>   For this, my humble cloud of smoke,
> For this, my three lowly torches,
>   For this, my three humble candles,
> I go to beg holy pardon,
>   I go to beg divine forgiveness ...
>
> (Laughlin 1980:216–17)

> The hot ones,
>   The warm ones [i.e., the ancestral gods who are believed
> to contain the maximum possible amount of heat],
> Those gathered together,
>   Those joined together,
> With their gifts,
>   With their travails.
> I only wish the same, my Father,
>   I only wish the same, my Lord ...
> May I not yet reach the mountaintop,
>   May I not yet reach the hilltop,
> May I not yet clothe myself with dirt,
>   May I not yet clothe myself with mud.[1]
>
> (Vogt 1993:53–54)

The shaman then leads a procession counterclockwise to each of the inside four corners of the new house, where three pine tips from the bundle held by the house owner are planted and decorated with red geraniums; he plants and lights candles (usually two white wax ones for the ancestral gods and one tallow one for the Earth Lord) and prays at each corner (fig. 2.3).

The shaman likewise pours chicken broth and sugar-cane liquor on the four corner posts and on the center of the four walls. Assistants then climb onto the ceiling joists and "feed" the meal to the roof. Beginning with the

After chanting another long prayer at the house cross, the members of the procession depart for the mountains in rank-order: the miscellaneous assistants out front, then the flower carrier, the candle carrier, the wife of the house owner, the house owner, and the shaman at the rear. Ordinarily, four sacred mountains are visited—*san kishtoval, mushul vits, sisil vits,* and lastly *kalvario* (where the ancestral gods are believed to have their meetings). At the foot and summit of each of these sacred mountains candles, incense, liquor, and prayers are offered to the ancestral gods. The ceremony takes place in one day and ordinarily lasts several hours, but may be longer if the ritual group is required to wait in line behind other ritualists from different households to finish their rites at the mountain shrines.

Returning to the house cross, prayers are again chanted (see Laughlin 1980 for additional prayers in the ritual). The procession then enters the house, lights more candles, and prays at the center grave of the rooster. The men don their hats and black ceremonial robes and dance to the music of the violin, harp, and guitar. Finally, the formal part of the ceremony ends with a ritual meal (Vogt 1993:54).

For the next three days the house must be carefully attended, for it now possesses an inner soul and requires special care, "just like a newborn child" or "a sick person" following a curing ceremony. The small cross remains at the grave of the sacrificed rooster; it is later removed and used for various purposes—for example, to protect the corn stored in the house (Vogt 1992:257). In these days following the ritual, the family members must all remain at home and begin to place their hair combings in the cracks of the walls, signifying their occupancy and belonging in this new house (Bardrick 1970).

Upon reading the house dedication rites, perhaps the first question that arises concerns what elements are from Spanish culture of the sixteenth century and which could be pre-Columbian Mayan. Unquestionably, much of the paraphernalia used in the rites and some of the words in the prayers were introduced by the Spaniards: chickens, sugarcane liquor, wooden crosses, candles, red geraniums, and the words for God, Jesus Christ, and the saints in the prayers. But a case can be made that chickens replaced the aboriginal turkeys (and/or iguanas: see Tozzer 1941:148) and that distilled sugarcane liquor was a successor to pre-Columbian fermented *chicha.* The form of the cross, signifying the world tree, was clearly present among the Classic Maya, for example, in the iconography at Palenque (Vogt 1992). As for the wax and tallow candles, we know that the pre-Columbian Yucatec Maya gathered beeswax (Tozzer 1941:193), but the only references to candles are post-Conquest, so they must be reckoned as a Spanish introduction. On the other hand,

the Zinacantecos clearly conceptualize the candles as tortillas, and we know both from the chronicles (Tozzer 1941:148) and from contemporary ethnographic reports (e.g., Redfield and Villa Rojas 1934:129, 146) that the Yucatec Maya offered tortillas to the gods and still do so. While the red geraniums were clearly introduced from Europe (Vogt 1993:70), the Highlands of Chiapas have many varieties of native red flowers that could have been used in pre-Conquest times. Although many Tzotzil prayers now begin with references to God and Jesus Christ, they move on to words and concepts that have little or nothing to do with Catholic theology or cosmology. Indeed, the Christian terms seen to serve as a kind of frame to convey the impression that the prayers are Catholic, much as the presence of hundreds of crosses in Zinacantán conveys the false impression that the Zinacantecos must be among the most Catholic people in the world (Vogt and Vogt 1980:517).

Once we account for these various introduced elements, the basic forms and meanings of the house dedication rites appear to me to derive from ancient Mayan concepts and practices.

INTERPRETATIONS OF HOUSE RITUALS

Apart from the hints I have offered in the description, what symbolic meanings are conveyed by these dedicatory rites for a new house? At this more abstract level of analysis, I suggest three critical sets of meanings.

First, it is clear that the dedication rites employ symbols representing reciprocal transactions between the Zinacantecos and the Earth Lord: Offerings are made in an effort to compensate him for incursions into and the use of materials from his domain. The candle offerings made inside the house always consist of both white wax (symbolizing tortillas) and tallow (symbolizing meat) candles, because, as the Zinacantecos put it, the Earth Lord, being like "a fat and greedy Ladino [descendant of the Spanish conquerors]," craves meat with his tortillas. By contrast, candle offerings at the house cross and to the ancestral shrines at the foot and summit of the sacred mountains are entirely white wax: The ancestral gods are Indians who always eat tortillas, but who eat meat only rarely.

But offerings of candles are not enough. If the Earth Lord does not receive other gifts, he may someday capture the souls of the inhabitants of the house and put them to work as slaves for many years, until the "iron sandals he gives them all wear out." At the very least, he will make the "earth move" under the house and frighten its inhabitants. Thus, chickens, symbolizing the residents of the new house, are offered as substitutes. In the Holy Candle rite, the chickens suspended from the peak of the house and beheaded over the central hole are a gift of "souls" as their blood flows directly into the Earth Lord's domain. Although their flesh is consumed in the ritual meal, the heads and feathers are placed in the hole, so that in the end the substitutes are the property of the Earth Lord.

The black rooster is a symbolic replacement for the male owner of the house, the person ultimately responsible for this incursion into the Earth Lord's domain. It represents a prestation of both body and soul—an unblemished, undivided whole—as it is ritually interred in the "grave" in the center of the earthen floor of the new house.

Second, the house rites focus on an important ritual transition: Materials belonging to the Earth Lord are transferred into the Zinacanteco social order or, in Lévi-Strauss's (1966) terms, from Nature to Culture. Just as fences and gates constructed later will emphasize the property rights of the family and protect against outsiders who seek to impose or interfere, so the ritual circuit around the four corners inside the house delineates the area safe from "demons" and from the Earth Lord. The close attention paid to the exact center of the house at both the ground and roof levels serves in part to protect against the "demons," which try to enter especially at these places because, being farthest from the corners, they are least protected (Bardrick 1970). After a successful house circuit, the Earth Lord can never capture the souls of family members who happen to fall down inside the house, nor can demons enter the house.

Placing the house cross (through which communication with the soul of the house takes place) in the patio during the dedication ritual symbolizes the transformation of a mere physical structure into one with a soul, with a place in and significance for society. Note that the cross itself is kept apart from the territory of the Earth Lord by being tied to a stake pushed into the earth rather than inserted directly into the ground. The pine needles strewn in front of the cross for ritual occasions further demarcate the domain of the Earth Lord from that of the living Zinacantecos by creating a dividing carpet. Prayers that refer to the house as "my eyes' awakening" and "my heart's repose" also emphasize the safety and the civilized nature of the space.

Such boundary-defining activity—"framing," in Douglas's terms (1966:63–64)—of houses serves to protect, to keep in and nourish the souls of houses, and to shut out demons, the evil, powerful symbols of disorder. The process of socialization in these rites is similar to the "embracing" performed by godparents in the baptismal rite, by shamans in a curing ceremony, and by parents toward their young children. In each case, objects or persons not fully incorporated into the Zinacanteco social order are looked after, cared for, guided into their proper role in society. Continued "embracing" necessitates an order within, a sustained orderliness on the part of the person or thing embraced, and the person or thing must ceaselessly conform to the principles of civilized order endorsed by the ancestral gods. Thus the house ceremonies not only create social order, but also perpetuate it in the family shelter that is crucial for Zinacanteco life (Vogt 1993:59).

Third, houses and their dedication rituals also provide visual small-scale models of the quincuncial universe in which the Zinacantecos live. According to the Zinacantecos, the universe was created by the *vashak-men*, gods who support it at its corners and who designated the center, *mishik' balamil*, "navel of the world," in Zinacantán Center. Houses have corresponding corner posts and precisely determined centers, which are strongly emphasized in the dedicatory rites.

Houses also provide an image of the vertical divisions in the universe: The Earth Lord who lives in the Underworld is represented by the earthen floor and the area beneath where the sacrificial chickens are buried. A second vertical division consists of the majestic sacred mountains, which house the ancestral gods and rise to peaks above, and in opposition to, the domain of the Earth Lord. This mountain part of the universe is mirrored in the structure of the house roof, not only in the striking visual similarity between mountain and roof shapes but also, more significantly, in the use of identical body terms for the two. *Yok,* "its foot," refers to both the foot of a mountain and the foundation of a house; *sch'ut,* "its stomach," is the midpoint of a mountainside as well as the wall of a house; *schikin,* "its ear" or "its corner," refers to the corners of both houses and mountains; and *shol,* "its head," can be a mountaintop or a housetop (Vogt 1993:58).

Rising above the holy mountains is a quincuncial space with the three layers of *vinahel,* "sky": in the lowest the female moon traverses the sky each night, in the middle are the stars that provide light above and below, and in the uppermost layer the male sun travels along his path each day. Similarly, a Zinacanteco roof structure has three conceptual "layers," marked by the three sets of joists. These are emphasized during the *hol chuk* rite when ritualists climb to each layer and offer chicken broth and liquor to the gods at each of the all-important corners and the center (the peak of the roof).

The critically important binary opposition between rising and setting sun is symbolically represented in the allocation of space inside a Zinacanteco house: the men's side is toward the "rising sun," with the house altar against the eastern wall; the women's side of the house, with the hearth and the metates and the cooking pots and *comales,* is toward the "setting sun." The men's side (in this patrilineal, patrilocal social system) symbolizes maleness, hotness, aboveness, oldness, and higher rank; the women's side, femaleness, coldness, belowness, youngness, and lower rank (Gossen 1972).

Termination Rituals

The most important termination ritual in Zinacantán consists of the rites that take place at the death of a person. Death, in the view of the Zinacantecos, does not result from "natural causes." It may result from soul loss; from having one's animal spirit companion released from its corral and shot in the woods; from having one's innate soul sold irrevocably to the Earth Lord; or, much less commonly, from physical injury.

Most Zinacantecos die on their reed mats on the earthen floors of their houses. At the moment of death, whichever of the thirteen parts of the innate soul remain in the body depart. The scarf (for a man) or the shawl (for a woman) is placed over the head, covering the mouth. An old man or old woman with a different surname (i.e., from another lineage) is called upon to bathe the corpse with laurel and myrtle leaves before it becomes too stiff to handle. A very elderly person is selected because there is always a danger that the soul of the deceased will take others to the grave with him.

The corpse is dressed in either clean or new clothes and placed on a petate that is turned upside-down and covered by a blanket that is turned wrong side to the body. The head is placed toward the setting sun—the opposite of the sleeping position of living Zinacantecos—and the area is fenced off within the house by household articles.

A pine coffin is purchased from a local carpenter either in Zinacantán Center or in San Cristóbal de las Casas. While awaiting its arrival, relatives and neighbors gather in the house to contribute money, which is placed in a plate by the body. The money is later used to purchase candles for rituals at the cemetery. Then, if anyone knows the Catholic Pater Noster—and few do—it is recited. Three musicians—violinist, harpist, and guitarist—are summoned to entertain the soul of the deceased.

When the coffin arrives, the body is placed in it with head toward the rising sun, unless it is an unbaptized child, in which case the head points toward the setting sun. A rooster's head is set in a bowl of chicken broth beside the head of the deceased along with some tortillas and salt. Three small bags of money are placed with the body, one tied at the belt where a Zinacanteco purse is normally carried, the other two hidden at the sides. At the foot of the corpse are set a small bowl and a gourd with water; these are the drinking dishes needed by the soul. A small sack of charred, ground tortillas (food unlike that consumed by the living) is added for food. An all-night wake follows, during which the musicians play, sugarcane liquor is served, and a ritual meal is provided at which the rooster (whose head was placed in the coffin) is eaten (Vogt 1969:217–218). During the wake, many address the dead in ritual speeches. The following is an example of a ritual speech a wife uses (in part) to mourn her dead spouse:

Oh God, what are you doing?
    Oh God, why are you dying?

Oh Lord,
    If you abandon me here all alone,
If sickness can be resisted no longer,
    If the end can be avoided no longer,
My husband,
    My companion,
Who will I talk with here,
    Who will I speak to here?..
Our fathers,
    Our mothers,
Let our fathers patiently open their hearts,
    Let our mothers patiently open their hearts,
Perhaps into eternity,
    They do not die,
    They do not pass away,
May they plant their corn,
    May they plant their roots ...

(Pope 1969:8–9).

At dawn another ritual meal is served, and preparations are made for the trip to the cemetery. All in the house cry openly and loudly to express their grief. The coffin is closed and carried outside, where it is fastened to two long poles that will rest on the shoulders of the four pallbearers. If the deceased was a married woman, her husband is expected to state publicly whom he plans to marry as the coffin is being removed from the house. (A Zinacanteco man does not know how to make tortillas and would starve to death without a wife to prepare these essential food staples.) Since there is a strong belief that the soul of the deceased wishes to take family, friends, and possessions with it, there are ritual acts to protect the survivors and block off the channels to the Underworld. An adult woman is asked to lead in these rites, which consist of spitting saltwater on the spot where the coffin has been located during the wake, as well as in all the places around the house and patio where the deceased has worked, walked, and slept, "in order to loosen the soul from the house" and prevent it from returning. In some hamlets, the house cross is also pulled up and set against the fence at the side of the patio to remove the ritual entrance into the house so that the soul cannot find its way back.

The funeral procession is led by the musicians; then comes the coffin, carried by the pallbearers (who are compadres or neighbors of the deceased, specifically not brothers or close relatives); next the men, including the assistants who will dig the grave; then the women (led by the widow, if the deceased was a man); and finally the young women and children (whose souls are least firmly attached to their bodies). There are always customary, fixed resting places along the route to the cemetery at which the procession stops. At these places the coffin is opened, candles are lighted and prayers are said, the corpse is given water to drink by an old woman, either from a red geranium or with her finger, and everyone drinks cane liquor.

Upon arrival at the cemetery, the coffin is set down and another round of liquor is served. The gravediggers start digging the grave; when it is half-finished, another round of cane liquor is served. Any bones encountered from previous burials are kept on the side to be buried again with the coffin. Several symbolic actions are taken to discourage the dead from returning and taking more souls away. After the grave is finished, a pick and shovel are left crossed on top of the grave while the workers drink *pozol* (uncooked maize dough mixed with cold water). Every half-hour or so the deceased is given another drink of water to relieve his thirst. The children who are present step up to the open coffin and kick the side so that the deceased will not take their souls with him.

As the coffin is closed for the final time and lowered halfway into the grave, with its head pointed to the setting sun, another round of liquor is served. The coffin is then lowered the rest of the way, and all present throw three handfuls of earth over it.

The filling of the grave is done in "six strips." When it is half-filled (three strips), the grave objects are put in, just on top of any bones that have been unearthed from previous burials. These objects (which have been removed from the coffin before it is closed for the final time) include, for a man, his hat with the edges burned and the black bands ripped in three places ("so they won't turn into snakes") and his sandals with the high backs cut ("so they won't turn into bull's horns and gore the soul"). For a woman, the woolen shawl is cut at the corners ("so it won't turn into a ram"). Additional grave objects include a cup, a plate, a needle and ball of thread, a married person's rosary, a woman's hair comb, necklaces, blankets, and old clothes, as well as any special mementos prized by the deceased—all of which are said to possess the soul of their owner.

Finally, the grave is completely filled and covered with fresh pine needles. A simple wooden cross is erected at the head of the grave and adorned with pine tips and red geraniums. Three candles are lighted in a pit (to prevent them from being blown out by the wind) in front of the cross: two of white wax and one of tallow, to feed both the ancestral gods and the Earth Lord. The grave is now called "the house of the dead"; in some hamlets, boards, or even a thatched roof, are erected over the grave.

There are some major variations in these patterns as described here. A pregnant woman has the fetus removed before burial; a deceased woman's weaving is finished for her. If a cargoholder dies, he is buried in the clothes in which he was sworn into office, and two *regidores* (second rank of cargoholders) come to the house to swear him out of office. Anyone killed violently is buried without grave goods and without a day of rest before burial (Vogt 1969:220).

After the soul leaves the body, it retraces the course of its life in the body, gathering up all pieces of flesh, hair, or nail left behind. The journey keeps the potentially dangerous soul away from the house during the wake. This first journey is followed by another, more arduous, to *k'otebal*, "the place of arrival"; here the soul must cross a large river on the back of a black dog and follow a trail to a junction marked by a cross shrine. It learns from the crow of the black rooster (whose head was buried with the body) whether it will continue on the broad road to *k'atin-bak*, "place warmed by bones," a deep hole inside the earth, or on a narrow crooked path to *vinahel*. Unless a person has seriously deviated from the moral code of the Zinacantecos, his soul may take the path to *vinahel*, which is much like an earthly Zinacantán with similar social responsibilities. If someone has sinned and is condemned by his kinsmen and neighbors as a witch or is murdered, public denunciation and ritual neglect may characterize the funeral, and the soul is banished to *k'atin-bak* (Vogt 1993:23).

A great deal of ritual activity continues to be directed toward creating and maintaining a new relationship with the immortal innate soul of the one who has died. Cemeteries are visited on Sundays, especially by the women in the family of the deceased, and candles, copal incense, and prayers are offered. On All Saints' Day special rituals are performed focused on this interaction between the living and the dead. All Zinacanteco families spend a day in the cemetery placing gifts of food and liquor on the graves, burning incense, lighting candles, and praying to their dead, as the three usual musicians play and sing, and all drink cane liquor. Miniature tables (loaded with food and liquor) and chairs are set up in the house for return visits by the souls of the dead on the following day. (For more details on the funeral and burial rites see Pope 1967, 1969.)

As for Spanish versus Maya elements in these ceremonies, I have found it difficult to sort out the cultural derivation of the various episodes. For while a Catholic priest is never involved and the Pater Noster is seldom recited, many of the ritual sequences are performed in funerals and burials in Spain and among the Ladinos in Chiapas. The elements and sequences that appear to be more Mayan than Catholic Spanish are these: the use of copal incense; the relatively elaborated customs about grave goods, including food and drink and vessels in which to consume these; the cutting, burning, or breaking of many items of the grave goods associated with the deceased; and the spreading of pine needles over the grave.

INTERPRETATIONS OF DEATH RITES

The first episodes in the death rituals provide a setting for the grief process of the bereaved to play out, but at the same time they move quickly and systematically to close the conduits between the world of the living and that of the dead. The spitting of salt (which serves as a barrier or insulator, unlike cane liquor that opens channels of communication between humans and between humans and gods in Zinacantán); the turning of reed mats upside down and blankets inside out; the ripping of hats; and the charring of tortillas: These are all actions to differentiate the dead from the living and to close the portals to the afterlife.

Once the soul of the deceased has completed its journeys (with the aid of water and food provided by the survivors) and has been safely locked into the other world, the deceased is transformed into an honored ancestor, and the continuing rites emphasize an ongoing interaction between the living Zinacantecos and their ancestral gods. Not only are offerings of food and prayers provided each Sunday for the dead, but at All Saints Day each November the living take generous offerings of food to the graves and spend a whole day in the cemeteries with the dead while musicians play and sing. Then the ancestors come to visit the living in their homes, where more offerings of food and liquor are set out on miniature tables with chairs for each of the remembered deceased relatives. (The food is especially generous for the dead who have left rights to land to their successors.) This rite "provides for the dead's rightful re-entry into the world of the living—it transforms a deceased person from a potentially destructive ghost into a welcome and beneficent ancestor" (Pope 1969:56). Furthermore, there is daily interaction between the living and the dead in the form of dreams in which the souls of ancestors regularly communicate with the souls of people and provide advice, warnings, and prophecies. Since the traditional Zinacantecos believe that the ancestors are models of ideal behavior and decorum and possess infinite knowledge about the world, the ongoing interaction between the living and the dead looms large in the maintenance of contemporary Zinacanteco society.[2]

ACKNOWLEDGMENTS

I am indebted to Robert M. Laughlin for comments and criticisms of this paper.

NOTES

1. These last four lines refer to a human burial in a cemetery; cemeteries are almost always located on hilltops or mountain ridges.

2. Other termination rituals in Zinacantán, which I do not have space to describe here, include the interesting end-of-office rites performed by cargoholders in the ceremonial center. For example, when a *mayordomo* finishes his year in office, there is a ceremonial dismantling of his house altar that is accompanied by special prayers, songs, and dances, with wailing and sobbing, which speak about the "seating" place of the saint with whom the *mayordomo* is especially associated (Laughlin 1980:278–282). Likewise, when the year of service ends for the four *regidores,* they cry with sorrow over ending their cargos, and then break and burn their staffs of office (Vogt 1969:512).

REFERENCES CITED

Bardrick, J. Lauren
 1970 Face to Face with the Gods: A Study of Ritual Order and Holiness in Zinacantán." Summer Field Report, Harvard Chiapas Project, Peabody Museum, Harvard University.

Bricker, Victoria R.
 1989 "The Calendrical Meaning of Ritual among the Maya." In *Ethnographic Encounters in Southern Mesoamerica: Essays in Honor of Evon Z. Vogt, Jr.,* edited by Victoria R. Bricker and Gary H. Gossen, 231–50. Austin: University of Texas Press.

Douglas, Mary
 1966 *Purity and Danger.* London: Routledge and Kegan Paul.

Gossen, Gary H.
 1972 "Temporal and Spatial Equivalents in Chamula Ritual Symbolism." In *Reader in Comparative Religion: An Anthropological Approach,* 3rd ed., edited by William A. Lessa and Evon Z. Vogt, 135–49. New York: Harper and Row.

Laughlin, Robert M.
 1980 *Of Shoes and Ships and Sealing Wax: Sundries from Zinacantán.* Smithsonian Contributions to Anthropology 25. Washington, D.C.: Smithsonian Institution Press.

Lévi-Strauss, Claude
 1966 *The Savage Mind.* Chicago: University of Chicago Press.

Pope, Carolyn C.
 1967 "Good for the Soul: Cemeteries in Zinacantán." Summer Field Report, Harvard Chiapas Project, Peabody Museum, Harvard University.
 1969 "The Funeral Ceremony in Zinacantán." A.B. honors thesis, Harvard University.

Redfield, Robert, and Alfonso Villa Rojas
 1934 *Chan Kom: A Maya Village.* Chicago: University of Chicago Press.

Tozzer, Alfred M.
 1941 *Landa's "Relacion de las Cosas de Yucatan."* Papers of the Peabody Museum of American Archaeology and Ethnology 28.

Vogt, Evon Z.
 1969 *Zinacantán: A Maya Community in the Highlands of Chiapas.* Cambridge: Harvard University Press.
 1990 *The Zinacantecos of Mexico: A Modern Maya Way of Life.* Forth Worth: Holt, Rinehart and Winston.
 1992 "Cruces Indias y Bastones de Mando en Mesoamerica." In *De Palabra y Obra en el Nuevo Mundo 2: Encuentros Interetnicas,* edited by Manuel Gutierrez Estevez, Miguel Leon-Portilla, Gary H. Gossen, and J. Jorge Klor de Alba, 249–94. Madrid: Siglo XXI de España Editores, S.A.; Mexico City: Siglo XXI Editores.
 1993 *Tortillas for the Gods: A Symbolic Analysis of Zinacanteco Rituals.* Norman: University of Oklahoma Press.
 1994 *Fieldwork among the Maya: Reflections on the Harvard Chiapas Project.* Albuquerque: University of New Mexico Press.

Vogt, Evon Z., and Catherine C. Vogt
 1980 "Pre-Columbian Mayan and Mexican Symbols in Zinacanteco Ritual." In *La Antropologia Americanista en la Actualidad: Homenaje a Raphael Girard,* 1:499-523. Mexico City: Editores Mexicanos Unidos.

Warfield, James P.
 1966 "La Arquitectura en Zinacantán." *Los Zinacantecos: Un Pueblo Tzotzil de Los Altos de Chiapas,* edited by Evon Z. Vogt, 183–207. Mexico City: Instituto Nacional Indigenista.

CHAPTER THREE

Seven Ingredients in Mesoamerican Ensoulment
Dedication and Termination in Tenejapa

Brian Stross
University of Texas at Austin

Many peoples in the western world believe that only humans have souls, while all other things, animate and inanimate, lack them. Spaniards arriving in Mesoamerica even questioned for a time whether the indigenous Mesoamerican peoples themselves had souls. Native Mesoamericans, however, attributed a soul to all living things and considered all of nature to be alive.[1]

Early Mesoamericans, and among them the Mayans, surely reckoned, as do their modern descendants, that the souls of useful natural things—entities such as maize, deer, fruit trees, caves, and lakes (Alcorn 1984:78)—are protected by deities and need nourishment, encouragement, and respect (Laughlin 1975:155). When harvested or otherwise used by humans, these things were and are accorded continuing respect. Then as now, products of human manufacture, such as temples, houses, altars, and censers, also required nourishment, encouragement, protection, and respectful treatment—but first they had to be animated or imbued with life. Accordingly, they were ceremonially given a soul and sometimes a heart. According to such a world view, the entire world is alive. For cultural artifacts to become useful parts of the world, they must be brought to life—given a soul—and then nourished. Sometimes cultural artifacts simply acquire the souls of their owners.[2] In this essay, I argue that for Mesoamericans the process of creating and animating cultural artifacts was and is analogous to the birth process, while abandoning or destroying such artifacts was akin to death.

These interpretations of ancient world view and behavior, of dedication and termination events that took place in the past, for which only archaeological remains can give direct testimony, are profoundly informed by modern ethnographic data on similar events occurring in indigenous communities of Mesoamerica (see Freidel et al. 1993). The depth and resilience of the Mesoamerican world view persisted in spite of the invading Spaniards, who never conquered that aspect of the indigenous heritage.

To indigenous Mesoamericans—including the Mayans of today as well as the Classic Maya living more than a millennium ago—the life cycle from birth to death and back characterizes all things having souls. In the case of a building, the dedication is the ritual practice marking its figurative birth, while the termination ritual indicates its metaphoric death. Therefore, a knowledge of the birth process and of ritual practices attending birth can meaningfully inform our interpretation of dedication rituals, which share ritual elements metaphorically related to those attending other births. Similarly, death and mortuary customs lend insight into termination rituals.

Beyond looking to dedication and termination rituals in modern Mayan societies for information on their meaning for the Classic Maya, we can also look at the human life cycle and its social construction by modern Maya for information relevant to the forms and meanings of Classic Maya dedication and termination rituals. In the remainder of this essay, this claim is examined and illustrated with relevant Tzeltal Mayan ethnographic data on house dedication, birth customs, and death ritual.

ANIMATING THE INANIMATE

Of major importance for understanding the place of dedication (or animation) and termination (or de-animation) rituals is knowing how one goes about animating the various material things made by humans. In Mesoamerica this is accomplished by performing several actions, perhaps better viewed as processes. These actions may be manifest or latent, fully expressed or attenuated, overt or covert, and they are usually expressed ceremonially through ritual. As Monaghan (this volume) emphasizes, while rejecting the word *ritual*, these actions inform every step of the construction. They include seven chief components, ingredients, or processes.

1. *Purifying, cleaning, and sweeping.* These are different words for what might be seen as a single element in the ritual animation and dedication of an artifact. Usually this is accomplished by fasting, sweeping, censing, or some combination of these, but other means are known, including chanting, dripping water, and washing with special soap.
2. *Measuring.* To measure a thing is equivalent to giving it a place in space (and time), assigning it boundaries that can be defined in other terms. Measurement need not be done as overtly as with a tape measure; all that is necessary is to have some culturally relevant means of comparing the length and/or position of the artifact with something else.
3. *Naming.* To assign a name to a thing is equivalent to giving the thing a place in the human mind, thus assigning it mental boundaries. Names may be given to the parts of a thing in replication of the process of manufacture, as a metaphorical process of gestation and birth. Names may be spoken or pronounced in the form of chanting or singing, as with the Yekuana of South America, who sing their woven baskets into existence (Guss 1989).

4. *Assigning guardianship.* To assign guardianship of a thing means to give it an owner and protector—a deity, parent, or owner. Whereas a child's parents are assigned according to relatively inflexible rules by the society into which the child is born, deities or ancestor spirits assigned to guardianship over a manufactured item may be chosen somewhat more freely by the person making the assignment, often a shaman. The names of these deities or ancestors are ritually announced in a formulaic way, thus linking them to the item and its destiny.
5. *Transferring or transmitting "animateness."* To transfer to the manufactured item the quality of "animateness" from a human, animal, or other living entity is equivalent to bringing an artifact to life—in other words, giving it a soul. This can be accomplished simply by using the item (Laughlin 1975:139) or by having life blown, breathed, or spit into it by a shaman. Sometimes the life quality is transmitted by touching or laying on of hands. The life force may be even be painted onto a thing with real or symbolic blood (see McGee, this volume). Sometimes the life force is transferred from one entity to another by sacrificing the first. For example, in Mesoamerican communities where a pole symbolizing the World Tree is ceremonially erected on the village plaza to enact the *volador* ceremony, a living chicken is crushed to death at the bottom of the hole as the pole is erected, which transfers its life force to the World Tree. Tzeltal, Tzotzil, and Tojolabal Mayan consultants have said that similar sacrifices with human victims have taken place in historical times as a final phase of bridge construction in Chiapas, in order to provide the bridge with a soul, giving it strength to withstand the forces of nature.[3]
6. *Clothing the thing.* To clothe something is equivalent to giving it protection by means of a covering or shield that functions also as a boundary between the thing and the rest of the natural world. When human beings put on clothes, we are covering particular parts of the body and showing that we are social beings. Sometimes our clothing embellishes or draws attention to the parts of the body that are covered, but here the covering function is more important. Covering something—clothing it—functions to protect or hide it, or both, and that is why we can see it as a protective shield. Just as our clothing establishes a social

as well as a physical boundary between our bodies and what is outside of our bodies, the covering of a thing constructed and then animated establishes its boundaries and mediates its relationship with the external world.

7. *Feeding.* To feed something is equivalent to maintaining its animateness. All that is animate must be sustained or maintained with some sort of feeding. The "food" may seem surprising on occasion. For example, Zinacanteco Tzotzil Mayans consider the smoke from white candles to be "tortillas" for the gods, while the smoke from burning copal incense is referred to as their "cigarettes" (see Vogt 1993 [1976]:1, this volume). Nevertheless, such items are legitimate and appropriate sustenance that serve the ritual purpose.

Animating rituals often incorporate several of these seven elements, as illustrated, for example, by a special chant recited by the Lacandon over rubber humanoid figures to animate them so they can be burned in sacrifice (see McGee, this volume). One chant recorded by Davis (1978:137–40; reproduced in McGee 1990:91) names them as rubber figures using several metaphorical designations and also names the body parts that were created for them one at a time. The chant locates the figures on sacred boards, telling them where their "house" is; it invokes the names of deities destined to make use of the figures once sacrificed (their guardians) and also designates as their "mother and father" the shaman who created them. The actual transmission of the life force to the rubber images is accomplished by painting them red with symbolic blood derived from annatto seeds (this was formerly done with human blood). McGee (this volume) illustrates the same point about animating rituals, but with respect to incense burners among the Lacandon.

The generalized elements or processes noted here that obtain for Mesoamerican construction activities related to dedication and termination are grounded in fieldwork in a Tzeltal Mayan community located in the central highlands of Chiapas, Mexico (map 3.1). This fieldwork provides the basis for presenting some of the key elements in birth, death, and house animation.

The Tenejapa community of some ten thousand Tzeltal speakers is located about 33 km northeast of San Cristóbal de las Casas. On the other side of San Cristóbal are communities of Tzotzil speakers—closely related to

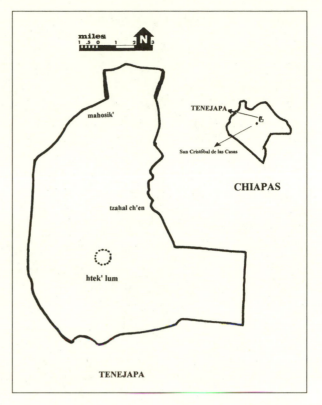

Map 3.1.   Outline of Chiapas, Mexico, with Municipio of Tenajapa enlarged. Author did primary fieldwork in the Parajes of Mahosik' and Tzahal Ch'en, labeled.

Tzeltal speakers—including the Zinacanteco Mayans discussed by Vogt (this volume). One of seventeen closed corporate Tzeltal communities distributed among twelve municipios of Tzeltal speakers, Tenejapa is composed of twenty-one dispersed patrilineal hamlets. These hamlets, housing the majority of the population, are linked through a ceremonial center *(htek lum),* the seat of municipal government, in which reside approximately a hundred mestizo families and a small permanent Indian population.

TENEJAPA TZELTAL HOUSE ANIMATION

In Tenejapa the process of house construction incorporates most of the seven elements involved in animating

Fig. 3.1.   Musical accompaniment to a ritual housewarming in Tenejapa.

the inanimate, and the process spans a week or more, incorporating several ritual occasions (fig. 3.1). When constructing a new house, Tenejapa Tzeltal Mayans first measure out the place where it is to be located. Then they level the ground for the house floor and outside patio, and measure the house dimensions with a rod the length of outstretched arms from fingertip to fingertip. Next the vertical posts and horizontal frame beams are placed, the roof frame is constructed, and thatching applied to clothe the roof. Finally, a drainage ditch is dug around the house, the siding boards are put in place, and a door is installed. Offerings are made at several points in this construction process, as Monaghan (this volume) and Vogt (this volume) have pointed out for the Mixtecs and Zinacantecos, respectively.

Once the house has been constructed to this point, it still needs to be animated. To this end three hearthstones are placed in the center of the house floor and a fire started. Then a cross is constructed of pine wood, crowning a newly prepared altar of pine boughs, candles, candleholders, and censers placed next to one wall. Then a chicken, usually a rooster, is hung by its feet from the center of the house, and its head is cut off to let blood drip into the hearth (see Vogt, this volume, for similar activities described in more detail). Alternatively, the bird may be hung with its feet down until it is dead (Berlin et al. 1974:150). The chicken is censed, cooked, and eaten. Part of the chicken is buried in each corner of the house to placate the plants used in the house construction, and sugarcane liquor is poured on the ground.

Prayers, candles, and incense are offered at the altar, invoking the protection of several deities who will watch over the house and its occupants. The owner of the house does not eat on the day of its animation, or dedication.

Cleansing, measuring, assigning guardianship, transferring animacy, and feeding are all present in the process of contemporary Tzeltal house creation and dedication, but there is no obvious evidence that the house is named. However, naming is perhaps the best attested element in temple construction and dedication by the Classic Maya. The temples are named by glyphs in the Classic Maya script, many of which have been deciphered (Schele and Freidel 1990). There is also evidence, if less direct, that the Classic Maya must have used measuring instruments.[4] Cache "offerings" can be interpreted as a way of animating the building by inserting a "heart" that in some cases may replicate the cosmos with representatives from each cosmic level[5]—a heart that in all likelihood was ensouled and fed through blood sacrifice. Additionally, the Classic Maya temple was "clothed" in red paint or lime whitewash (see Greene Robertson 1979:149 for detailed examples) and may have been further adorned with cut vegetation.

In this connection, one might view the layers of thatch with which the contemporary Tzeltal house is roofed as its "clothing." It is notable too that the Yucatec Maya community cross, which is painted green and represents the World Tree (the *axis mundi*, which is also symbolized by the *ceiba* tree, Yucatec *yax che'*, literally "green tree"), is also "dressed" by being adorned with the shirtlike garments called *huipils*. Tzeltal and Tzotzil Mayans dress their crosses with green pine boughs rather than green paint (Vogt 1969). Tzeltal and Tzotzil ritual renewal and veneration of cult objects—now including saints—involves censing the object and its clothes. This action can be seen both as purifying and as feeding the object. Its clothes are also ritually washed and changed. In an archaeological context we can view the resin-bound cinnabar covering many Mayan jade funerary objects as a kind of "clothing." The layers of red and white earth that cover—or clothe—Classic Maya burials, abandoned temples, and even Preclassic Olmec tombs (Kent Reilly, personal communication 1992) show the endurance of this practice through the centuries. Comparison of such practices with the saint-veneration practices of today suggests the application of native beliefs to places where Catholicism has engaged indigenous material culture.

Tenejapa Tzeltal Birth

A house or temple, a cross, a mask, a wooden idol, or a "god pot" (incense burner): each, to be made functional, must undergo animation procedures (see, for example, McGee, this volume; Thompson 1970:190–191; Vogt, this volume) that empower it as an agent of appropriate activity. The same holds true for a newborn child, who must be given a sociocultural position constructed in terms dictated by the ideological systems of the society in which it is born. Although the infant is born animate in a natural sense, it still needs to be animated in a social sense—that is, incorporated into the societal body. Further, its soul needs to be "fixed" so that it will be retained by the corporeal body and not wander excessively. The procedures used by the Tzeltal Maya differ in only minor respects from other societies in Mesoamerica.

In Tenejapa, gestation is accompanied by several kinds of birth preparation, including various purification and strengthening rituals. These are accomplished through praying by the curer and drinking of a potion by the woman; the woman also observes various restrictions on food and activity (Stross 1969:25–27).

When the infant drops from the mother onto the house floor, a midwife picks it up and gives it to the weakened mother, thereby officially assigning guardianship. The infant's eyes and nostrils are opened and cleansed of birthing mucus, allowing for free breathing. A thread ties the umbilical cord close to the baby's stomach, and the measure of the distance between outstretched thumb and middle finger (a *hoht*) is applied to the cord from the thread to where the cord is cut. The afterbirth is then dried by the fire and burned.

The midwife cleans and purifies the newborn baby in warm herbal water with soap from a soaproot plant *(ch'opak)*, then censes it with the smoke from copal incense while praying. After the baby is dressed, the core of a chile pepper is rubbed softly on its lips, or the mother puts a small piece of chewed chile in its mouth. Then the baby is allowed to breastfeed. Shortly thereafter the whole family participates in finding a name for the newborn infant. A boy baby may well be named after the paternal grandfather as his "replacement" *(s-helol)*. A girl baby is usually named after a paternal grandmother or aunt.

Naming prayers are made in front of the family altar, usually by a curer, and then candles and incense are burned. A small piece of beeswax is stuck on the middle of the top of the baby's head so that evil spirit beings won't molest the infant. A blue thread may be tied around its neck to avert illness. On the afternoon of the birth, a rooster is sacrificed and eaten by the family. After that several postpartum restrictions are observed for twenty days and more, and the baby is kept in the house, protected from the gaze of strangers.

Just as a house is dedicated, a newborn child is socially confirmed in its animation by means of ritual cleansing, measuring, naming, feeding, clothing, guardianship, and transfer of animacy. In like manner, a mask, a censer, a trail shrine, and an altar are all animated through similar ritual means in Tenejapa, although in abbreviated form.

Tenejapa Tzeltal Death

In Tenejapa death is accompanied by several kinds of ritual preparation, beginning even before the moment of death, in the same way that the birth moment is preceded as well as followed by ritual. For things of human manufacture, termination rituals are de-animating, disposing of the object's soul in ways that avoid danger to humans. For humans themselves, death ritual is also largely concerned with disposition of the soul in ways that avoid danger to the humans remaining in this world (see Vogt, this volume). The ritual actions performed include variations on the same elements already mentioned in connection with dedication and birth.

Upon death, the body is placed on its back on planks in the house where relatives can visit, be fed, and mourn. The house fire is kept burning briskly, and candles are placed near the corpse's head and lit. Candles must remain burning for three days, the length of time that the house cannot be swept with a broom.

The face and feet of the corpse are carefully washed, using soaproot—the same as used to clean a newborn infant—rather than soap. Then it is dressed in new clothes, the old ones being thrown away, and a new extra shirt is folded under the head. A white wool blanket is draped over the body, and the sides of a new reed mat are folded up and tied together with string to enclose the body. The corpse lies on its back, arms at its sides with palms inward, and feet aligned with the toes up.

A small, new, but flawed net bag, holding a gourd, and a new tortilla bag containing charred tortillas as well as some Mexican coins are placed on one side of the body, and a water bottle is put on the other. Once the gravediggers arrive at the house, the body is measured with wet bark from a *bat* tree (*Heliocarpus donnell-smithii*). The measuring cord made of bark is then used to carefully measure the dimensions at the gravesite, which is located near the house if possible. A single knot on the bark cord distinguishes length from width by dividing the cord into two unequal parts, one for length and one for width. The grave is excavated while onlookers drink sugarcane rum, smoke cigarettes, and reminisce about the deceased.

The grave is dug to a depth of more than a meter. At that point a 15 cm ledge is left along each side, the length of the grave, and then another 75 cm of soil is excavated, thus forming channels that hold a bed of poles to surmount the body in the grave. Before the poles are all placed, the body is brought to the grave on a pole litter and placed on planks at the bottom, with the head toward the east. The time for lament is just before the body is lifted from the litter and lowered on its reed mat into the grave. The poles are replaced over the body, forming a chamber. Dirt is replaced in the grave a couple of centimeters at a time and tamped by foot and stone until it has formed a low mound over the grave. About 20 cm from the top of the mound the measuring cord was balled up and stuck in the middle. Once burial is accomplished, six candles are placed in the earth across the width of the grave over the chest area and lit.

Prayers are said over the grave, asking the deceased's soul to come to the grave and not to return to the house out of habit, where it could molest the surviving family members. Earlier, in the house of the deceased, a family member had said similar prayers before taking three pinches of earth from each of the four sides of the corpse and putting them in the bottle of water to be buried with it. Then the corpse was lifted to bring it to the gravesite. A family member brushed where it had lain with his or her hand, formed a cross there on the ground with leaves and stems of a bush, prayed, and brought a censer with embers and chile to prevent harm from befalling the family living in the house.

Following the burial a candle must burn constantly in the house for three nights, the house floor cannot be swept with a broom for three days, the gravedigging tools cannot come near the house for three days, and some or all of the deceased's family must stay awake all night for three nights. The basket used in digging the grave is thrown away.

Purifying with smoke, cleaning with soaproot, and sweeping with the hands are all part of Tenejapa Tzeltal mortuary customs. Also prominent are actions of measuring, dressing, feeding, and assigning guardianship (in the prayers to the soul). Naming also occurs, as the deceased is repeatedly named as the soul is addressed. The timing of lamentations, just before the body is lowered into the grave, suggests a communion or at least communication between the soul of the deceased and the souls of those left behind, and may reference a transmission of life force between the world of the living and the Otherworld.[6]

DEACTIVATING THE ANIMATE

In mortuary ritual we can identify many, and perhaps all, of the elements described above in connection with birth ritual. One difference between social constructions of birth and those of death lies in the focus of concern for the soul: At birth, the concern is to nurture and protect the soul in this world so that it will stay with its designated owner, while in death the major concern is to release the soul from this world and keep it satisfied—or at least too busy to stay with, and thereby cause harm to, the individuals whose souls interacted with it in this world before its owner's death.

Similar considerations obtain for manufactured items, such as food utensils and tools. The souls of such things are often associated with the individual who makes or owns them, and they must be released from the objects in order to accompany the individual's soul in the other world. In the Tzotzil village of Zinacantán, "clothes and objects associated with the dead person are placed in the grave, each somehow cut, burned, or broken" (Vogt 1993 [1976]:23). In a Veracruz Nahua village attendants "remove the plates, cups, and machete that were with the body and ... break them ... to release the *yolotl* souls in the objects so that they could accompany the deceased's soul to *Mictlan*" (Sandstrom 1991:298). Huastec Mayans of San Luis Potosí likewise smash plates and bowls of the deceased (Alcorn 1984:146). Furthermore, among the Huastecs, "when their owner dies, domesticated plants either also die or they fade into the *alte'* (which is metaphorically equivalent to death)" (Alcorn 1984:96). This is completely consistent with Eliade's contention that "the food plant is not *given* in nature; it is the product of a slaying, for it was thus that it was created in the dawn of time" (1959:103). In the case of the Classic Maya at Yaxchilan, evidence found on the ball court's hieroglyphic stairway indicates that the world itself was created by a beheading of the maize deity. This seems analogous

to the destruction of buildings at the death of a Classic Maya ruler (Mock 1993) and similar to the overturning of stelae under related circumstances.

Smashing objects constitutes one way of deactivating, or de-animating, them and releasing the soul. Other means, also done in a ritual context, include drilling or punching a hole through the object, preserving its formal integrity but invalidating its function. Archaeologists have long been familiar with such "kill holes" found on the edge or in the center of ceramic vessels. Manufactured images based on human or animal forms are found in Mesoamerica with the left eye and sometimes the mouth mutilated, or else decapitated, and it is likely that these are methods of releasing the soul of the object. The soul is not dealt with solely by being released; its journey is sometimes directed by blocking access to places where its influence is not desired (as among the Huichol, Tojolabal, Tzotzil, and Tzeltal). A soul will naturally travel along pathways frequented by people, and certain paths can be ritually and symbolically blocked with sticks or other articles, such as "god's eyes," to prevent the passage of the soul and direct it to where it is supposed to go.

Ritual abandonment of houses in Mesoamerica involves pulling down one or more corner posts, and often the roof, usually accompanied by copal incense purification, prayers, and other offerings. In Classic times the Maya also smashed artifacts as part of the abandonment procedure. Schele and Freidel note similarities in form and content between termination and dedication rituals in the archaeological record, much like the similarities in the form and meaning of ritual actions attending birth and death of humans, discussed here.

> Archaeologically, there is some evidence supporting the association of termination and dedication rituals with the act of reestablishment or founding. Both kinds of rituals are similar in form and content (Freidel 1986b). Termination rituals involving the smashing of artifacts of pottery, jade, and other materials, and the layering of these materials in white earth, are found not only upon the occasion of the permanent abandonment of buildings, but also at their reconstruction. At Cerros, the first place this ritual activity was identified and documented in the Maya region ... it is clear that the same unbroken ritual offerings which terminate a building can be part of the dedication ceremony of the new building. (Schele and Freidel 1990:459)

For modern Mayans the creation of the world (cosmogonic ritual), the birth of a person (birth and afterbirth ritual), and the creation of a building (construction and dedication ritual) share important features. In a sense, as processes, they are cut from the same cloth and must be attended by homologous if not always formally similar ritual behavior. The crucial shared features are ensouling, the trapping of a soul in some "vessel," and travel by transformation from one level of existence to another through a portal linking levels (see also McGee 1990:107). The ensouling process encompasses most or all of the seven distinct components identified above.

Likewise, destruction of the world, death of a person, and abandonment of a building are similar. The crucial shared features are desouling, release of the soul from its "vessel," and travel by transformation from one level of existence to another through a portal linking levels. The same seven components described above can frequently be found in the process of desouling.

Dying and getting born are sometimes lengthy and complex processes (illness and death, gestation and birth) that culminate in differently named, and therefore differently categorized, events, but the events themselves share significant features: They are perceived as occurring in a "portal" or "pathway" between worlds, and they entail a transformation of state or level, a change in form and in location. Humans facilitate the transformations occurring in a portal by means of ritual activity that can be expressed with social constructions, discussed above as seven elements of animation (and de-animation).

Elements of rituals attending the dedication and termination of manufactured objects can be profitably understood in terms of analogous events in the life cycle of humans and in terms of the social constructs that extend birth and death processes to everything with a soul. Life, its inception and termination, constitutes an integral part of the world view, presumably in all human societies, so that animation of inanimate objects (ensouling) and de-animation of things that have been animated are ritual activities of great importance (see also, for example, Daniel 1984:119; Masson et al. 1992). Here dedication and termination have been seen to share several meaningful processes that are part of ritual observance. Since creation of one thing necessarily involves destruction of something else that provided the materials for its construction, perhaps it should not be surprising that so much is shared in cultural perceptions of these processes.

The Classic Maya and other Mesoamericans of ancient times almost certainly perceived creation of the world, birth of a person, and creation of a building as sharing significant features. They must also have viewed destruction of the world, death of a person, and abandonment of a building as similar—just as their descendants do today. The usefulness of ethnography in informing archaeological interpretation—as argued here and by Freidel and colleagues (1993)—is due to the interrelationship of past and present in Mesoamerica and to the formidable resilience of indigenous world views, even in the face of more than fifteen hundred years of adaptation to changing social and natural environments, including five hundred years of subordination to the Spanish heritage. To the extent that the core world view discussed here has persisted in its major outlines, ethnographic descriptions of social activities attending birth and death (in addition to descriptions of dedication and termination ceremonies) can provide valuable insights about past practices of ancient Mesoamerican societies investigated primarily with archaeological techniques. Seven elements or processes have been isolated here as attending "birth" and "death" as social constructions, and if they describe the present, they may also be said to describe the past.

NOTES

1. My fieldwork in different Mayan and other Mesoamerican communities supports this generalization, and similar conclusions are documented by other researchers (e.g., Guiteras-Holmes 1961; Laughlin 1975; McGee, this volume; Monaghan, this volume; Sandstrom 1991; Vogt 1993 [1976], this volume).

2. The Tzotzil Mayan word *ch'ulel*, for example, means "soul (of everything naturally created, and of manufactured objects that have been used and so receive soul of owner)" (Laughlin 1975:139).

3. According to numerous traditions, "not only the cosmos ... comes to birth in consequence of the immolation of a primordial being and from his own substance, but also food plants, the races of man, or different social classes. It is on this type of cosmogonic myth that building sacrifices depend. If a 'construction' is to endure (be it house, temple, tool, etc.), it must be animated, that is, it must receive life and a soul. The transfer of the soul is possible only through a blood sacrifice" (Eliade 1959:55–56).

4. Indirect evidence includes (1) the measuring cords currently in use for housebuilding and other purposes by Mayan groups, including Tzeltal, Tzotzil, Yucatecs,

Chorti, and Cakchiquel; (2) references to measuring cords in early Colonial period documents referring to pre-Columbian times, such as the Quiché book *Popol Vuh* and the Yucatec *Chilam Balam of Chumayel,* and also the Yucatec *Ritual of the Bacabs;* (3) the fact that the proportions of most Classic Maya temples that have been carefully measured demonstrate the use of a measuring cord such as those in use today (Christopher Powell, personal communication 1993).

5. The heart of a thing is its central part, its middle. Annabeth Headrick (personal communication 1992) has suggested that there are two kinds of caches. One, the important main one in the center of a building, is its heart. When the building is abandoned or built over, sometimes the heart will have to be removed and the building symbolically killed. Thus we find that caches are sometimes "looted" in antiquity. The central cache is the heart, the cosmos, and the animating force.

6. In other cultures and contexts, laments serve a variety of purposes, one of which is to provide a ritual channel for the necessary step toward reincorporation of the newly structured community. When humans were deliberately killed—as during the Maya Classic period, when sacrifice was done by means of decapitation or heart removal—the life force was more obviously transferred from one entity to another.

References Cited

Alcorn, Janis B.
1984   *Huastec Mayan Ethnobotany.* Austin: University of Texas Press.
Berlin, Brent, Dennis E. Breedlove, and Peter H. Raven
1974   *Principles of Tzeltal Plant Classification.* New York: Academic Press.
Daniel, E. Valentine
1984   *Fluid Signs: Being a Person the Tamil Way.* Berkeley: University of California Press.
Davis, Virginia D.
1978   *Ritual of the Northern Lacandón Maya.* Ph.D. diss., Tulane University.
Eliade, Mircea
1959   *The Sacred and the Profane.* New York: Harcourt, Brace.
Freidel, David, Linda Schele, and Joy Parker
1993   *Maya Cosmos: Three Thousand Years on the Shaman's Path.* New York: William Morrow.
Greene Robertson, Merle
1979   A Sequence for Palenque Painting Techniques. In *Maya Archaeology and Ethnohistory,* edited by N. Hammond and G. R. Willey, 149–71. Austin: University of Texas Press.
Guiteras-Holmes, Calixta
1961   *Perils of the Soul.* Glencoe, Ill.: Free Press.
Guss, David. M.
1989   *To Weave and Sing: Art, Symbol and Narrative in the South American Rain Forest.* Berkeley: University of California Press.
Laughlin, Robert M.
1975   *The Great Tzotzil Dictionary of San Lorenzo Zinacantán.* Smithsonian Contributions to Anthropology 19. Washington, D.C.: Smithsonian Institution Press.
Masson, Marilyn A., Heather Orr, and Javier Urcid Serrano
1992   "Building Dedication, Nahual Transformation, and Captive Sacrifice at Monte Alban: Programs of Sacred Geography." Paper presented at the 57th Meeting of the Society for American Archaeology, Pittsburgh.
McGee, R. Jon
1990   *Life, Ritual, and Religion among the Lacandón Maya.* Belmont, Calif.: Wadsworth Publishing.
Mock, Shirley Boteler
1993   "Ritual Passages: Dedication and Termination Events in the Archaeological Record of Mesoamerica." Paper presented at the 92nd Annual Meeting of the American Anthropological Association, Washington, D.C.
Sandstrom, Alan R.
1991   *Corn Is Our Blood.* Norman: University of Oklahoma Press.
Schele, Linda, and David Freidel
1990   *A Forest of Kings.* New York: William Morrow.
Stross, Brian M.
1969   *Language Acquisition by Tenejapa Tzeltal Children.* Language-Behavior Research Laboratory Working Paper 20. Berkeley: University of California.
Thompson, J. Eric S.
1970   *Maya History and Religion.* Norman: University of Oklahoma Press.
Vogt, Evon Z.
1969   *Zinacantán.* Cambridge, Mass.: Belknap Press.
1993 [1976] *Tortillas for the Gods.* Norman: University of Oklahoma Press.

CHAPTER FOUR

The Lacandon Incense Burner Renewal Ceremony
Termination and Dedication Ritual among the Contemporary Maya

R. Jon McGee
Southwest Texas State University

Recent research suggests that the ancient Maya conceived of their temples and pyramids as animate, and that they awakened these structures in dedication rituals marked by human sacrifice and bloodletting, and the caching of valuable objects, such as pottery, jade jewelry, and obsidian. Impressive strides in the decipherment of Maya hieroglyphics have allowed us to read of these activities, the individuals who conducted them, and the timing of the rites. When the buildings were renovated or replaced, they were ritually killed in rites that often involved defacing their façades and breaking valuable items, such as jade jewelry and pottery, covering the fragments in a layer of white marl, and burying them. A contemporary parallel to these ancient dedication and termination rituals is the incense burner renewal ceremony of the Lacandon Maya. Incense burners are the Lacandon's medium of communication with their gods. Just as the ancient Maya ritually animated their temples, so too the Lacandon ceremonially animate their god pots through special prayers, and with offerings of humanoid figures made of rubber and symbolic human flesh and blood. When these god pots are replaced, the old ones are killed and buried as the final act of the ceremony. Thus, a more thorough understanding of ancient Maya cosmology may be obtained by comparing the archaeological record and hieroglyphic texts with ethnographic evidence from this contemporary Lacandon rite.

ETHNOGRAPHIC BACKGROUND

The Lacandon Maya are swidden horticulturalists who live in the *Selva Lacandona* of southeastern Chiapas, Mexico. If the observer looks past the use of modern items—a community truck, tin-roofed houses, wristwatches, and battery-powered radios—their lives are little different from those of the common Maya people of antiquity. They work their milpas, hunt game in the forest, and worship their gods. Their lifestyle would immediately be familiar to any archaeologist who has excavated Mesoamerican living sites. Lacandon communities are made up of patrilineal house clusters. Individual families typically live in one-room, thatched-roof structures with packed earthen floors (only recently have younger men started building homes with tin roofs and cement floors) and a kitchen hut next door. Meals are cooked over the ubiquitous three-stone hearth, and items are stored in containers of clay, woven net bags, and baskets. A person's life is regulated by the seasons and the agricultural cycle, and the passing of time is measured by the phases of the moon. The primary crops are corn and beans, along with a variety of other vegetables, which men supplement by hunting deer, monkey, and turkey, and fishing. Women typically oversee the domestic side of life, supervising children, weaving, preparing food, and helping with planting and weeding in the milpas.

Lacandon Religion

The Lacandon are particularly significant for modern ethnohistorical and archaeological research because their religious practices have dramatic parallels with prehispanic and, in some cases, Classic Maya religion. As I have described in detail in earlier work (McGee 1990), the Lacandon are the last of the fully non-Christian Maya. Virtually no element of Christian belief or ritual practice has been assimilated into their religious beliefs. Contemporary Lacandon gods and mythology are all directly related to ancient Maya beliefs (see McGee 1984). Ritual implements described by sixteenth-century observers or uncovered by modern archaeologists—such as incense burners, *xikals* (paddle-like incense boards), and flint blades for bloodletting—are still a part of Lacandon religion. Offerings such as copal incense, ritual foodstuffs, and the beverage *balché* are identical to those used by the prehispanic Maya. Additionally, elements of contemporary Lacandon mythology, such as the journey of ancestral folk heroes through the Underworld, reflect elements of prehispanic Maya mythology described in the Quiché Maya chronicle *Popol Vuh*.

Most compelling of all religious parallels is the Lacandon's retention, in symbolic form, of the sacrificial practices of their ancestors. Although autosacrifice (by piercing the earlobes with a flint blade) was discontinued about a generation ago, symbolic human sacrifice and bloodletting remain an integral part of most Lacandon rites. In particular, Lacandon elders speak of an ancient people called the *Nuki Nahwahto*, who were said to kidnap people for sacrifice, cut out their hearts, feed the victim's heart and blood to their incense burners, and then feast on the victim's body. In contemporary Lacandon rites, a red dye made from seeds of the annatto tree *(Bixa orellana)* represents human blood, and the Lacandon paint their ritual hut, implements, and themselves with this dye. Additionally, food offerings made from corn, such as the ceremonial tamale *(nahwah)*, represent human flesh; the Lacandon dip these in the symbolic blood and feed them to the gods by placing pieces of the offerings in the mouths of their god pots, clay incense burners with faces modeled on the front. Although the Lacandon deny any connection to the *Nuki Nahwahto*, after they have fed the gods their symbolic flesh and blood, participants in the rite sit down to feast on the remaining offerings—

thus imitating the ritual sacrifice and cannibalism of their prehispanic ancestors as described in their mythology.

CLASSIC PERIOD DEDICATION AND TERMINATION CEREMONIES AND LACANDON RELIGION

It has long been known that the Maya intentionally buried caches of valuable goods and human sacrificial remains within structures as dedicatory offerings during construction of the buildings (see, for example, Coe 1959; Freidel et al. 1993; Smith 1972). Freidel and Schele (1989:236) surmise that these dedication rituals not only marked the completion of construction, but also were conducted with the purpose of animating the building or activating the "portal" through which kings communicated with the supernatural.

As structures were animated through dedication rituals marked by caching and human sacrificial rites, so too the spiritual force within buildings was diffused through termination rituals when a building was abandoned or renovated (Schele and Freidel 1990:313). These termination rituals are marked in the archaeological record by the scattering of objects, such as pottery or jewelry, that had been smashed or broken and covered in white marl (Garber 1989), and by the defacing of monuments and mask façades on buildings (Freidel and Schele 1989:239).

Are there parallel beliefs in contemporary Maya religious practices that can provide further insight into this subject? Vogt observed that Zinacanteco shamans perform the *Ch'ul Kantela* ceremony after construction is completed on a new house. Similar to the ancient dedication ceremonies, the rite includes as significant features the planting of a house cross, the offering of candles and incense, and the sacrifice of chickens, one of which is buried in the center of the floor. The purpose of the rite is to animate the house, which is then carefully watched for the next three days, for it has been given a soul and must be cared for like a sick person whose soul has been restored by a curing ceremony (Vogt 1969:461–64).

Although the Lacandon do not have dedication and termination rites for their ritual structures (*yatoch k'uh,* "god house"), which are simple thatched huts, they do practice elaborate rituals surrounding the construction, animation, and abandonment of their most important ritual implements, the god pots. This ceremony is the modern analogue of the ancient Maya dedication and termination rituals and provides one more avenue for examining ancient Maya cosmology.

The Lacandon are not the descendants of ancient Maya aristocracy. In all probability, their ancestors watched from the periphery as the lords of the great Maya cities constructed their temples and monuments, and performed their elaborate sacrificial rites. Given their heritage and simple lifestyle today, it is not surprising that it is the construction of their most sacred implements, the god pots, rather than the building of structures, that most concerns the devout Lacandon man. Lacandon incense burners, called *läkil k'uh,* literally "god pots," are the central focus of all Lacandon ritual activity. They are the most significant ritual implement because they are the medium of communication between gods and men, and the vehicle for transmitting offerings. During a ritual, gods descend to the god house, partake of their offerings of symbolic flesh and blood, and drink their *balché* when it is placed on the outthrust lip of the god pot dedicated to them. Thus, just as temple doorways were the gateways through which ancient Maya shaman/kings entered the supernatural realm, god pots are the portals through which Lacandon men communicate with their deities.

Although not thought to be accurate depictions of gods, god pots are conceived as corporeal replicas of the gods to whom they are dedicated. The pots are animated during the incense burner renewal ceremony. During construction of a new god pot, five cacao beans are placed in the bowl to represent the heart, lungs, liver, stomach, and diaphragm. Furthermore, specific facial features, such as ears with earrings, eyes, nose, and mouth, are molded on the head of the god pot. The front of a god pot is called its chest, and the bottom its feet (Davis 1978:73). God pots are painted white with vertical black stripes for males and in crossing vertical and horizontal stripes for females. They are further spotted red with annatto in the places that correspond to where men paint themselves during the incense burner renewal ceremony: the forehead, chin, chest, and feet (see fig. 4.1).

When making or replacing a god pot, one of the most important elements is not the burner itself, but a small object that is placed in the bottom of the bowl. According to Tozzer's observation at the turn of the twentieth century, the Lacandon placed "idols" in the bowls of the newly made god pots, and these figures were then covered in copal incense (1978a:140). Today small stones taken from nearby Classic period ruins are deposited in

the bowl. The Lacandon compare these stones to radios (Davis 1978:74), and it is through this medium that a man's prayers and offerings are transmitted to the gods. Thus there is a clear parallel between the ancient and contemporary practices. Ancient temple caches comprised jade, pottery, and human sacrificial remains; caches of nonelites contained more mundane items, such as pottery, jade or shell beads, and flakes of chert (Driver et al. 1992). By the early twentieth century, god pot caches had been simplified to figurines, and today they are simply stones from Classic ruins. It appears that the Lacandons' placement of items in a god pot as part of its animation ritual is the contemporary equivalent of the ancient Maya's placement of offerings in the foundations of structures as part of the ritual surrounding the dedication and animation of buildings. Just as dedication ceremonies "ensouled" ancient Maya ritual places, so too god pots are ceremonially "awakened." Consequently, understanding the ceremonial process by which the Lacandon animate their god pots will help us to better comprehend the cosmological themes that unite ancient and contemporary Maya peoples.

The Incense Burner Renewal Ceremony

Just as incense burners are the ritual implements of central significance, the most elaborate of Lacandon rituals is the incense burner renewal ceremony, and it provides the clearest parallels between ancient Maya dedication and termination rites and contemporary Lacandon rituals. Many Classic period religious themes are still reflected in this rite. Other than the hieroglyphic texts on monuments dedicated to recording these events, the only historical record of this ritual is found in Landa's *Relación de las cosas de Yucatán,* written c. 1566. In this account, Landa describes a ritual he calls "Oc Na," which he says means "renovation of the temple in honor of the Chacs" (Tozzer 1978b:161). After periods of sexual abstinence and fasting, new idols were made, and "they *rebuilt the house or renovated it, and they placed on the wall the memorial of these things, written in their characters*" (Tozzer 1978b:161; emphasis added). Landa's account of this rite provides the transitional link between Classic Period and contemporary Lacandon practice. Although sparse in detail, Landa's account clearly describes a temple renovation ceremony marked by the dedication of the structure through hieroglyphic inscriptions on the walls of the building, much as the Classic Maya erected stelae or carved lintels to commemorate significant

Fig. 4.1. The god pot Äk Nah, "Our Mother," wife of the Underworld Lord. This god pot is used only during the incense burner renewal ceremony.

events and ritual actions of the nobility. More important, Landa states that this rite was accompanied by the construction of new incense burners; thus, the ritual he describes must have been similar to the contemporary Lacandon incense burner renewal ceremony.

Landa speculated that the Oc Na rite was an agricultural ceremony dedicated to the rain gods, because it was held during the months of Chen and Yax and involved first-fruit offerings from the fields. It was actually a rite held to renew the incense burners and, in Landa's time, to renovate and rededicate ritual structures. The ceremony is held in the late summer because that is when the yearly agricultural cycle permits men the time necessary to perform the rite. It is only when crops are ready for harvest that men have the one to two months necessary to conduct the ceremony, in the time between harvesting and clearing the next season's milpa.

Up until about 1970 the Lacandon performed the incense burner renewal rite yearly, as the Maya had done during the sixteenth century. The rite was also performed after eclipses of the sun. Today, however, the rite is preformed infrequently, the last two occasions occurring in 1970 and 1991. Our knowledge of the ceremony comes from Bruce's brief eyewitness description (1982), Tozzer's turn-of-the-century observations (1978a), and interviews with informants who have participated in the

rituals. This ritual is the longest and most intricate of the ceremonies in Lacandon religion. Over a period of one to two months, the participants are secluded in the god house where they eat, sleep, pray, and purify themselves for the construction of the new god pots. According to Bruce (1982:30), all benches, hammocks, clothing, and other personal possessions were either made new or scrubbed clean in preparation for the ceremony. No nonparticipant was allowed to touch them. Although women of the community continued to prepare the participants' food, they left it on neutral ground where the men retrieved it, and the men's diets were severely restricted. During this period, men are also required to abstain from sex as they perform the arduous rituals that culminate in the awakening of new god pots.

The new god pots are made in a temporary shelter constructed away from the village, for only the participants may witness their construction. In addition to the god pots, small offering bowls called *sil* are made, as well as a special god pot with arms called *Äk Nah* (Landa's "Oc Nah"), "Our Mother," who is the wife of the Lord of the Underworld (fig. 4.1). This god pot is used only in renewal ceremonies on the day the new god pots are awakened; food offerings are placed in its hand, rather than in the mouth, as is done with other god pots.

The creation and decoration of the new god pots and the decommissioning or killing of the old, along with the accompanying prayers and offerings, make up most of the activities during the one- to two-month ritual. Having described the *balché* and *nahwah* offering rituals in much greater detail elsewhere (McGee 1990), here I will say only that providing the gods with daily rounds of offerings—copal incense, *nahwah, atole,* annatto, meat, bark cloth bands, *balché, k'ik'* (humanoid figures made from natural rubber), and *xikals*—occupies most of the participants' time during the day. Tozzer (1978a:136) further observed that when men were intoxicated on *balché* they sometimes pierced their ears with a stone arrow point and dripped the blood down onto the god pots.

During the transitional period before new god pots are completed, the old incense burners, which are about to die, are taken down from their storage shelf in the god house, placed on a mat of palm leaves facing east, and fed daily offerings. The new god pots are fashioned by hand, dried for several days, then fired in the coals of a "virgin fire" *(suhuy k'ak'),* which is kindled for that purpose. After firing, the incense burners are painted white and black with red spots, as described above.

Once the new incense burners are completed, they are carried to the god house from the shelter where they were made. The old god pots are fed offerings one last time, the stone concealed in their bowls is removed, and the pots are placed in a corner of the god house facing west and covered, an action that symbolizes their death. The next morning, the new god pots take their places in the god house. They are fed their first offerings of *balché*, the sacred stone is placed in their bowls, and immediately the stone is covered with copal incense. A special chant is sung to awaken the god pots, and they are struck with special blue, red, and black clay beads that are believed to have been made by the gods for their necklaces (Davis 1978:77). I include here portions of the chant recorded by Davis (1978:78–83), along with my own translation:

ka kuren in wäsik	sitting, I awaken it
he' ku na'akah ähsähk'in	here the morning star [Venus] rises
he' ku na'akah ähsähk'ab	here the evening star rises
ti' u Yumbirika'an[1]	for the lord of the sky [Hachäkyum]
bahon Äkyantho'[2] ka kurih	everyone Äkyantho' sits
ka yan saih in wäsäbeh	again here are beads my awakeners
Äkyan u sukun in yum	Äkyantho' older brother of my lord
ka lukih ka saih in wäsäbeh	get out your beads my awakeners ...
tan u sa'astar tik yum	it is clearing [the sun is rising] for the lords ...
eh u yurika'an	Oh lord of the sky
eh Äyyantho'	Oh Äkyantho'...
tu wenen 'okor	they [the new god pots] sleep inside
ti u wenen 'okor	for those who sleep inside ...
su'uy k'in	the virgin [new/pure] day
su'uy ku lik tu yok ti k'in	the virgins [new god pots] rise to their feet for the sun
ahen	awaken
ka pit ah wich ah wirik	you open your eyes and see
ah wo'och buliwah	your food bean tamales
tan ah wuyik tan u xultan tik yum	you are hearing it, the ending of the world for our lords [the old god pots]
tan ka likcheh	you are standing
ah wilik manan ah wilik	you will see it come to pass ...

As described in the prayer of awakening, the new god pots are shown to the gods and fed offerings of *balché, nahwah,* and annatto. Thus, just as the ancient Maya animated their temples with offerings of blood, sacrificial victims, and caches of valuable objects, so too the Lacandon awaken their god pots with symbolic blood and flesh, and the ritual intoxicant formerly used in bloodletting rites.[3] After this initial round of offerings has been fed to the new god pots, annatto is used to repaint the red designs on the god house and the container in which *balché* is brewed. Next, the god pots are painted with a spot of red on their foreheads and chins, and the ritual participants paint themselves at the corresponding locations and then spot their tunics all over with the red dye, much as the clothes of a person who had pierced his ears or genitals in an act of bloodletting would be spattered with blood.

For the next several days, the men are occupied with feeding the new god pots a variety of offerings. These comprise principally *balché,* incense, and some of the first foods prepared from products newly harvested from the fields, such as tamales, beans, and tobacco. On the final day of the ceremony, the new pots are put away on their storage shelf in the god house, and the ritual hut is swept clean. The old incense burners, which have sat covered in a corner for the past several days, are carefully collected and taken to a dry limestone cave about an hour's walk from the community. There, amid the smoke from burning incense, the god pots are covered with palm leaves and abandoned. The symbolism associated with death is striking in these final acts. Just as the painting of new god pots is part of the ritual that brings them to life, old god pots have their paint burned off. One informant described this process as "washing them with fire." The paint represents the clothes and skin of the god pots, and it is the removal of this paint, rather than the breaking of the incense burners, that signifies their death. Abandoned god pots are called *u bäkel äk yum,* "the bones of our Lords." The vessels are left in caves, which are considered sacred and dangerous places because they are passages to the Underworld. Furthermore, the covering of the god pots with palm leaves corresponds to the palm-thatch shelter that is erected over a fresh gravesite during Lacandon funerals.

The Lacandon incense burner renewal ceremony is clearly a modern version, though in simplified form, of the ancient Maya dedication and termination rituals. In the time between the Classic period and conquest by the Spaniards, these rituals were greatly simplified, as shown by Landa's description of the Oc Na ceremony. Nevertheless, the Lacandon god pot renewal ceremony and the Zinacantecan *Ch'ul Kantela* rite lend ethnographic support to the belief that the ancient Maya conceived of their ritual structures as animate beings that were ritually awakened when buildings were constructed and eventually killed when buildings were abandoned or renovated. As indicated by hieroglyphic texts and archaeological evidence, this process was accomplished through prayer, human and animal sacrifice, bloodletting, and the caching of valuable objects. In the same fashion today Zinacantecos animate the souls of their homes through prayer and the sacrifice of chickens, while Lacandon men awaken new god pots through special prayers, offerings of *balché*, extensive feedings of tamales and annatto symbolizing human flesh and blood, and deposition of sacred stones in the bowl of the burners. Like the ancient Maya structures that were "deactivated" when they were abandoned, with the valuables in their caches smashed and scattered, old incense burners are ritually killed and symbolically buried in hidden cave shrines once new god pots have been constructed.

Notes

1. *Yumbirika'an,* "Lord of the Sky," is another name for Hachäkyum, who in Lacandon belief created human beings.

2. *Äkyantho'* is the Lacandon god of foreigners and foreign things. Additionally, he is the older brother of Hachäkyum.

3. It is interesting to note that Venus, which the ancient Maya associated with warfare and sacrificial death, is mentioned several times in the chant.

References Cited

Bruce, Robert D., and Victor Perera
1982   *The Last Lords of Palenque.* Boston: Little Brown.

Coe, William R.
1959   *Piedras Negras Archaeology: Artifacts, Caches, and Burials.* Philadelphia: University Museum.

Davis, Virginia Dale
1978   "Ritual of the Northern Lacandón Maya." Ph.D. diss., Tulane University.

Driver, David W., James F. Garber, Lauren A. Sullivan, and David M. Glassman
1992   "Ritual Activity at the Site of Blackman Eddy, Belize." Paper presented at the 57th Annual Meeting of the Society for American Archeology, Pittsburgh.

Freidel, David A., and Linda Schele
1989   "Dead Kings and Living Temples: Dedication and Termination Rituals among the Ancient Maya." In *Word and Image in Maya Culture: Explorations in Language, Writing, and Representation,* edited by William F. Hanks and Don S. Rice, 233–43. Salt Lake City: University of Utah Press.

Freidel, David A., Linda Schele, and Joy Parker
1993   *The Maya Cosmos: Three Thousand Years on the Shaman's Path.* New York: William Morrow.

Garber, James F.
1989   *Archeology at Cerros, Belize, Central America, Vol. 2: The Artifacts.* Dallas: Southern Methodist University Press.

McGee, R. Jon
1984   "The Influence of Prehispanic Maya Religion in Contemporary Lacandón Ritual." *Journal of Latin American Lore* 10:175-187.
1990   *Life, Ritual and Religion among the Lacandón Maya.* Belmont, Calif.: Wadsworth.

Schele, Linda, and David A. Freidel
1990   *The Forest of Kings: The Untold Story of the Ancient Maya.* New York: William Morrow.

Smith, A. Ledyard
1972   *Excavations at Altar de Sacrificios: Architecture, Settlement, Burials, and Caches.* Cambridge, Mass.: Peabody Museum.

Tozzer, Alfred A.
1978a   *A Comparative Study of the Mayas and Lacandones.* New York: AMS Press.
1978b   *Landa's Relación de las cosas de Yucatán.* Millwood, N.Y.: Kraus Reprint.

Vogt, Evon Z.
1969   *Zinacantan: A Maya Community in the Highlands of Chiapas.* Cambridge, Mass.: Harvard University Press.

CHAPTER FIVE

Dedication
Ritual or Production?

John Monaghan
Vanderbilt University

W<small>E KNOW FROM MANY AND DIVERSE SOURCES THAT</small> the ancient Maya marked the construction of their temples, palaces, and other buildings with elaborate ceremonies, which scholars have labeled "dedication rituals." These rituals involved blood sacrifice and the caching of objects under and around the construction. Because the Maya perceived palaces, temples, and other buildings as living things, dedication appears to have been designed to animate the things they built, while corresponding termination rituals served to withdraw them from use, or de-animate them (Freidel and Schele 1989; McGee, this volume; Mock, this volume; Vogt 1969, this volume; Walker, this volume).

If we turn to the Mixteca region of Oaxaca, we would be hard pressed to find evidence for the Maya pattern of dedication among contemporary Mixtec people. Although certain elements correspond to Maya dedication (formal requests to Earth for permission to build the house, ceremonies predicated on the house as a model of the cosmos), the key act—ensouling the structure—appears to be absent. In Mixtec pantheism, everything in existence is alive: In the Mixtec town of Santiago Nuyoo, where I conducted fieldwork, the only things I could discover that people *didn't* view as alive were rocks that had been burned by fire (and the people who held this view were a distinct minority). Given this, it is difficult to see why a product would have to be ceremonially endowed with

life. In Mixtec terms, by definition a house is alive since it is made up of materials that are alive. Why make special efforts to bring about a state of affairs that already exists?

This might suggest that the concept of dedication is of limited value outside the Maya area. However, the manner in which dedication has been discussed by Mayanists suggests a perspective that will allow us to encompass both Mixtec practices surrounding new constructions and Maya dedicatory practices within a single analytic framework.

DEDICATION RITUAL

Over the years, the list of ceremonial practices and indigenous purposes that are labeled as "dedicatory" has gradually expanded; the term now includes things that appear quite different from one another. For example, while some dedication rites have the aim of setting aside objects for sacred use, others seem to mark a ruler's reign, record a period in the calendar, commemorate a military victory, or indicate a rite of passage of some kind. Moreover, we now see dedication as being performed for the construction not only of buildings, but also of plazas, stelae, benches, and even ceramic vessels. With regard to buildings, dedication is now seen as occurring at different stages of construction and not just at completion.

The broad application of the term *dedicatory* to Meso-american religious practices threatens the analytic use-fulness of the concept—after all, anything that explains everything in the end explains nothing. But there is an-other alternative to seeing the expansion of the number and kinds of things labeled as dedication rituals solely as the result of our overenthusiastic application of the idea of dedication: We can also see the problem as the result of the limits we place upon ourselves by calling all these practices "ritual."

"Ritual," like so many other elements of our sociologi-cal vocabulary, is not an unproblematic concept, even though we use the term with great frequency. Attempts to define ritual as a distinct form of action have given way to the realization that the classification of any behav-ior as "ritual" in opposition to other activities is not possible. As Edmund Leach wisely pointed out more than forty years ago, even the most profane act has aesthetic, non-functional, and symbolic dimensions, so that it too has a ritual quality (Leach 1954:12–13).

Turning to Mesoamerican conceptions of "ritual," it is not at all clear that a discrete category of ritual action ever existed. It is usually the case that the terms trans-lated as "ritual" refer either to specific ceremonies or to a class of acts—such as "ordering," "feeding," or "plant-ing"—that are not confined to religious ceremonies. More-over, in the Mixtec-speaking town of Santiago Nuyoo, people do not separate the creation of objects into "prac-tical" versus "ritual" aspects. In building a house, for example, people usually start by digging into a hillside to create a level surface or terrace, since the area is so moun-tainous. Before doing this, the builders request permis-sion from Earth by making offerings of *pulque* to the *nu ñu'un* that reside in the spot (local deities whose name translates as the "face" or "place" of Earth; for more de-tails, see Monaghan 1995). Meanwhile, the cross-beams for the roof are cut—but this is done only when the moon is waning *(nijia)* and the wood hardens *(nijia)*. Of course, Mixtec people see that the acts of pouring *pulque* over the earth, digging into the mountainside with a pick, and cutting down trees for beams are different from one another. Yet, as one man explained to me, not making an offering would be like putting down roof shingles with-out nailing them to the cross-beams. Just as the shingles would blow away or fall, the *nu ñu'un* might be angered without the offering and cause the earth to settle in such a way that the walls of the house would crack or the beams, also being *yute* (tender, soft) like the moon, would rot. In

other words, each of these activities—making offerings to the *nu ñu'un*, cutting the beams during certain phases of the moon, nailing shingles to the cross-beams—is necessary for the successful completion of the project. And the things we call "ritual"—prayer, ceremony, obser-vances—not only take place at the end of the project, but also inform every step of the construction (see Freidel and Schele 1989, on ancient Maya constructions).

The Mixtec example suggests that our use of the term *ritual,* though helpful for some purposes, can get in the way of our understanding of Mesoamerican conceptions of how houses—and other things—are built. Accord-ingly, in discussing dedication rituals in the remainder of this essay, I have chosen to omit the term *ritual* and in-stead to view the sacrifices, prayers, and taboos that characterize dedicatory acts as part of a local theory of *production*: a set of ideas about how people create and maintain the conditions of their existence. As several essays in this volume show, such ideas inform creative acts in a variety of contexts (McGee, this volume; Mock, this volume; Stross, this volume; Vogt, this volume; Walker, this volume). Diego Durán hinted as much when he complained, "Heathenism and idolatry are present everywhere: in sowing, in reaping, in storing grain, even in plowing the earth and in building houses; in wakes and funerals, in weddings and births" (Durán 1977:55).

More generally, the argument that we view "dedica-tion" as production requires that we move beyond the view that the logic of production is encompassed by technology, or is defined solely in terms of its material utility (Gudeman 1986:30, 90, 127, 141; Sahlins 1976:169–70). Once we do this, it becomes clear that the "factors of production" that Mesoamerican people draw upon in reproducing their existence—labor, capital, resources—are mediated by ideas about the body, work, gender, and nature. Such a perspective is implicit in the many essays in this volume that contextualize the Maya concept of "dedication"—the process of bringing to life or "ensoul-ing" things made by human hands—by viewing it in terms of Maya ideas about the universe in which we live, Maya theories of birth and death, and (in discussions of the exclusion of females from dedicatory acts; e.g., McGee, this volume) Maya constructions of gender and sexuality.

The benefits of viewing Maya dedication as produc-tion become especially clear in a comparative context. As I have already pointed out, the Maya concept of dedica-tion has only limited applicability to the Mixtec area. But instead of simply leaving the matter there, we can use the concept of "production" to pinpoint the differences between the two areas, by specifying how production is mediated by Mixtec, rather than Maya, ideas about the body, gender, and cosmology.

COOKING

Key to the Mixtec logic of production is the notion that what people are doing is cooking something. To return to our example of housebuilding, the first step, as we saw, involves digging into a hillside to create a terrace. Nuyootecos describe this action as "cooking" the site. But the act of cooking has a significance in the construction that goes beyond simply leveling a building site. Smith notes that in sixteenth-century Mixtec *chiyo*, a term we might translate as "cooked," was also the Mixtec word for "altar," "house site," or "foundation." In the ancient writing system this notion was usually represented by a temple platform with stairways to one side (Smith 1973:45, 47). If we sometimes describe structures by foundational acts (e.g., the word *building* in English), then this appears to be true for the ancient Mixtec as well, only that the foundational act involved "cooking."

Just as in the case of Maya dedication ritual, where the act of ensouling is related to the symbolism of birth (see Stross, this volume; Vogt, this volume), so too the process of cooking something in the Mixteca is informed by cultural constructions of human physiology. But instead of the act of birth, what appears to be the focus is gestation. For Mixtecs today a child is first created when the man's semen (*nute kuiji*, "white liquid") fills a woman's womb (*soko*). Semen, people say, is blood (see López Austin 1980:331) that flows from all over a man's body when he becomes "hot" during the sexual act. It is partly for this reason that the penis is called *tuchi yii*, "man's vein," and the vagina *tuchi si'i*, "woman's vein." When semen enters a woman in sufficient quantities, it slowly thickens (*nakujio ini*) "like chocolate mixed with water" and begins to grow. The sexual act must be repeated up to ten times for a woman to receive enough semen to allow her to become pregnant.[1] Women are considered colder than men, and men must heat up women with their life-giving fluids to the point where the process of gestation can begin. As this suggests, the woman is a kind of receptacle in which the fetus grows; she does not contribute in any significant way to the make-up of the child at this stage in its development. It is male blood, in the

form of semen, which is crucial. However, a woman must be young enough to bear children, or no amount of semen will produce a child. As people in Nuyoo say, she must be able "to cook," that is, she cannot be postmenopausal (*nijia*, "matronly," "firm," "mature").[2]

Inside the mother's womb, the fetus slowly grows for nine months, where it "swims" in "female liquid" (*nute si'i*) and feeds off its mother's blood. While in this state, the mother is said to be *yute*, a term that is also used to refer to plants that have not ripened yet and whose fruit remains green, immature, and full of water. Like these fruits, the blood of pregnant women is said to be bitter. It is also said to be "sickly" (*niñi va tivi*), and pregnant women are *ca'vi*, a term that translates as "sick" and "wounded" but that also refers to the splotches that appear on a woman's face and body when she first becomes pregnant (these are also called *pintu* and *veru*, and appear on boys when they reach puberty). Most significantly, pregnant women's blood is said to be cold *(viji)*. Consequently, pregnant women should avoid cold foods, such as pork, cherries, certain kinds of bananas, and avocados (see Mak 1959, for a list of foods that Mixtec people identify as cold). A woman should also eat as many "hot" foods as possible, such as beef and chicken. A woman is coldest just after her child is born (or, as Mixtecs put it, "when it falls to the ankles of its mother"), and she is *ki'mu*, "weak, thin, and cold from the loss of blood." Her excessive coldness must be actively counterbalanced by "hot" things, to move her to the midpoint between hot and cold. For this reason, the midwife gives the mother and her child a sweatbath to heat up her blood (*nasaa niñi*) and "recook" her veins (*na chi'yo tuchi*). This heating of her blood and cooking of her veins is to make her "hard" or "mature" (*nijia*) and has the important effect of converting her blood into a form suitable for the child to feed upon outside her womb—that is, breast milk. Note that the materials used in making a house— in particular, the wood and the cross-beams—are only usable if they are prepared while the moon is waning. At this time they are hard and mature (*nijia*); at other times they are *yute*. It is as if the house materials must "cook," like a fetus, before they can be completed.

Because they are in a state of excessive coldness, pregnant women have negative effects on a range of things. Some say pregnant women can injure others because they have the evil eye *(nuu sheen)*. More common is the notion that pregnant women cause things to cook improperly (*ndu chi'yo, nsa's tiu'in*, "remain raw"). Thus pregnant women should not approach the metal pots where pork rind is frying, since their presence will make it come out heavy with fat and sticky.[3] Pregnant women should avoid the places where tamales are being boiled, since they will cause the tamales to cook only on one side. The same is true for meat and ground corn cooked in underground ovens, or the ovens where men make lime. In pottery-making communities, pregnant women should avoid kilns where pottery is being fired, for the same reason.[4] Even tortillas will be affected, since pregnant women will cause them to grow mold after only a half-day—something also related to their being improperly cooked. By extension, pregnant women should also avoid contact with bananas, since they will cause the fruit to mature on only one side, while the other side remains green.

These examples indicate that pregnant women, who are "cooking," should avoid contact with things that are also being cooked (baked foods, pork rinds fried in fat, lime made in ovens, pottery fired in kilns).[5] But the negative effects that they cause also highlight the analogies the Mixtec draw between these acts and show how cooking as a metaphor for production can be extended beyond bringing something in contact with fire (as in the example of the ripening bananas, which are also "cooking").[6]

What can the focus on cooking tell us about dedication? It shows that what is at issue in the Mixtec construction of houses is *transformation*. Just as the fetus is transformed in a woman's womb, or limestone is transformed into lime, or clay into a pot, a building is similarly something that is the result of the combination and transformation of materials—a dish that has been cooked, to follow the Mixtec metaphor. Of course, cooking is a very widespread metaphor for transformation, and part of what is going on in the Mixteca is a very Lévi-Straussian conveyance of things of the Earth (nature) to human control (culture) (see Monaghan 1995; see also Vogt, this volume). Yet what is most interesting from the standpoint of this volume is how the Mixtec logic of production contrasts with that of the Maya. Instead of a wholly new beginning—the creation of new life through the ensouling act, so that ideas of birth inform the erection of new buildings (and those of death govern the destruction of buildings)—we have a focus on changes in state, the combination of elements that are themselves undergoing transformation. Accordingly, cultural constructions of gestation, of metamorphosis, of "cooking" become important in Mixtec discussions of the building of new houses and other structures.

The concept of production has the advantage of encouraging us to view the rites and practices surrounding dedication not as phenomenologically distinct kinds of activity, occurring apart from the rest of life (as we usually understand ritual), but as one of a set of activities through which people create and maintain the conditions of their existence. It also allows us to view Mixtec and Maya practices within a single framework and thus come to a fuller understanding of the differences between the two areas. But can a perspective derived from ethnographic sources help us to make sense of the archaeology of the region? Clearly, in a diverse area such as Oaxaca there is abundant room for ethnic and historical variation in the conception of and practices surrounding construction. In any event, based on the material from Nuyoo, one very general hypothesis would be that given differences in the logic of production between the Maya and the Mixtec, we should expect to find differences in the remains associated with the construction of ancient buildings. While in the Maya area each new construction would have to be separately ensouled—as attested in the archaeological record by numerous and systematically deposited offerings—in the Mixteca a single offering to the Earth (so that the builders could use the construction site) would be all that was required. Although much more excavation would have to be carried out in the Mixteca before we could confidently point to any major differences between the two areas, there does seem to be some support for this hypothesis. Based on published excavation reports, caches associated with constructions in the Mixteca are rare compared to those found in the Maya area (e.g., Lind 1979). They also seem to be much less systematically interred than in the Maya area (Art Joyce, personal communication 1993; Randall Spores, personal communication 1993).

Another hypothesis concerns the iconography of offerings and other items associated with construction. While drawing on ideas about the body, as in the Maya area, in the Mixtec area the iconography would be associated not with birth and death, but with gestation, mutation, and transformation. Again, based on the work of Masson and Orr (this volume), there appears to be some support for this hypothesis in the Oaxaca material. They note that in Monte Alban the objects marking new construction seem to be associated with "nagualism," the idea that humans maintain a transformational relationship with an animal or celestial object. In Nuyoo the noun designating the transformed version of the self (e.g., *kiti nuvi*) is also a verb meaning "metamorphosis," and it can be applied to all sorts of things that change from one state to another—such as a tadpole into a frog or someone who is ill into someone who is well, or even a collection of beams, shingles, and adobe bricks into a house.

Notes

1. This notion is widespread in Mesoamerica (see López Austin 1980:337).

2. The idea that women of child-bearing age cook is also found in the Maya area (Blaffer 1972:122–23).

3. While in the Mixteca pregnant women can spoil cooking meat, in Chiapas pregnant women can keep raw meat from spoiling. Thus during Carnival ritual advisers will search out women who are pregnant. They are requested to bite the brisket of the slaughtered bull three times to protect the meat from flies and from spoiling (Bricker 1973:107).

During earthquakes, the Nahuas covered up pots or even broke them, so that pregnant women would not abort (López Austin 1980:275), suggesting a connection between the vessels where food is cooked and the womb.

5. Among the contemporary Maya of Chiapas, should a woman approach a place where men are making lime, she will affect the fire so that it burns out from the chimney where the stones are piled, toward the oven entrance (Blaffer 1972:122). In Tlaxcala, men are responsible for making and baking *pan de muerto*, while women are forbidden to handle the bread until it is ready to be placed on the altar (Nutini 1988:122).

6. Other activities that may be informed by this same paradigm of production include fishing among the Mixe (Lipp 1991:32) and the dyeing of thread in coastal Oaxaca (Johnson et al. 1983; see also Prechtel and Carlson 1988).

References Cited

Blaffer, Sarah L.
1972 *The Black-man of Zinacantan: A Central American Legend.* Austin: University of Texas Press.

Bricker, Victoria
1973 *Ritual Humor in Highland Chiapas.* Austin: University of Texas Press.

Durán, Diego
1977 *Book of the Gods and Rites of the Ancient Calendar.* Translated and edited by Fernando Horcasitas and Doris Heyden. Norman: University of Oklahoma Press.

Freidel, David, and Linda Schele
1989 "Dead Kings and Living Temples: Dedication and Termination Rituals among the Ancient Maya." In *Word and Image in Maya Culture: Explorations in Language, Writing and Representation,* edited by William Hanks and Don Rice, 233–43. Salt Lake City: University of Utah Press.

Gudeman, Stephen
1986 *Economics as Culture.* London: Routledge and Kegan Paul.

Johnson, Andrea, Sara Stark, and Julián Mendoza García
1983 *Xemblu Cuenda Ra Cahyi Yuhva.* Mexico City: Instituto Lingüístico de Verano.

Leach, Edmund
1954 *Political Systems of Highland Burma.* Boston: Beacon Press.

Lind, Michael
1979 *Postclassic and Early Colonial Mixtec Houses in the Nochixtlan Valley, Oaxaca.* Nashville, Tenn.: Vanderbilt University Publications in Anthropology.

Lipp, Frank
1991 *The Mixe of Oaxaca: Religion, Ritual and Healing.* Austin: University of Texas Press.

López Austin, Alfredo
1980 *Cuerpo humano e ideología: Las concepciones de los antiguos Nahuas.* Mexico City: Universidad Autónoma de México.

Mak, Cornelia
1959 "Mixtec Medical Beliefs and Practices." *America Indigena* 19:125–50.

Marcus, Joyce
1983 "Zapotec Religion." In *The Cloud People: Divergent Evolution of the Zapotec and Mixtec Civilizations,* edited by Kent V. Flannery and Joyce Marcus, 345–51. New York: Academic Press.

Monaghan, John
1995 *The Covenants with Earth and Rain: Exchange, Sacrifice and Revelation in Mixtec Sociality.* Norman: University of Oklahoma Press.

Nutini, Hugo
  1988   *Todos Santos in Rural Tlaxcala.* Princeton, N.J.: Princeton University Press.
Prechtel, Martin, and Robert Carlson
  1988   "Weaving and Cosmos amongst the Tzutujil Maya of Guatemala." *RES* 15:122–32.
Sahlins, Marshall
  1976   *Culture and Practical Reason.* Chicago: University of Chicago Press.

Smith, Mary Elizabeth
  1973   *Picture Writing from Ancient Southern Mexico.* Norman: University of Oklahoma Press.
Vogt, Evon Z.
  1969   *Zinacantan: A Maya Community in the Highlands of Chiapas.* Cambridge, Mass.: Harvard University, Belknap Press.

PART TWO

Archaeological Evidence from the Maya

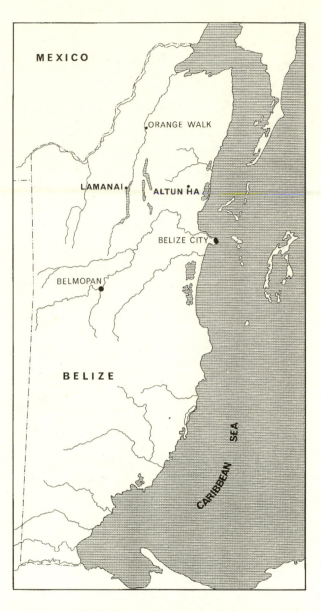

Map 6.1.   Belize, showing locations of Altun Ha and
Lamanai.

CHAPTER SIX

Intercessions with the Gods

Caches and Their Significance at Altun Ha and Lamanai, Belize

David M. Pendergast
Royal Ontario Museum

Excavations at Altun Ha between 1964 and 1970 (Pendergast 1979, 1982a, 1990a) and at Lamanai from 1974 through 1985 (Graham 1987; Pendergast 1981a, 1982b, 1986a, 1986b, 1990b, 1991) yielded a sample of caches of very substantial breadth in form and even more striking variety and richness in contents. The 119 artifact offerings from Altun Ha and the 126 from Lamanai illustrate forcefully the parallels and contrasts between two near-neighbor centers, while at the same time they provide evidence regarding conservatism and innovation in both material and nonmaterial culture over time. Of greatest importance, however, is the significant light that the data shed on the determinants and the motivations that encompassed offering activity at the two sites (map 6.1). In very large part, the understanding of cache deposition that emerges from the Altun Ha and Lamanai information can, I believe, be extended to the entirety of the southern Lowlands and very probably to the Maya area as a whole.

Part of the contrast between the sites is unquestionably a real reflection of different avenues pursued by neighboring but separate polities. At the same time, part of the contrast is the product of the considerable difference in occupation span. At Altun Ha the period represented by offerings extends from mid-Preclassic times to the early years of the Postclassic, while at Lamanai the span is much greater, with a beginning date of c. 1500 B.C. and a terminal point sometime after A.D. 1641. It would be instructive to examine the particulars of change through time at each site, but such an effort is far beyond the scope of this essay, as is intersite comparison of the exceedingly plentiful cache contents. Instead, I propose to concentrate on the broad strokes in the picture of cache composition and deposition patterns at the two centers, in order to illustrate the general nature of the data base from which it may be possible to draw conclusions regarding the significance of offerings.

The caches at both sites can be separated into three categories on the basis of context. By far the largest class occurs in communally built structures that were dedicated to the public weal; as we shall see, caches in this context predictably are the most consistent across sites in location, if not in contents. The second group occurs in residential structures, where offerings presumably had the same function but usually or always with single-family focus, and with generally greater freedom both in position and in makeup. In each of these two categories there is a significant division on the basis of specific context (see below). The final category comprises monument-related offerings, which are absent from the Altun Ha sample and are comparatively few in number at Lamanai. Owing in part to context, this third group of caches appears to differ materially from the other two, but in fact it is quite likely to have resembled other offerings in function.

THE HISTORY OF CACHE ACTIVITY AT ALTUN HA AND LAMANAI

The Preclassic

The earliest evidence at either site of what can surely be identified as offering activity occurs at Lamanai, but it includes no artifacts, and its context is somewhat obscure. The data are nevertheless significant because of their implications regarding evanescent offering activity—events highly unlikely to be discernible in the archaeological record except with the greatest of luck. In an apparent harbor near the north end of the site, a concentration of corn pollen far greater than normal for the site, with absolutely no indication of architectural or other cultural association, points to offering of whole young corn plants tossed into the waters from a boat, raft, or platform. The radiocarbon date of 1500 B.C. from wood stratigraphically associated with the pollen may indicate complex offering activity very early in the Preclassic, though not necessarily the deposition of caches as they are normally defined.

Not until the Late Preclassic, probably 400 B.C. or later, are there data from both sites on offerings in architectural context, which at this stage means structures that are communal and ceremonial in nature. Unfortunately, the source of Preclassic caches at Altun Ha is a round platform (Pendergast 1982a:186–89, fig. 98), which offers much less in the way of architectural definition than do buildings of other forms, though certain features identify its front. At issue is the relationship of the cache to the primary axis of the structure—one of two factors critical to assessment of prescriptions and proscriptions that structured offering activity. Although the primary axis can only be loosely defined for the Altun Ha platform, it is fairly clear that in the Preclassic—in contrast with later times at the site—this structural lifeline did not serve as the determinant of cache location. Although the inclusion of jade objects had become a significant part of Altun Ha offering practice by about 450–300 B.C., the stipulations regarding position that marked subsequent events evidently were not yet in force.

At Lamanai a northern suburb structure yielded a two-vessel cache with marine shells and obsidian that exemplifies the pattern of primary-axis placement, the typical occurrence of caches without surrounding cribbing or other protection, and the use of pottery in caches that remained the rule at the site until at least Early Postclassic times. Elsewhere at the site during the Preclassic, ceramic caches occur both on and well away from the primary axis. In addition, some are accompanied by a feature common at Lamanai from Preclassic through Terminal Classic times: the empty pit, often on or very near the primary axis, with every indication that use as a cache container was either contemplated or actually carried out. Such pits, which we came to know as "Lamanai Holes," were maddeningly common. The frequency of their occurrence suggests that they were not incorrectly placed offering pits for which correction was subsequently made, a phenomenon that may be in evidence at Altun Ha (Pendergast 1990a:252). Pits of this character also occur without associated caches nearby; this observation, together with the occasional presence of a thin basal stratum of organic decay product or evidence of burning, suggests their use for offerings that were composed entirely of perishable objects, either artifacts or natural materials.

Late in the Preclassic it is possible to discern in Structure N10-43 the beginnings of a perdurable approach to offerings in major Central Precinct structures that sharply distinguishes Lamanai from Altun Ha. Although it is very risky to attempt to assess cache significance on the basis of contents, the Lamanai evidence suggests that logical determinants of cache placement were not operative in the community. Neither architectural size and complexity nor the degree of change wrought by modifications was necessarily reflected in primary-axis offerings of an appropriately sumptuous nature, or even in the presence of an offering in any form.

Put simply, the approach to offerings in major communal structures at Lamanai seems exceedingly parsimonious when compared with that at Altun Ha. Witness the Late Preclassic structure in the N9-56 sequence: Though it was obviously an undertaking of very considerable significance, and was embellished with highly important stairside outset masks, it boasted no offerings, as far as we could discover from our extensive excavations along the primary axis and deeply into the core of the platform. The first two major modifications to the primary structure of N10-43, also of Late Preclassic date, likewise appear to have gone unaccompanied by cache deposition or other dedicatory activity.

Only at the beginning of the third reconfiguration of Structure N10-43, which resulted in a new stair and significant changes in the main lower landing area, was work on the structure dedicated in proper fashion with an offering placed in a pit cut into the plaza floor at the base of the original stair. Situated on the primary axis, the cache was unquestionably a dedicatory effort in advance of the new construction. Still, it scarcely raised the wealth level represented by its earlier counterpart. It did, however, commence a subtheme within the pattern of ceramics in Lamanai caches that persisted through much of the Classic: the use of paired dishes as lid and container for small objects of various sorts.

Although the evidence that bears on Preclassic offertory practice is severely limited, it shows quite clearly that the focus in the early centuries of Lamanai's occupation was on pottery vessels (fig. 6.1) as the principal, and often the only, element in caches. With the exception of a single jade bead and a jade bib-helmet figural pendant from N10-43 (fig. 6.2), no material imported from any great distance seems to have played a part in cache assemblages. One could deduce from the evidence that Lamanai's trade connections were limited in the Preclassic, but the shaky foundation for such a deduction is readily apparent. It is equally likely that the seemingly parsimonious approach adopted for Preclassic offerings was simply a matter of preference, and in fact much of the later record appears to bear out this interpretation of the earliest cache data.

The Classic

During the opening years of the Classic, both sites saw a considerable amount of building renewal and probably some building starts. As in earlier times, and indeed throughout the history of Lamanai, there was clearly no hard and fast rule regarding placement of offerings along the primary axis of new construction, or in any other context. A building renewal might contain an offering although its predecessor had none, and the presence of such an offering certainly did not dictate similar deposition in succeeding modifications. If we were to use Altun Ha as the yardstick, we would judge that the builders of Lamanai disregarded far more than half the opportunities for cache placement. Furthermore, if we were to adopt Altun Ha cache contents (fig. 6.3) as the standard—a serious error, beyond question—we would be forced to conclude that the inhabitants of Lamanai rarely if ever attained the lofty heights of cache wealth that were commonplace among their coastal neighbors.

Fig. 6.1. Blackware cylindrical vessel container (height 20.2 cm), Lamanai Cache N10-43/6; 100 B.C.–A.D. 100.

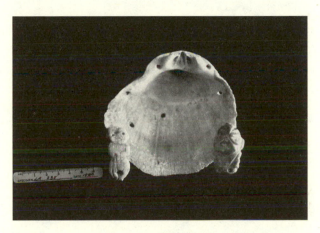

Fig. 6.2. Contents of Lamanai Cache N10-43/6. Height of jade bib-helmet pendant is 4.7 cm.

Fig. 6.3. Altun Ha Cache F-1/1, probably c. A.D. 600. Pit diameter is 40 cm.

Fig. 6.4. Lamanai Cache N9-53/1, c. A.D. 500–550 (?): *left,* with lid vessel in place; *right,* with contents exposed. Diameter of lid vessel is 29.3 cm.

Lamanai's Classic offerings resemble those of Altun Ha in one respect: they conformed to no pattern whatsoever, except during a brief period in the Middle Classic, and then probably only in two neighboring structures. The absence of patterning in cache contents, combined with the seemingly erratic distribution of offerings, leads all too easily to the assessment of cache characteristics as a reflection of the relative importance of various construction efforts: A building modification with a cache must have been more important than one without, and a large offering must have reflected greater importance than a small one. In fact, we have no knowledge of the rationale that determined cache size, or of the basis for choice of one piece of construction as an offering site and rejection of another. The variety in both of these matters is so great that it might as easily be laid to caprice as to conscious choice in ritual practice. Whether caprice or choice, however, there is no question that the determinants were adhered to with far greater frequency at Altun Ha than at Lamanai.

Examination of the full panoply of Altun Ha's Classic offerings and the more limited but equally intriguing range at Lamanai would require at least an entire volume. However, it is worth noting here that while the Classic period at Altun Ha shows evidence of single, highly varied offerings in association with structural modifications, the Classic at Lamanai was marked by a brief period of near uniformity in cache containers, among which was a group of five pairs in a single stair modification. In middle to late Early Classic times, Lamanai's builders introduced paired, unslipped, large round-side bowls as container and lid, which were unquestionably made specifically for cache use (fig. 6.4). It is curious in the extreme that the development of some standardization in containers was accompanied by one of only two deviations from the pattern of single structure–associated caches encountered at the site.

Multiple offerings also occurred in Structure N10-9, but in a form that differed in almost every respect from all other offerings at the site. In the core of the upper part of the stair, the builders placed two separate mosaic objects, of which one, a large mask, survives nearly intact. Unfortunately, the other object, which was of smaller total volume and was probably not a mask, consists largely of patternless fragments.

Late Classic offerings at Lamanai were marked by departure from earlier patterns and also by greater opulence. Such offerings often retained paired vessels but replaced vessel contents either with groups of large ceremonial flints (fig. 6.5) or with obsidian in quantities as large as 15.6 kg. For perhaps as much as two and a half centuries, offerings at Lamanai appear to have made as forceful a statement regarding the site's prominence as did those at Altun Ha, though with materials generally a bit further down the scale of ceremonial value than many from caches at Altun Ha.

The Postclassic

Near the artificial separation between the Late Classic and the Early Postclassic at Lamanai came a variety of dedicatory activity that, together with what may have been the largest single construction effort ever mounted at the site (Pendergast 1986a:231–32), bespeaks very considerable community vigor. The construction work was set in motion to the accompaniment of one of the largest offerings known at Lamanai, which involved massive amounts of burning as well as numerous specialized vessels (Pendergast 1981b:4). Slightly earlier, the deposition of a much smaller but highly important offering of vessels and mercury beneath the marker disk of a small ball court (Pendergast 1982c) testified eloquently to Lamanai's socioeconomic strength in a time of chaos in many other southern Lowlands centers.

The middle and later years of the Postclassic, a time of reshaping and concentration of the community in the southern portion of the Central Precinct, were marked by a shift away from use of quantities of artifacts in dedicatory offerings. The focus from the thirteenth century onward was, instead, frequently but not uniformly on single vessels (fig. 6.6) or other objects, which were deposited both in units under construction and in or on ruined buildings. The change may have been partly a reflection of decreasing size of the Lamanai polity, but evidence of continuing internal and external economic vitality suggests that reduced cache size resulted from a shift in values rather than a decline in means. Part of this evidence consists of offering contents from the early and middle parts of the time span.

From the thirteenth to the early fifteenth century, the inhabitants of Lamanai deposited some fairly opulent smash-and-scatter offerings on the surfaces of buildings either long abandoned or in their final days of use (Pendergast 1981a:44, 51). Here the prodigal disposal of high-value objects in termination rituals attained a level equal to that of earlier times, especially in the case of thirty or more locally made and imported Mayapan-related figurine censers spread over and around Structure N9-56 (Pendergast 1981a:51, fig. 27). The contrast between such termination deposits and many of the dedicatory caches suggests that the importance of dedication offering had

Fig. 6.5.   Lamanai Cache N10-9/8, probably ninth century. Note vessel at left.

Fig. 6.6.   Vessel from Lamanai Cache N10-43/1. Vessel (diameter 19.0 cm) was deposited with a single jade bead in collapse debris at the base of the structure.

Fig. 6.7. Lamanai single-object offerings from immediate pre-Conquest and post-Conquest contexts. Height of left figure is 9.2 cm.

Fig. 6.8. Lamanai Cache N11-4/1, one of several Contact Period representations of a mythical crocodile, here with God N in its mouth, probably post-1641. Length is 22.7 cm.

diminished by at least the Middle Postclassic. There is, however, no solid reason to assume that smaller amounts of material indicate reduced ritual importance of the activity, or that the value of the objects offered was not entirely commensurate with the importance of the construction or other endeavors involved. The truth is that in this respect as in others, the Postclassic was a time of change that must be understood in its own terms rather than by comparison with earlier patterns (Pendergast 1990b).

The Contact Period

The Historic period was marked by the first significant disruption of offering practices whose fundamental principles had remained constant since the Preclassic. The disruption was occasioned by the intrusion of Europeans into the Maya world, which began in Belize about 1544 (Graham et al. 1989:1256). From the outset until the Spanish hold on Lamanai was permanently shaken loose in 1641 (López de Cogolludo 1971:book 11, chap. 13), it appeared that Christian precepts had largely swept aside indigenous beliefs and practices. Superposition of the first Christian temple atop the ruins of a native one, however, was accompanied by deposition of one pre-Columbian–style offering (Pendergast 1991:343), and the persistence of related activity is documented by numerous references to idolatry in the ethnohistorical record. Lamanai served as a center for reduction of the surrounding territory and hence had a varied and only partly stable population. As a result it very probably experienced more resistance to Christianity and recurrence of pre-Columbian practice than existed in some other Spanish-period communities.

Part of the evidence that pre-Contact values and techniques remained generally powerful as part of a joint Maya/Spanish accommodation (Graham et al. 1989:1257; Pendergast 1993) consists of continuity in offering practice. Once freed of Spanish presence, the Maya reasserted earlier attitudes (figs. 6.7, 6.8), but in contexts that in some instances were determined at least in part by Christian considerations (Graham et al. 1989:1257; Pendergast 1991:346–347, 1993). The strongest expression of the resurgence of pre-Columbian practice in a partly syncretic form was the placement of a stela with accompanying substela cache in the ruined nave of the second church. The cache contents were of classes that would have been chosen before European contact, but the sacred space in which the activity took place was now defined by Christian belief.

Similar conjoining of Christian sacred space and pre-Columbian cache practice is reflected in at least three of the other six caches placed within the nave and at the face of the masonry chancel of the church. The remaining three offerings comprised one group of miniature animal figurines and two ceramic mythical crocodilian creatures, surely a restatement of the crocodile association reflected in the name of the community (Pendergast 1981a:31–32). The close resemblance of the figurines to ones deposited elsewhere in the community more than a century earlier is direct physical evidence of the maintenance of the pre-Columbian tradition alongside Christian belief.

In contrast with the profusion of church offerings, axial and other caches are nearly absent in what is very likely to be either a Spanish-period or a post-1641 settlement zone at the south end of the site (Pendergast 1985:2). The scarcity of offerings may indicate diminished concern with dedicatory matters in residential context, but it is equally likely that it reflects an overall reduction in resources or the closing off of trade in some classes of material. Full consideration of such complex issues goes well beyond the bounds of the present discussion. There is no question, however, that offering practice in the Historic period bespeaks a Maya dedicatory tradition that was durable enough to withstand and accommodate the onslaughts of a new belief system, and to survive into the post-European period with most or all of its essential elements intact.

Cache Placement and Cache Meaning

The data from Altun Ha and Lamanai clearly present a solidly documented opportunity to move beyond description to a characterization of the modal aspects of dedicatory activity at the two sites. Although neither center is fully representative of southern Maya Lowlands prehistory—and indeed in the Maya context it would be foolish to seek a holotype—I suggest that the general statements that follow are very likely to be widely applicable in the Maya world.

The Role of the Primary Axis

It is abundantly clear from the record at both sites that the primary axis was the principal determinant of cache position in communally built structures. Evidence suggests that the Maya established this vital structure lifeline by visual identification rather than precise measurement. As a result, offering position might deviate slightly from a true measured axis, and the deviation was likely to be greater in upper portions of a structure than at the base, presumably because those depositing an offering there found fewer visual keys to axis position.

One of the aims in placement of a cache on the primary axis can surely be understood as support for or enhancement of the function of the axis itself, which appears to have been dual. The primary axis was, first, an identifier of the structure, distinctive of that building and maintained as an entity that, though invisible, was perceptible as physically separate from the axes of any facing structures. This concern accounts for the offsetting of facing buildings in the otherwise symmetrical configurations that usually border plazas and other platform surface areas. In its relationship to the axis as structural identifier, a cache can be seen as purely dedicatory, especially if it lies beneath or at a low level within new construction. It is readily apparent that continuing focus on the primary axis should have led to rededication with every significant remodeling of the structure, but the histories of both Altun Ha and Lamanai show that this seemingly logical approach did not obtain in either community. The actual significance of a given construction effort, as opposed to the archaeologist's assessment of it, may be at issue here. Significance was surely a ceremonial matter for the Maya, while our judgment is with rare exceptions rooted in engineering and traffic-flow concerns because there are no readable clues to ceremonial impact.

The second aspect of the primary axis is its function as the main avenue of communication with a deity. In this respect, the midline is very likely to have been understood as extending not only beyond the foot of the stair and across the plaza but also beyond the summit into the heavens, presumably for an unimaginable distance in both directions. Although this would appear to have offered the opportunity for axial caches well beyond the limits of a structure—in one direction, at least—the evidence indicates that the building was perceived as the proper vessel for all axial offerings. The power of the axis was no doubt understood to be self-generating, but it was surely reified by the presence of one or more offerings along the vital line. A basal or preconstruction cache might well have served both to dedicate the structure and to amplify the axial communication system; caches at higher points in the building seem more likely to have been focused on the latter function.

It is far more difficult to identify primary-axis caches in residential structures, largely because domestic structures often had more than one major access and sometimes were laid out in a way that thwarts efforts to identify the midline. Still, there are numerous instances of unquestionable or probable primary-axis caches in residential structures at both Altun Ha and Lamanai, and it is likely that the dedicatory purpose in this context was generally similar to that in communal structures. It is often true, however, that dedicatory activity in residential structures had more of a topping-off quality than is standard for public structures: Domestic offerings frequently occur immediately beneath room floors or walls, rather than at stair bases or elsewhere in the platform core. This suggests that the particulars of domestic axial offerings may have differed from those at a community level, a conclusion that is scarcely surprising.

Subsidiary Axes

In both public and domestic contexts, there are also offerings that are away from the primary axis. Caches of this class may fall on apparent transverse axes, which are usually more easily identified in communal than in residential structures. The basis for identification in either setting is often a matter of exclusion: If the offering is not associated with a feature of the antecedent or the new construction, we may assume a link with an otherwise unidentifiable subsidiary line. Vertical location may indicate whether dedication or amplification was the primary motive of the cache, but unfortunately, there is still considerable room for speculation.

Feature-linked Caches

The final subcategory of caches in both residential and community contexts comprises offerings clearly related to an architectural feature and therefore not linked to any axis of the structure. Though far more likely to occur in elite residences and in communal structures, feature-linked caches are also found in less elaborate domestic buildings. In all instances the purpose of the cache is very likely to have been recognition of the importance of the feature to which it is linked. In communal buildings the importance was surely ceremonial, while in residences it may have been established either by ceremony or by sentiment. It is very probably significant that in cases where no ceremonial aspect can be discerned in the feature honored, caches contain great varieties of low-value objects—just what one might expect in a purely household endeavor without ties to a deity.

Monument-associated Caches

Monument-associated caches at Lamanai may well have had both the functions ascribed to primary-axis caches in communal structures. Uncertainty regarding this point arises from our limited knowledge of the intended functions of the monuments themselves. If they were seen solely as statements on the part of rulers, associated caches are most likely to have had a purely dedicatory intent. If, on the other hand, either the power of the ruler or the power of a deity to whom the ruler was linked also resided in the monument, then something of the amplification purpose may also have been served by a cache.

The Aims of Dedicatory Activity

With very limited exceptions, all the hopes and intentions that I have thus far suggested as embodied within caches were focused on the maintenance of the future. A few, to be sure, looked backward by focusing on an element of a structure about to be concealed beneath a new building, but even so the offering may have been making a statement about the structure to come. Offerings that lay on a primary axis maintained over many reconfigurations of a building surely also embraced a consciousness of the past, but their main focus was forward rather than backward. To ensure the success, and perhaps even the durability, of a building itself by an appropriate offering within its core was to relinquish wealth in an effort to ensure the years ahead. To give physical expression to the pipeline between humans and their gods by placing offerings along that line was to express both the need to have a deity's ear and the hope that what the deity heard would be continually pleasing.

In all such endeavors there was a very large measure of reciprocity, either actual or anticipated. As the gods had given, so offerings in their temples and in residences gave back to them; as it was hoped the gods would continue to give, so the offerings would help to convert hope into reality. In whatever form and whatever context, caches were for the Maya a physical means of staving off the descent of the great Monty Python-esque foot that could obliterate the best of human efforts in one final, awful instant.

ACKNOWLEDGMENTS

Excavations at Altun Ha were supported by the Canada Council, the Wenner-Gren Foundation, the *Globe and Mail* of Toronto, and research funds of the Royal Ontario Museum. The Lamanai work also received support from the Canada Council (later the Social Sciences and Humanities Research Council of Canada) and Royal Ontario Museum research funds, with capital equipment grants from the Richard M. Ivey Foundation of London, Ontario.

REFERENCES CITED

Graham, E.
1987   "Terminal Classic to Early Historic Period Vessel Forms from Belize." In *Maya Ceramics: Papers from the 1985 Maya Ceramic Conference,* edited by P. M. Rice and R. J. Sharer, 73–98. BAR International Series 345(i). Oxford, England: BAR.

Graham, E., D. M. Pendergast, and G. D. Jones
1989   "On the Fringes of Conquest: Maya-Spanish Contact in Colonial Belize." *Science* 246:1254–59.

López de Cogolludo, D.
1971   *Los tres siglos de la dominación española en Yucatán, o sea Historia de esta provincia.* Facsimile of 2nd ed., Mérida-Campeche 1842–1845. Graz, Austria: Akademische Druck und Verlagsanstalt.

Pendergast, D. M.
1979   *Excavations at Altun Ha, Belize, 1964–1970.* Vol. 1. Toronto: Royal Ontario Museum.
1981a   "Lamanai, Belize: Summary of Excavation Results, 1974–1980." *Journal of Field Archaeology* 8:29–53.
1981b   "Lamanai 1981 (II): Buds, Sweat and Gears." *Royal Ontario Museum Archaeological Newsletter,* n.s. 199.
1982a   *Excavations at Altun Ha, Belize, 1964–1970.* Vol. 2. Toronto: Royal Ontario Museum.
1982b   "Lamanai, Belice, durante el Post-Clásico." *Estudios de Cultura Maya* 14:19–58.
1982c   "Ancient Maya Mercury." *Science* 217:533–35.
1985   "Lamanai 1985: Stop Me before I Dig Again." *Royal Ontario Museum Archaeological Newsletter,* ser. 2, 11.
1986a   "Stability through Change: Lamanai, Belize, from the Ninth to the Seventeenth Century." In *Late Lowland Maya Civilization: Classic to Postclassic,* edited by J. A. Sabloff and E. W. Andrews V, pp. 223–49. Albuquerque: University of New Mexico Press.
1986b   "Under Spanish Rule: The Final Chapter in Lamanai's Maya History." *Belcast Journal of Belizean Affairs* 3(1–2):1–7.
1990a   *Excavations at Altun Ha, Belize, 1964–1970.* Vol. 3. Toronto: Royal Ontario Museum.
1990b   "Up from the Dust: The Central Lowlands Postclassic as Seen from Lamanai and Marco Gonzalez, Belize." In *Vision and Revision in Maya Studies,* edited by F. S. Clancy and P. D. Harrison, 169–77. Albuquerque: University of New Mexico Press.
1991   "The Southern Maya Lowlands Contact Experience: The View from Lamanai, Belize." In *Columbian Consequences,* edited by D. H. Thomas, 3 vols., 3:336–54. Washington, D.C.: Smithsonian Institution Press.
1993   "Worlds in Collision: The Maya/Spanish Encounter in Sixteenth and Seventeenth Century Belize." In *The Meeting of Two Worlds: Europe and the Americas, 1492–1650,* edited by W. Bray, 105–43. London: British Academy.

CHAPTER SEVEN

Maya Dedications of Authority

Sandra Noble
FAMSI Director
Foundation for the Advancement of
Mesoamerican Studies, Inc.

Hieroglyphic records of dedicatory events were fairly common throughout the Classic Maya area, and somewhat more prevalent at Copán, Honduras, than at other sites, especially during the latest known sociopolitical era (c. A.D. 760–800). At that time dedicatory rites for stone benches became one of the most commonly recorded events. It is my thesis that at Copán, the documentation of one's personal participation in the dedication of one's *seat of authority* became the public and permanent validation of one's *position of authority*. To show this, I compare the benches and dedicatory texts of Copán to examples drawn from a broader spectrum of Maya seats, images, and records of dedication rites.

Although we can't know the actual sociology of ancient political material goods, by tracing the similarities of commissioned choices through time and through space, we can determine what forms were repeatedly selected for communication of concepts via material objects. Recognizing the significant variations within these repeated choices or "conventions" allows us to detect elite accommodations to changing sociopolitical circumstances. Additionally, as Chartier (1989:171) suggests, "the notion of selective appropriation [of elements] makes it possible to appreciate the differences in cultural apportionment ... the creative invention that lies at the very heart of the reception process." Thus we should "focus attention on the differentiated and contrasting uses of the same goods, the same texts, and the same ideas."

Precisely this sort of distinctive and reductive use of ritual imagery and text characterizes the latest sculptures of Copán, and it may imply a distinction between intended messages of the later monuments as opposed to messages conveyed by more standardized texts and images from earlier eras. As noted in previous searches for evidence of original sculptors' intent in the Copán area, design, decoration, and construction of architecture provide a visual statement of power (Hendon 1992:895).

For most of Maya history as documented in dynastic monuments, text and image operated together as complementary "scripts" for validating authority. The conventional glyphic data, usually on the sides or backs of sculpture, were juxtaposed with equally conventional figural images on the frontal faces of stelae. Comparison of Maya monuments and pottery from the Preclassic through the Late Classic (c. A.D. 100–900) reveals three major forms of imagery: standing human figures, seated personages, and depictions of reptilian monsters (figs. 7.1, 7.2, 7.3). In the texts accompanying these images, the most frequently documented rituals, or traditions of ceremony, were birth, heir designation, public celebrations of war conquests, completion and renewal of time cycles, and what Mayanists have termed "dedication rites."

Fig. 7.1.   Copán, Stela 6. (Barbara Fash in Urban and Schortman 1986:21)

While we have solid reasons to suspect that Maya "dedications" served a similar function to twentieth-century "cornerstone laying," we cannot be certain what particular aspects of consecration rites were being referred to by the Maya. That is, were artists referring to an initial "sod turning," to a final "ribbon cutting," or to any number of possible occasions in between? About a dozen different "dedication verbs" occur in Maya texts. Some have been deciphered, including the verbs for "self-sacrifice," "fire rites," "setting in place of monuments," and "caching of offering" (see Schele 1992 for decipherments by Linda Schele and David Stuart). Although archaeological remains of dedication and termination rituals suggest a standardized sequence of events, the textual records of such activity are often more general than specific. For this reason, in the following pages I shall boldly assume that for the Maya, "dedication verbs" referred to some or all of the following dedicatory practices, which collectively sanctified, consecrated, and animated architectural structures and space:

-self-sacrificial bloodletting for offerings
-the burning of blood-spattered papers and/or incense
-the conjuring of supernatural cloud/smoke monsters
-the appearance and intervention of gods/ancestors
-the sealing of paraphernalia in caching vessels
-the burial of offerings in floors or staircases, or under seats
-the oration by dignitaries to conclude the sanction

Through the epigraphic and ethnographic work of many scholars (for an extensive bibliography, see Schele and Freidel 1990), it has become ever more apparent that the major role of dedicatory rites was to manifest and involve supernaturals for the witnessing and divine sanctioning of human actions. Both ethnographic records and hieroglyphic inscriptions frequently feature the conjuring and appearance of deities, the creation of supernatural space, and the animation of that space. In this way, dedicatory ritual seems to include a reenactment of mythical creation, often conceptualized as a journey from chaos to order, and/or a passage from one state to another.

Although the correspondence of particular images with particular textual references is not absolute, at Copán there is a gradual shift to clear preferences for interrelationships of the figural reptilians with the associated glyphic records of dedication. Along with the selected major image (either a standing or a seated figure), there is often a subsidiary image, one of several reptil-

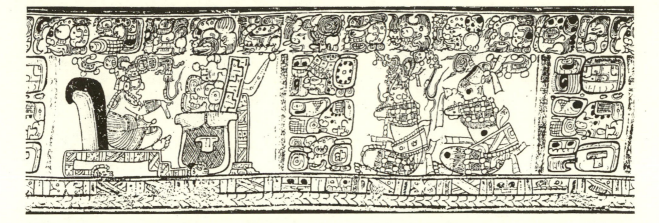

Fig. 7.2. Roll-out photograph by Justin Kerr (K1183). (Kerr 1989:65)

ians. These have been variously called the Bicephalic Monster (Cohodas 1982), the Vision Serpent (Schele and Miller 1986), the Planetary Band (Carlson and Landis 1985), or the Celestial Cosmic Monster (Schele and Miller 1986). Analysis of Maya reptilians reveals several versions, with subtle semantic differences indicated by distinguishing iconographic characteristics (Cohodas 1982). However, these zoomorphs may be perceived as essentially equivalent images, with an essentially equivalent cluster of associated meanings. They are all versions of shared origins: serpentine bodies, some with two iden-

tical snakeheads, others having two different heads. They also share equivalent, if not identical, contexts.[1]

The interrelationship of dedication ritual and serpentine imagery, so prevalent in the late sculpture of Copán, appears to stem from the earliest representations of serpentine monsters, commonly included as secondary symbols of authority (Hauberg Stela or Bonampak Lintel 4). This originally subsidiary, serpentine element later becomes the major focus of Copán's sculpture. Standing rulers, as on Copán Stela 6 (fig. 7.1), often carry a double-headed serpent bar with reptilian deities emerging from

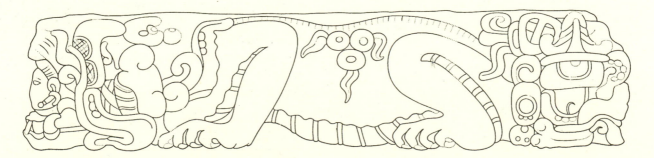

Fig. 7.3. Copán, Altar 41. (After Maudslay 1974: pl. 14)

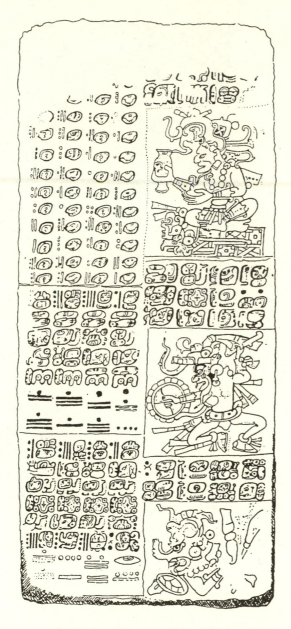

Fig. 7.4. Codex Dresden 46A. (After Villacorta and Villacorta 1930)

the maw of opposed heads. This emphasis on emergence via the serpentine body (symbolic regurgitation) is metaphorically equivalent to birth, to creation, and to the moment of accession to political office (that is, the moment of significant change in status).

Human figures are frequently shown seated on serpentine forms or sky band forms, and occasionally on composites of both those forms (figs. 7.2, 7.4). These "seats of power" signal a supernatural environment and probably imply some measure of sanction of the seating/accession by the serpentine/reptilian represented.[2] Significantly, although these serpentine forms may vary in some respects, the basic components of a supernatural, serpentine, bicephalic deity is shared through Maya time and space. We can never know precisely how this creature was once received or how it once asserted authority, but its strong association with sociopolitical authority is clearly evident. Ethnographic analogy, as well as Maya history, myth, and historiography, provides "some understanding of just what they took as the point of what they were doing" (Geertz 1983). The serpentine-reptilian seems to be a physical representation of a conceptual vehicle of change associated with transformation from one state to another (for example, deceased to reborn), or from one realm to another (Otherworld to seen world, for example). Such transformations may be conceived as taking place within the body of the bicephalic Cosmic Monster whose front and rear heads mark portals of the Otherworld: the entrance into, and exit out of, the sacred realm of gods and ancestors.

At Yaxchilan, to illustrate the sacred validation of the ruler's inauguration, artists created an image portraying a conjuring of Yaxchilan's ancestral founder through the body of a two-headed serpent (fig. 7.5). Years later at the same site, artists imitated that composition, this time (fig. 7.6) to sanction the actual birth of an heir, the grandchild and namesake of the initial patron of the image.

At Palenque the Oval Palace Tablet, located above a major "accession seat," is encircled with the body of a serpent. Thus, like the Piedras Negras accession stelae, the Palenque scene of the passage of power or inauguration of the ruler is enveloped with the supernatural sanction of the reptilian (fig. 7.7). Elsewhere at Palenque,

Fig. 7.5. *Facing page.* Yaxchilan, Lintel 25.
(Ian Graham, in Graham and Von Euw 1977, 3:56)

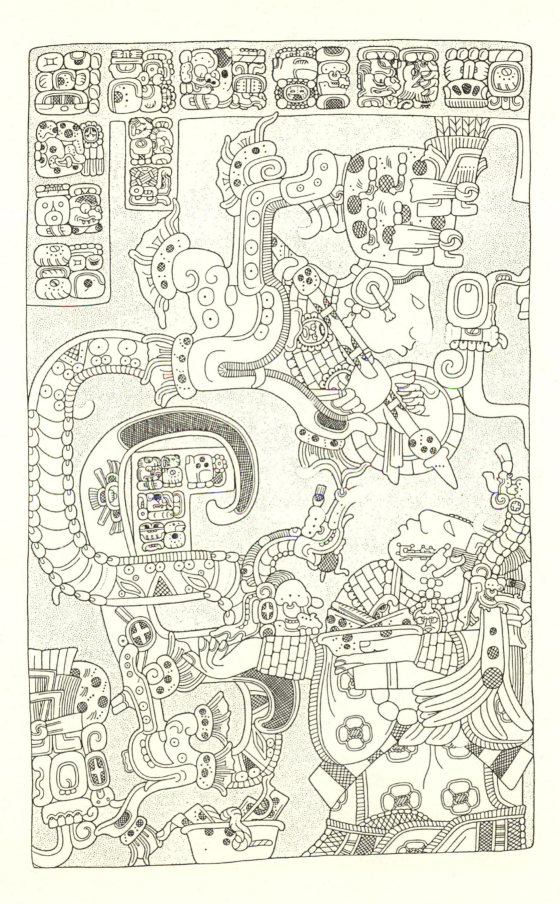

Fig. 7.6.   Yaxchilan, Lintel 13. (Ian Graham, in Graham and Von Euw 1977, 3:50)

builders of Pacal's tomb constructed a hollow serpentine form leading from the sarcophagus up the stairway, terminating at the central doorway with a serpentine maw. This three-dimensionally modeled serpent connects the dark tomb with the bright outdoors, thereby ensuring an eternal passageway between the underworld realm of the deceased and the upperworld realm of the living, via the limestone "body" of the serpentine monster.

At Copán, Stela D of c. A.D. 735 presents a conventional image of a standing ruler and a conventional hieroglyphic text commemorating the end of a Maya time period, along with a conventional record of the "dedication rites" for this stela (fig. 7.8). However, there is an unusual iconographic addition to this monument, an addition now recognizable as a precedent for the later

emphasis at Copán on bicephalic reptilians and supernatural sanctioning rituals of dedication (c. A.D. 765). On Stela D double-headed serpents intertwine up and down both sides and over the top of the stela, terminating with paired, disembodied, reptilian-head glyphs. These glyphs and the accompanying Planetary Bands as serpentine bodies are included as locative references to portals of the Underworld (fig. 7.8).[3] This juxtaposition of the serpent heads with corresponding glyphic references to Underworld locations portrays again, as on Palenque's Oval Palace Tablet, a Maya ruler enveloped "within" the supernatural sanction of the double-headed reptilian.[4]

This ideal of sanction, accomplished through ritualized conjuring of the serpentine body, was employed some thirty years later by several members of Copán's

Fig. 7.7.   Palenque, Oval Palace tablet and bench. (After Robertson 1985:92)

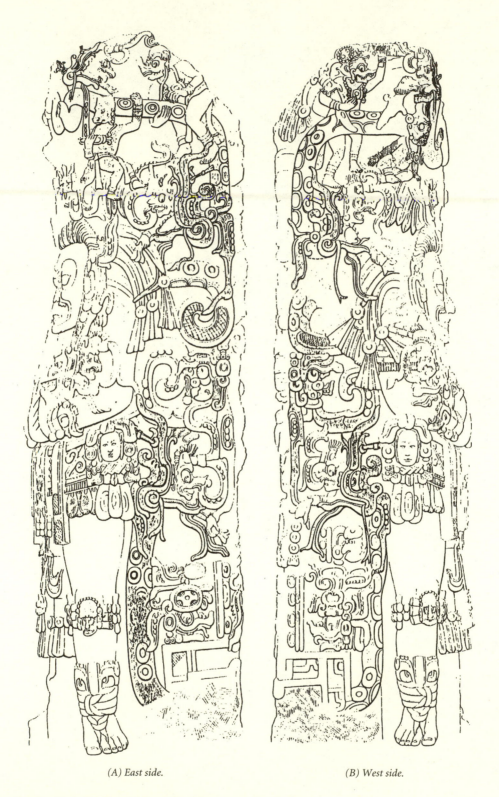

(A) East side.　　　　　　　　　　　　　　　*(B) West side.*

Fig. 7.8.　Copán, Stela D sides. (After Maudslay 1974: pl. 46)

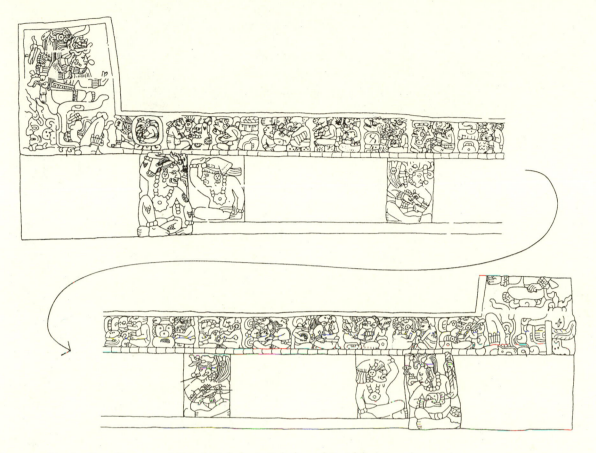

Fig. 7.9.   Copán, Sepulturas seat. (Linda Schele, in Schele and Freidel 1990:331)

nobility as visual validations of their having acceded to some position of authority. So much has been written about Copán's benches in recent years that they have practically become one of the world's wonders, particularly the bench from the suburb known today as Sepulturas. This Sepulturas seat (fig. 7.9) is one of the most widely publicized Maya sculptural artifacts. The texts and images of this bench have been interpreted by some scholars (Bardsley 1990; Fash 1991; Schele and Freidel 1990) as signals of sociopolitical disturbance, an explanation based in part on the elaborate iconography and the equally ornate hieroglyphic inscriptions. With a presumed correspondence between the degree of elaboration of the seat and the degree of status of its owner, Copán's Sepulturas seat has been interpreted as an at-

tempt at usurping of royal prerogative by nonroyal suburban lords. That is, the commissioning of this seat and the recording of presumed "royal" rituals by "nonroyals" have been viewed as indications of resistance to rulership, of intensified class conflict, and of revolt by suburban nobility.

Changes in sculptural form, inscription, and image once did suggest nonroyal imitation, and hence contestation, of royal power. However, consideration of regional patterns of dedicatory monuments suggests to me now, by contrast, that the benches in Copán's suburbs should not be interpreted as evidence of dissent. Rather, their texts, images, and positions may be viewed as conforming to expected regional and social patterns of replication. During the final few reigns at Copán, sculptural

Fig. 7.10.　Copán, Altar U. (Linda Schele, in Schele and Freidel 1990:333)

choices changed. Instead of traditional stelae, altarlike sculptures and benches became the most common carved monuments at Copán. Imagery focused on composite reptilian monsters (figs. 7.9, 7.10) rather than on customary royal portraits. Further, sculptures in suburban areas were now elaborately decorated, much like those of the downtown core. Hieroglyphic inscriptions involving single verbs and dates written in shorthand script now substituted for the long and detailed texts of earlier monuments. And perhaps most significant, the previous textual emphasis on genealogical and political history was supplemented by shorter inscriptions documenting dedicatory ritual, performed in most cases by subordinate nobility and nonroyals.

Such changes, however, are expected aspects of urban growth and do not necessarily indicate abrupt shifts in sociopolitical organization. As Geertz claims, "the relevance of historical fact for sociological analysis rests on the perception that though both the structure and the expressions of social life change, the inner necessities that animate it, do not ... political authority still requires a cultural frame in which to define itself and advance its claims" (1983:143). Although the stelae portraits of human figures were replaced at Copán with nonhuman images of two-headed monsters, Copán's serpentine bench-monsters must have continued to represent some

primary aspect of a cultural frame—to represent, and be received as, the animation of political power.

Comparison with other Maya benches is helpful in attempting to understand such a cultural frame. Many benches are depicted as being supported or held up by aged deities, named in the texts as *bacabs*. This title can be translated as "the standing-up one" and refers to actual ritual and to recorded mythology. Briefly, the event of Maya cosmic origin is a separation of sky from earth, the bringing of light (the sun) into existing darkness. *Bacabs* are supernaturals whose job is to support the sky. As clearly evident on the unpublished Lintel 4 from Lax Tunich (fig. 7.11), the sky-band bench is often depicted as an enormously heavy load, a burden.[5] This concept—exemplified by several elaborate Maya stone benches and by painted depictions of benches also upheld by aged *bacabs*—reveals, in my opinion, the idealized framework from which the sculptured Sepulturas bench derives.

Fig. 7.11.　*Facing page.* Lax Tunich, Panel 4. (Unpublished photograph in author's possession)

In distinguishing standardized traditions for monumental sculpture at Copán, it is also necessary to recognize which aspects of more traditional compositions were omitted from the latest benches and seats of the Maya center and, more especially, which elements were retained. Altars U and 41 and the Sepulturas bench illustrate the considerable reductions of text and image as compared to earlier monuments at the site. In later sculpture the normalized tradition of the two-headed reptilian is present, but the typical standing or seated ruler is absent; the normalized tradition of a dedication record is present, but the typical records of genealogical and political history are absent. In these latest monuments of the Copán area, especially the Sepulturas seat (fig. 7.9), visual validations of political power are reduced to an image of the serpentine body as the source of, and the seat for, authority. Furthermore, the hieroglyphic record of the dedication rites for that seat also clarifies some of the interwoven semantic aspects of benches, seats, and the dedication ritual.

Textual and figural references to "seating" occur within all periods of Maya society. The *chum-wan,* "seating," glyph itself originates in a profile sketch of a seated figure (see Schele and Miller 1986). Carved objects of many eras depict personages seated upon cushions, benches, and serpentine monsters. As derived from later and longer texts, the ceremony of accession seems to have involved several stages: announcement of one's appointment to some office, adornment with some regionally accepted symbol of authority, commissioning of some marker of that ceremony, and the dedication and setting up of that marker. I believe the bench is just such a marker, whether erected in a central city, a multi-room complex, or a single-room structure. The bench is a symbolic referent to the series of accession events and to the physical locus of those events.

Although pictographic glyphs describing seats have been identified for some time, only recently has a group of epigraphers identified a phonetic form that seems to name a seat (see "Altars" Z, T, U, and 41; also see remarks by Barbara MacLeod, Dorie Reents-Budet, Sandra Bardsley, and Khristaan Villela in MacLeod n.d.). That glyphic compound can be deciphered as *kuch* (T174.528) and can be translated variously as "a seat," "a territorial locale of political control," "a person charged with leadership responsibility," or "a burden, a heavy load, an encumbrance."

In other words, *kuch* describes a seat of authority, a place of authority, a person of authority, and a concept of burdensome authority (Bardsley 1996). On Altar 41 at Copán (fig. 7.3), full-figure glyphs were used by the head of state in a record of his having "set up" or dedicated this particular bench. Through the punning possible in a text written with full-humanoid figures instead of only phonetic signs, it is apparent today that the ancient Maya perceived the elevated status of a territorial *kuch* not only as a seat of authority but also as a burden of leadership responsibility. These nominal readings of the Copán benches as seats of authority imply that whoever performs and records the dedication rites for a seat has been validated as having the position of authority in that specific territory or realm of authority.

This further implies that not all representations of seated figures necessarily refer to a specific individual. Rather, I suspect that seated personages unidentified by nominals and/or titles may be significations of a more generic sociopolitical power—an authority associated with physically and ritually seated persons, persons validated for occupying a seat of authority. Additional evidence may be seen in the ancient Emblem Glyphs for the sites of Tonina and Machaquila. Their main signs, determined by Peter Mathews (1985) as signifying an autonomous political unit, are in these two cases pointed references to a territorial seat of power: for Tonina, the *po,* or "mat-covered seat"; for Machaquila, the *kuch,* or "seat and site of power." Thus, the rulers of these sites may once have been known as "the sacred lords of the territorial seat of power."

The elaboration of benches in subsidiary areas of Copán for subsidiary lords has suggested to some an attempt by the secondary members of society to usurp centralized status by appropriating "downtown imagery" for commissions of their own carved benches as local displays of elite power. Diachronic and synchronic comparison of Maya benches and their contexts suggests instead that although benches may signify status, such status is limited to specified realms. For this reason, elaborate benches commissioned by nonroyals in suburban settings do not necessarily indicate aggressive, illegal replication of royal prerogative. Rather, when viewed in relation to each other—including local, regional, and pan-Maya contexts—the benches merely indicate authority at some level, either within one's own lineage or within the group of regional lineage heads, each subservient to a supreme, royal lineage head. The notion of benches as tools of power refers to all representations of seats as instruments for both reflecting and re-creating sociopolitical relationships. This analogy suggests that other material objects of the ancient Maya may also have served as visual tools for the creation and maintenance of power relationships.

Aspects of sculptural style, environmental changes, and hieroglyphic format have suggested to Mayanists that the traditional organization of political control at Copán changed c. A.D. 760. This change has been described and understood as a shift from centralized control by a single divine ruler to a more conciliar government (Fash 1991) with political power shared among several elite members. However, while hieroglyphic texts of these monuments may mention accession of the nonruling patron to some political office as well as his affiliation with the ruler, textual records gradually come to focus primarily on the dedicatory date and associated ceremonies.[6] This gradual shift of hieroglyphic content is paralleled by iconographic shifts. Beginning with Altar Z, erected by one of the ruler's siblings (under the auspices of the ruler),[7] imagery no longer portrays a single, all-powerful ruler. Instead a nonhuman, Underworld reptilian becomes the prominent image, flanked at first by miniature depictions of elevated, seated humans (fig. 7.10), but eventually free of any figural reference to political portraits. It is also significant that at about the same time (c. A.D. 775) Copán's ruler himself renovated Structure 11 to include only minimal allusions to seated personages; these interior sculptures were extremely subsidiary to the colossal, double-headed reptilian on the exterior, public façade. The interior bench-row of Structure 11 with twenty figures ensconced on cushions may even refer to a political council as a general entity,[8] while the colossal, exterior serpentine monster (evidently upheld by equally colossal *bacabs/pahuatuns*) may refer to a specified supernatural source of all political power.

By c. A.D. 780 the royal human portrait was seemingly no longer employed at Copán, and hieroglyphic text consisted of an abbreviated date, a single dedicatory verb, and the name of the patron. Public validation of status and power was no longer accrued through one's dynastic and political history, as once displayed with lengthy textual records and larger-than-life portraits on stelae. Instead, by this time legitimacy was established primarily through records of one's having commissioned and dedicated a seat of power (a bench or "altar") elaborated with imagery of the primordial serpentine monster that originally facilitated the evolution of all Maya commoners and kings. The perception of power, formerly understood to reside solely in the person of the charismatic king and his lineage founders, seems to have been ad-

justed. While three major canonical images were once employed by all Maya rulers, by c. A.D. 780 at Copán those norms had been eliminated or reduced to bare minimum. Just as the dynastic system could no longer produce a single heir whose right to rule was unquestioned, the imagery formerly associated with that process was no longer viable.

The elimination of the royal portrait meant a new relationship among the standardized elements, for the ruler and his power were no longer one and the same. Power, thus separated from dynastic control, became a negotiable commodity. In place of the portrait of an enthroned ruler, whoever claimed power seated himself upon the seat of power. His dedication of this seat, involving the manifestation and intervention of serpentine supernaturals, sanctioned his right to rule. The sculptural reduction of text and image to normalized basics shows that the altered political organization and its compensating cultural frame required innovative compositions to document the ritual transfer of sacred power from the supernatural founders and ancestors to the human authorities.

ACKNOWLEDGMENTS

I appreciate the invitation from Shirley Mock and Debra Selsor-Walker to participate in the symposium that gave rise to this volume. I wish also to express my appreciation to the director of the Institutio Hondureno de Antropologia e Historia, the director of the Copán Acropolis Project, and the staff of El Centro Regional de Investigaciones Archeologica, each of whom kindly contributed to my study of ancient Copán. I am especially grateful to Anne Dowd, Barbara Fash, Ian Graham, Tom Jones, Justin Kerr, Alfred Maudslay, and Merle Greene Robertson for the fine quality of their drawings and photographs. I am indebted to Marvin Cohodas for giving so generously of his time and his thoughts. Investigations for this paper were supported also by a doctoral fellowship from the Social Sciences and Humanities Research Council of Canada.

NOTES

1. Note that it is the homophony of the Maya words *chaan*, "sky," and *chan*, "serpent," that allows and encourages the conceptual interchangeability and visual substitution of serpent bands and planetary bands as representations of the bicephalic Cosmic Monster.

2. This interpretation is strongly supported in the ancient hieroglyphic records of "the conjuring of a serpent, who is the way or naghual of so-and-so or such-and-such a place," and by more contemporary ethnographic documentation of similar situations (MacLeod 1991; see also Calvin 1994).

3. The disembodied Head 7 is a known locative indicator designating a sacred Underworld location (see Freidel et al. 1993:269; Naranjo Stela 22, Palenque Panel of the Cross, Jaina onyx vase), and as first proposed by Cohodas (1982:134), the glyphic Head 9 must refer as well to a supernatural location. It is possible that the paired heads refer to entrance and exit portals of a sacred Underworld realm.

4. The body of the bicephalic reptilian apparently alludes to the ruler's having negotiated a difficult passage to divine rulership—the journey that transformed him in the same way that all Maya originated via a transformation through the passageway or axis created when "the sky first separated from the earth" (MacLeod 1991). Note that Schele and Freidel (1990:66–71) have described the *wak-chaan* (a common Maya name for serpents) as the raised-up *chaan*, "sky," which they liken to the stood-up position of rulers as the tree of life or the vertical world axis. Schele (1992:121–210) has added to notions of Maya origin and creation with an interpretation of the Milky Way in its horizontal, east-west solstitial position across the sky as an astronomical version of the cosmic serpentine monster—a schema replicated in sculpture with the double-headed, horizontally aligned bench monsters of Copán.

5. It may be noted here that the concept of a sky-/serpent-band being upheld by supernaturals is common to Mesoamerica from the Early Preclassic (c. 1500 B.C.: San Lorenzo Monument 18) through the Late Classic (c. A.D. 1000: Chichén Itzá's "Atlantean Altars").

6. Note that these freestanding monuments commonly referred to as "altars" are often marked hieroglyphically as seating stones *(kuch)*.

7. The likelihood of Yax Pas having had at least four brothers or siblings who dedicated their own monuments is discussed by Bardsley (1990).

8. The reference to generic, successive power is emphasized because the iconographical elaboration of the seated figures of Temple 11 evokes that of the dynastic line of successors featured on Altar Q.

REFERENCES CITED

Bardsley, Sandra Noble
1990   "New Insights from 'New' Incensarios." *Copán Note 77.* Copán, Honduras: Copán Acropolis Project and the Instituto Hondureno de Antropologia e Historia.
1996   "Worked Benches and Power Tools at Copán." In *Debating Complexity: Proceedings of the 26th Annual Chacmool Conference,* Calgary, in press.

Calvin, Inga E.
1994   *Way Creatures: Images of Supernaturals on Classic Period Ceramics.* Master's thesis, University of Colorado at Boulder.

Carlson, John B., and Linda C. Landis
1985   "Bands, Bicephalic Dragons, and Other Beasts: The Skyband in Maya Art and Iconography." In *Fourth Palenque Round Table, 1980,* edited by Merle Greene Robertson and Elizabeth P. Benson, 115–40. San Francisco: Pre-Columbian Art Research Institute.

Chartier, Roger
1989   "Texts, Printing, Readings." In *The New Cultural History,* edited by Lynn Hunt, 154–75. Berkeley: University of California Press.

Cohodas, Marvin
1982   "The Bicephalic Monster in Classic Maya Sculpture." *Anthropologica* 24:105–46.

Fash, William L., Jr.
1991   *Scribes, Warriors and Kings: The City of Copán and the Ancient Maya.* London: Thames and Hudson.

Freidel, David, Linda Schele, and Joy Parker
1993   *Maya Cosmos: Three Thousand Years on the Shaman's Path.* New York: William Morrow.

Geertz, Clifford
1983   *Local Knowledge: Further Essays in Interpretive Anthropology.* New York: Basic Books.

Graham, Ian, and Eric Von Euw
1977   *Corpus of Maya Hieroglyphic Inscriptions, 3 (1).* Cambridge, Mass.: Peabody Museum of Archaeology and Ethnology, Harvard University.

Hendon, Julia A.
1992   "Status and Power in Classic Maya Society: An Archaeological Study." *American Anthropologist* 93(4):894–917.

Joyce, Rosemary A.
1991   *Cerro Palenque: Power and Identity on the Maya Periphery.* Austin: University of Texas Press.

Kerr, Justin
1989   *The Maya Vase Book: A Corpus of Rollout Photographs of Maya Vases, Vol. 1.* New York: Kerr Associates.

MacLeod, Barbara
1991   "Maya Genesis: The First Steps, North Austin Hieroglyphic Hunch #5, Notes on Maya Epigraphy." MS on file with author.

MacLeod, Barbara, Dorie Reents-Budet, Andrea Stone, and Khristaan Villela.

1993 "Notes on the T174 Compound." MS on file with authors.

Mathews, Peter

1985 "Maya Early Classic Monuments and Inscriptions." In *A Consideration of the Early Classic Period in the Maya Lowlands,* edited by G. R. Willey and P. Mathews, 5–54. Albany: Institute for Mesoamerican Studies, State University of New York at Albany.

Maudslay, Alfred P.

1974 *Biologia Central-Americana,* facsimile edited by Francis Robicsek. New York: Milpatron Publishing.

Robertson, Merle Greene

1985 *The Sculpture of Palenque, II: The Early Buildings of the Palace and the Wall Paintings.* Princeton, N.J.: Princeton University Press.

Schele, Linda

1992 *Workbook for the XVth Maya Hieroglyphic Workshop at Texas, March 14–15.* Austin: Department of Art and Art History and Institute of Latin American Studies, University of Texas at Austin.

Schele, Linda, and David Freidel

1990 *A Forest of Kings: The Untold Story of The Ancient Maya.* New York: William Morrow.

Schele, Linda, and Nikolai Grube

1993 *Workbook for the XIVth Maya Hieroglyphic Workshop at Texas, March 17–18.* Austin: Department of Art and Art History and Institute of Latin American Studies, University of Texas at Austin.

Schele, Linda, and Mary Ellen Miller

1986 *The Blood of Kings: Dynasty and Ritual in Maya Art.* Fort Worth: Kimbell Art Museum.

Spero, Joanne M.

1987 *Lightning Men and Water Serpents: A Comparison of Mayan and Mixe-Zoquean Beliefs.* Master's thesis, University of Texas at Austin.

Urban, Patricia, and Edward Schortman

1986 *The Southeast Maya Periphery.* Austin: University of Texas Press.

Villacorta, Carlos, and J. Antonio Villacorta

1930 *The Codex Dresden: Drawings of the Pages and Commentary in Spanish.* Laguna Hills, Ca.: Algean Park Press.

Webster, David, ed.

1989 *The House of the Bacabs, Copán, Honduras.* Studies in Pre-Columbian Art and Archaeology 29. Washington, D.C.: Dumbarton Oaks Research Library and Collection.

CHAPTER EIGHT

Smashed Pots and Shattered Dreams

The Material Evidence for an Early Classic Maya Site Termination at Cerros, Belize

Debra Selsor Walker
Florida International University

THE TENSION BETWEEN ARCHAEOLOGICAL REMAINS and their interpretation sustains a perpetual dialogue between present and past. As excavation informs our understanding of the past, so does knowledge about the past color our interpretations. The engine that drives archaeological theory building is fueled by analogy and material remains. New evidence can expand on current understanding or prompt the development of wholly new explanatory models. Like an unfinished conversation (Sullivan 1989), archaeological interpretation is punctuated by new discoveries and old beliefs. While the dialogue may be predictable for long periods, an occasional surge of new information can leave the discipline temporarily breathless. Nowhere is the current discourse more intense than among Mesoamericanists.

In Maya research, direct dialogue with the past began through recently deciphered texts left by ancient Maya scribes. As ideas came to light through hieroglyphic inscriptions, Maya prehistory became Maya history, seen through the eyes of the rich and powerful. We now know Maya kings and conquerors by name. Through their eyes, we are beginning to understand the dynamic Classic economy that drove intense political interactions and occasionally prompted devastating wars. As archaeologists analyze individual motivation in historical context, many of our interpretations have converged on Maya

religion as the medium for explaining poorly understood materials. Texts provide the link between past and present, allowing us to make better use of ethnographic analogy to explain ancient remains.

Interpretations of the Cerros data presented here owe much to the recent deluge of epigraphic research. This essay discusses the motives behind certain ritual actions that produced unusual material remains. As dialogue continues at the crux of Maya history and archaeology, we consider smashed pots to recover the shattered dreams of a community long forgotten.

CERROS AND ITS DEMISE

Cerros, Belize, is located on a small peninsula, Lowry's Point, that juts into Corozal Bay near the mouth of the New River (map 8.1). The Late Preclassic trading port has gained fame in recent years for its monumental architecture and painted stucco façades (Freidel 1985; Robertson and Freidel 1986). A small fishing/farming village first occupied in about 300 B.C. (Cliff and Crane 1989), the site center underwent large-scale construction beginning about 50 B.C. during the Tulix Phase (fig. 8.1). Materials dating to this period document a well-developed economy exhibiting the accumulation of considerable wealth. Due to its strategic coastal location near the mouth of two major rivers, Cerros

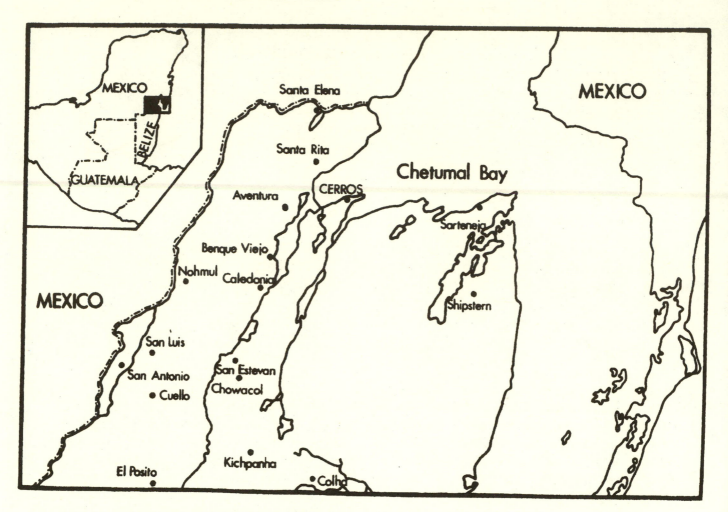

Map. 8.1.   Northern Belize, with location of Cerros.

is thought to have played an important role in interregional trade during the Late Preclassic (Freidel 1978; Garber 1989).

For reasons that remain obscure, Cerros saw an abrupt decline in residential population sometime after A.D. 200. This essay presents the results of recent research addressing the decline and collapse of the successful center. Based on patterned distributions of Early Classic material remains—Hubul Phase at Cerros—specific ritual events can be reconstructed. It is the thesis of this essay that these deposits reflect a sitewide rite of rededication and subsequent termination, performed within the bounds of a pan-Maya cosmology framing ritual behavior in sacred geography. After an introductory narrative of the events as they might have occurred, evidence is presented on which the interpretation is based.

NARRATIVE OF THE HUBUL EVENT

It was the nineteenth *katun* of the eighth *baktun,* a time of trouble at Cerros. People were abandoning the once vital port in droves, swept away by competition and conflict. War gripped Peten, and cities such as Uaxactun had fallen under the expansionist agenda of aggressive kings. Interior wars disrupted age-old trading partnerships up and down the river systems, wreaking havoc on the social order of Chetumal Bay. Some people had already left Cerros to join new settlements. Just across the Bay at Santa Rita Corozal, for example, opportunistic elites jockeyed for prime positions in the emerging regional market, while Cerros lost its economic edge.

There had been battles at Cerros as well, though time

had healed some of those wounds. Linked to political regimes in the interior, fighting in northern Belize had claimed many lives. The banner stone at the old pyramid had been knocked down without remorse (Reese-Taylor et al. 1996). People talked of those dark times with unnatural dread in their voices. Those who remained in the settlement struggled to keep up the city and its public facilities, but their efforts were inadequate. Poorly maintained canals were silting in, flooding fields and ruining crops. As structures in the site core crumbled, masons encased them in new buildings, conserving labor and resources whenever possible. The new monuments were bigger, but not as well made as the fine public buildings constructed a *baktun* ago by the founders.

With the completion of the eighth *baktun* at hand, Cerroseños decided to seek relief through supernatural mediation at the seam in time between two eras. Cut off from trading partners in the chaos following extended warfare, Cerros inhabitants attempted to revive the ancient center by calling on the supernatural power once housed in the holy portal at Structure 4, the tallest pyramid at the site. Toward that end, they organized a site-wide rite of rededication, performed in a last-ditch effort to rejuvenate the dying city.

Concentrating their efforts on the portal place atop the high temple, participants processed to the building carrying offerings. Replicating the actions of the First Father, *Hun-Nal-Ye*, they cached a bowl containing three tiny jade fragments (May*ak'ulel*; Schele 1989) inside the sacred mountain (Maya *witz*; Schele 1989). After sealing the cache in a matrix filled with pieces of bowls, dishes, and jars used in the rite, they offered incense atop three censer stacks arranged as the three-stone hearth of creation. This action opened a conduit through which supernatural energy could move. The portal was now open to receive their prayers.

As the shaman stood within the censer triangle naming the Creators, he offered prayers and incense to the Otherworld. Many in the dying community participated in the event, perhaps hopeful that their combined actions would please the lords of *Xibalba* and allow their city to be revived. The material remains of their participation, vessels that held food and drink for communal feasts, were intentionally broken in halves or quarters at the end of the rite and left strewn down the staircase and across the base of the temple. Following ancestral tradition, they replaced broken pots with new wares, symbolizing the birth of the ninth *baktun*. Censing and offering

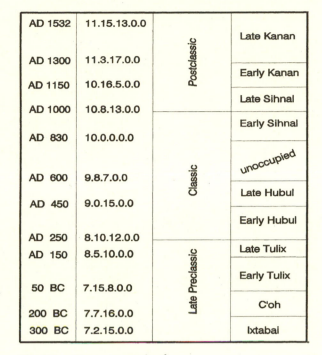

Fig. 8.1. Cerros ceramic phases.

AD 1532	11.15.13.0.0	Postclassic	Late Kanan
AD 1300	11.3.17.0.0	Postclassic	Early Kanan
AD 1150	10.16.5.0.0	Postclassic	Late Sihnal
AD 1000	10.8.13.0.0	Classic	Early Sihnal
AD 830	10.0.0.0.0	Classic	unoccupied
AD 600	9.8.7.0.0	Classic	Late Hubul
AD 450	9.0.15.0.0	Classic	Early Hubul
AD 250	8.10.12.0.0	Late Preclassic	Late Tulix
AD 150	8.5.10.0.0	Late Preclassic	Early Tulix
50 BC	7.15.8.0.0	Late Preclassic	C'oh
200 BC	7.7.16.0.0	Late Preclassic	Ixtabai
300 BC	7.2.15.0.0		

continued for days, weeks, even *winals*, as residents entreated providence on behalf of their troubled city.

As a symbol of the renewal rite, some participants collected handfuls of small sherds from the broken refuse of the ceremony, retaining them for later use. When they built new homes, they sprinkled small sherds in the white earth preparatory surface that formed a base for construction. Imbued with the same holy power (*k'ulel*; *ch'ulel* in Tzotzil) evoked in dedicatory rites, these sherds, like seeds, were planted below new households to ensure good fortune and prosperity.

Somewhat later, the vaulted portal building collapsed, sealing censer stacks in situ below fallen vault stones. Considering the forceful *huracanob* that plagued the community occasionally, this may have been a natural occurrence prompted solely by the elements. Or the collapse may have been intentional, when it became apparent that the rite had been performed in vain, for Cerros continued to lose population. Following Maya tradition, residents were compelled to close the portal once again before abandoning Cerros for the duration of the ninth *baktun*.

THE CASE FOR EMIC INTERPRETATION

Although this behavioral reconstruction of Hubul activities at Cerros may seem a bit fanciful, it is grounded in

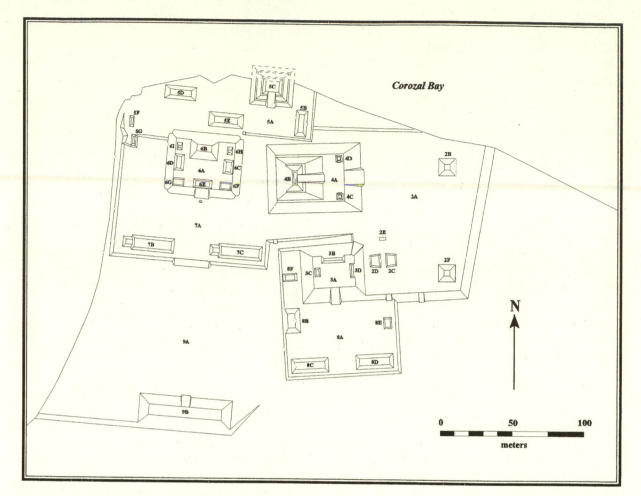

Map 8.2.   Cerros site core. (Drawn by Kathryn Reese-Taylor)

sound archaeological data and interpreted in light of recent epigraphic decipherments and iconographic analyses, which have established novel directions for Maya research. The new discipline of ancient Maya history undergirds cultural principles that are materially demonstrable at sites like Cerros. Archaeologists can now attempt the analysis of units that held symbolic meaning for the Maya, the emic perspective. At Cerros, we can seek points in the sacred geography of the ancient Maya landscape because the Maya left remains of their activities at those locales.

Maya sacred geography as a concept is based on an orthodox view of the cosmos described in the *Popol Vuh* (Tedlock 1986). In this perspective, creation took place at the *axis mundi,* which was a hearth containing three stones. This central location is called *ol* in Maya (Freidel et al. 1993), often written glyphically as three stones. Traditional Maya hearths still contain three stones. At creation, deities acted at the *ol* and propped the sky up over the earth with a giant *ceiba* tree, termed *wakah chan,* "raised-up sky" (Schele and Freidel 1990).

Freidel and colleagues (1993) note that the Maya replicated the cosmos in each settlement. In this view, the *ol* of any Maya community held a symbolic *ceiba* tree. The center was a focal point for defining sacred geography, around which humans organized themselves across the landscape. It was also a portal through which power could flow between natural and supernatural realms. Through ritual performance, a shaman or *way* (Houston and Stuart 1989) could access and manipulate supernatural power for the benefit of the community. Portals were opened and closed through ritual action (Walker 1990), and potential supernatural energy accumulated at particular loci through time. At Tikal, for example, Ruler A used the ancient power of the North Acropolis as the focal point for his Late Classic urban revitalization. Maya scribes have left us the names of these portal buildings in glyphic texts at Copan, Palenque, and elsewhere. Some portal buildings remained focal points on mental maps of a community's sacred geography long after the settlement was abandoned (Walker 1990:19).

Chamber 1, atop Cerros Structure 4B-1st, appears to have been one such point on the ancient sacred landscape (map 8.2), a hypothesis supported by the fact that the Maya left remains of certain dedicatory rites at this locus and nowhere else. Moreover, Maya visitors continued to leave offerings atop Structure 4 even after the site was abandoned as a residence. Known locally as The Bluffs, the Cerros Maya site takes its name from high mounds in the site core that are visible across the bay along the low-lying horizon. A likely landmark for prehispanic Maya mariners, the abandoned monumental center marked the rise on the horizon as a portal place in sacred geography built by the ancestors.

DEDICATION AND TERMINATION DEPOSITS

Although special deposits of various kinds have been a subject of interest for several decades (see Coe 1959), this essay focuses on the series of material remains consistently associated with the construction, burial, and abandonment of masonry buildings. Deposits associated with newly constructed or renovated buildings—often caches of whole vessels and other precious items—have been called the remains of dedication rites. Similarly, those associated with the abandonment of public buildings have been dubbed termination deposits. These remains are characterized by broken pots and fragmented bits of precious items (Yucatec k'ulel).

While rituals of both dedication and termination were investigated at Cerros, termination deposits are particularly well understood today because of the Cerros research. First noted in Late Preclassic Tulix contexts by Robertson (1983) and Garber (1983), termination deposits at Cerros constitute a material subcomplex that is consistently associated with the interment or apparent abandonment of public architecture. Material remains of these rites include fragmentary ceramic vessels of types and forms found together exclusively in this context. At Cerros, excavators sometimes uncovered jade and *Spondylus sp.* shell fragments, obsidian blades, hematite flecks, and evidence for burning in these deposits.

Tulix termination deposits generally were found banked against the lower façades of partly defaced public buildings, such as Structure 5C-2nd. Since Maya builders left these deposits in situ during subsequent renovations, excavators encountered them in sealed stratigraphic context and recognized them as a significant class of deposits because they made up a consistent part of the stratigraphic sequence. Interpretation of the last termination event at any Cerros building is more difficult, since it was not buried under subsequent construction. Left open to the elements for many years, pottery fragments were subject to erosion and redeposition, and may easily have been misinterpreted as squatters' debris or sheet midden. Detailed analyses of the Cerros contexts, however, illustrate the striking similarity of material elements in termination deposits, whether drawn from sealed or unsealed context.

Robertson (1983) identified the Tulix Phase ceramic subcomplex that was consistently associated with building interments and abandonments. Vessel forms that seem to be restricted to these termination contexts include Zapatista Trickle-on-Cream Brown three-handled jugs, Cabro Red and Chatoc Dichrome drinking mugs, and Sangre Red shallow bowls (fig. 8.2). Nearly always found broken and only partly reconstructable, these vessels were likely used in, then destroyed at the end of, a rite. Because some of the vessels were poorly smoothed, inadequately slipped, and fired at a relatively low temperature, Robertson has suggested that some pots were made specifically for use in a particular rite, after which they were destroyed. Fine-quality pottery was apparently not a requirement for one-time use. Based on ethnographic analogy, Robertson has suggested that the three-handled jugs once held *balche,* or mead, which was poured into drinking mugs for participants' use. Shallow red-slipped bowls, often found with their interiors burned, may have been containers for burnt offerings. These uses are consistent with ethnographically known rites, such as the *Ch'a-Chak* ceremony witnessed by Gann (1918) in northern Belize.

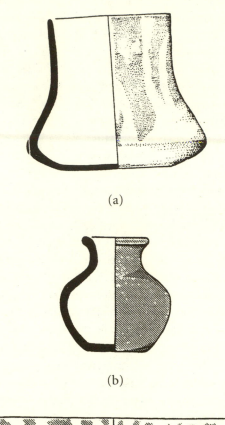

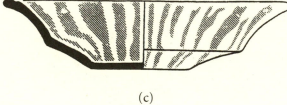

Fig. 8.2(a–c).   Vessel forms found in Tulix termination contexts (not to same scale).

A second ceramic constituent of the termination deposit is the censer complex. Variably defined in the literature, the term *censer* is used here to describe generally thick-walled, low-fired vessels, often made in unusual forms, which lack obvious utilitarian function. Tulix Phase censer vessels include Taciste Washed bowls with concave bases and hollow, tubular Cayman Modeled effigy censer stands with modeled anthropomorphic features (fig. 8.3). During use, a censer dish would have been stacked atop a censer stand. Copal incense, perhaps mixed with maize or a similar offering, was burned in the dish, forming a completed censer stack, as depicted on several Late Preclassic and Early Classic stelae (Freidel et al. 1988).

Like other vessels in the Tulix subcomplex, censer stands were found only in fragmentary form. A composite illustration for Tulix Phase was reconstructed based on analysis of fragments recovered from various buildings (Masucci 1983). Robertson (personal communication 1990) remarked on the difficulty of reconstructing such vessels because censer stand fragments recovered from various contexts at Cerros were all quite small, and few fits were identified. Typically, Cayman Modeled fragments were drawn from construction fill that had some association with a termination deposit. Robertson (personal communication 1990) speculated that the Cayman Modeled censer sherds were intentionally scattered to various locales; thus, only some ended up in the construction fill. Chase (1985) has postulated similar behaviors for the deposition of broken Postclassic effigy censers at Santa Rita Corozal. Although we cannot correlate Postclassic behaviors directly to Preclassic practices without demonstrating continuity, the consistent occurrence of unreconstructable censer fragments minimally demonstrates secondary context. If we then imply intentionality to the secondary deposition of such sherds, the pattern fits well with what we know about termination deposits: Vessels associated with them were ritually destroyed after use and deposited in specific locales.

It has been argued that an in situ censer stack defines a classificatory portal *(ol)* to the Otherworld, through which supernatural power can flow with shamanic assistance (Walker 1990:356). Censer stacks thus mimic the *wakah chan,* or *ceiba* tree, which defines the central place of any Maya community. Freidel and colleagues (1993) have delineated the origin of censer stacks more pre-

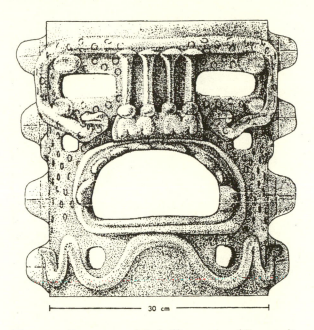

Fig. 8.3. Cayman modeled effigy censer. (Composite drawing by Karim Sadr)

cisely. According to them, the rationale for stacked censers stems from Maya creation mythology, evidenced by an account in the *Popol Vuh*. In this view, some effigy censer stands depict First Father, *Hun-Nal-Ye,* who acted with other deities during creation. According to the myth, First Father's decapitated head was hung on a tree in the Otherworld by the lords of *Xibalba*. From there he caused the birth of the Hero Twins who continued the creation story. His image on the censer stand is a symbol for the same tree of creation. Offerings deposited in the dish atop a censer stand reenact creation, imbuing the locale with the same supernatural creative force once wielded by *Hun-Nal-Ye*.

A Special Ceramic Deposit at Cerros Structure 4B-1st

Although several Tulix Phase termination deposits have been discovered at Cerros (Structures 2A-sub 4-1st, 3A-1st, 5C-2nd, 6B, and 29B), only Structure 4B-1st revealed Hubul Phase ritual remains. Maya ceramic remains from this epoch (referred to by some researchers as the Protoclassic or Terminal Preclassic) exhibit the innovative transitional forms that characterize calamitous eras. Since Maya long-count dates exist for the time range A.D. 200–

450, I have included Hubul Phase within the Classic era. At Cerros, Hubul ceramics echo the once robust tradition of Preclassic production and presage an emerging Classic tradition in innovative vessel forms and surface treatments.

The deposit considered here was drawn from two major operations conducted in the 1970s: Operation 25g at the base of the building (fig. 8.4) and Operations 20a–h, found inside the 4B-1st superstructure, Chamber 1. Subsequent research, beginning in 1993, revealed more of the deposit adjacent to Operation 25g. Analysis revealed that the entire deposit, from the 4B-1st summit to the base of its outset staircase, resulted from a discrete event or series of events spanning only a short time. This peculiar deposit exhibits five characteristics that distinguish it from Tulix antecedents: (1) the sherds date to Hubul Phase; (2) more halved and quartered vessels are represented; (3) a wider range of vessel forms is present; (4) a wider range of ceramic types is present; and (5) one whole vessel and several restorable censers are present.

Operation 25g

Structure 4B-1st is a pyramidal superstructure 13 m high that sits atop Structure 4A, a truncated pyramidal platform 9 m high. The entire complex faces east. Structure 4B-1st was first investigated in 1977, when a 2 m wide trench, Operation 25g, was placed immediately south of its outset staircase (fig. 8.5; Walker 1990:487). Subsequent excavations (Rich 1995) have revealed the entire lower east wall of 4B-1st. A stratum of marl melt representing the stucco façades that once decorated the building was contacted below humus, in turn sealing the special deposit beneath it. The stratigraphic sequence showed that sherds from this deposit had been left in situ after deposition, that the special deposit was laid down before the plaster façades fell into disrepair, and that the building saw no further architectural refurbishment until Terminal Classic Sihnal Phase. Broken pots lay in heaviest concentration near the base of the outset staircase, and their number diminished away from it. This distribution implies that some sherds fell to their final location from the staircase or upper terraces of the building. In sum, after the rite was completed, pottery fragments littered the entire central axis of 4B-1st.

Approximately six thousand sherds were recovered from the 6 m² deposit in Operation 25g; this number represents only a fraction of the total deposit at 4B-1st.

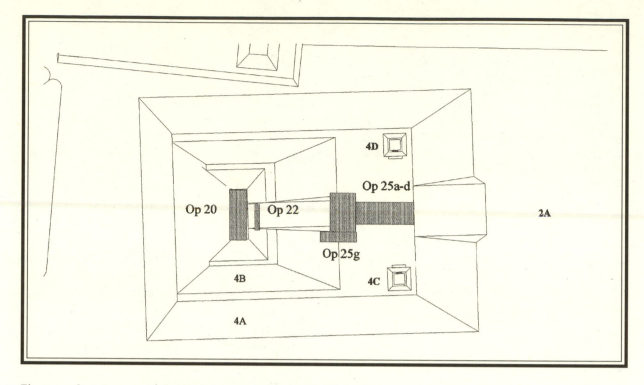

Fig. 8.4. Structure 4 with Operations 25g and 20a–h highlighted.

Fig. 8.5. (*Left*) Structure 4B-1st, Operation 25g trench after excavation.

As is characteristic of termination deposits, most vessels were fragmentary. Analysis of reconstructable vessels revealed that many pots had been broken in halves or quarters before deposition. In each case, refitting strategies failed to recover the balance of these pots.

Most vessel forms recovered from Operation 25g differ considerably from their Tulix Phase counterparts. Though some vessel forms were conserved through time, especially necked jars and shallow bowls, experimentation with pastes and slips is evident, and new modes occur. Flaring-walled serving dishes make up another component of the deposit. These are related to Tulix Phase special-occasion types (Robertson 1983), which seem to have been used for feasting and material display. Innovative forms, including a few mammiform, tetrapod, basal-flange bowls, help date the deposit to Hubul Phase. Overall continuities with local Tulix types are juxtaposed against obviously imported Early Classic types. Some types thus far identified include local varieties of Matamore Dichrome, Aguacate Orange, Manfredi Incised, Tigrillo Brown-on-Orange, various imported polychromes, and local imitations of them. No Hubul censer materials were recovered from the Operation 25g deposit. Censer fragments were recovered only from the interior of Chamber 1, the vaulted superstructure atop 4B-1st.

The relatively small percentage of imports may reflect Cerros's limited access to trade items during Hubul Phase. Technological heterogeneity found in locally produced vessels reflects a lack of standardization and, most likely, a range of potters with varying abilities. Based on some unsuccessful experimentations in form and materials, it is likely that Hubul potters had more limited access to high-quality pottery clays, tempers, and technological expertise than their Tulix ancestors. Such a breakdown in Hubul ceramic production mirrors the social turmoil in Early Classic northern Belize.

Operation 20

A deposit at the summit of Structure 4B-1st proved to be contemporary with the broken vessels strewn in Operation 25g. Operation 20 remains stem from the excavation of Chamber 1, an unusual feature situated atop Structure 4B-1st (fig. 8.6). At about 8 x 2 m interior space, this partly subterranean chamber once supported the only vaulted roof at Cerros. It is considered subterranean because its interior floor is approximately 1 m lower than the staircase leading up to it. Extant wall stubs rise about 1 m above the highest tread, or about 2 m above the floor.

Chamber 1 seems to have been built into Structure 4B-1st during its initial Tulix Phase construction, as the 4B-1st staircase abuts the east wall of Chamber 1. An eroded plaster floor shows that the vaulted chamber was in use for many years before its demise. Excavation below collapsed vault stones revealed a raised bench along the northern 2 m of Chamber 1. Although Hubul Phase modifications had been made to 4B-1st, most of the building, 13 m in height, was constructed earlier. Soundings into Chamber 1, 4B-1st, and the staircase of a poorly known interior structure, 4B-2nd, revealed that all three date originally to Tulix Phase.

Excavation of Chamber 1 revealed an additional oddity: The feature retained no evidence of a door. A solid masonry wall on the east face of the feature, two courses thick, abuts the staircase summit, running the full length of Structure 4B-1st. Chinking stones encountered between the two courses during recent stabilization work revealed that both courses were constructed simultaneously. A single-course western wall of similar length

Fig. 8.6.   Structure 4B-1st, Chamber 1, Operation 20 after excavation.

was also located. Both lacked any means of entry. These parallel walls, in turn, once supported a roof vault, though it had collapsed in antiquity. The summit stair thus led to a blank wall of indeterminate height that lacked apparent access to Chamber 1. While entry could have been attained through the north or south ends of the building, no end walls were encountered during excavation. These may have fallen outward when the vault collapsed, destroying any evidence for the original means of access. The orientation of pottery remains inside Chamber 1 suggests an original southern entry. Effigy censers that remained in situ on the building floor faced south, and would have been seen first on entry. The northern raised bench would thus have been hidden behind them.

Excavation of Chamber 1 revealed several discrete contexts on the building floor that appear to reflect the stages of an extended ritual performance (fig. 8.7). Participants first dug a long irregular hole into the raised bench at the north end of the building. In this trench they deposited Cache 4, a Dos Arroyos Orange Polychrome basal-flange bowl that held three jade fragments arranged in a triangle (fig. 8.8). Analysis revealed that the matrix surrounding the cache held fragments of the same types of vessels as those found at the base of 4B-1st in Operation 25g. Aguacate Orange shallow bowls and Manfredi Incised small jars are two identified types (fig. 8.9).

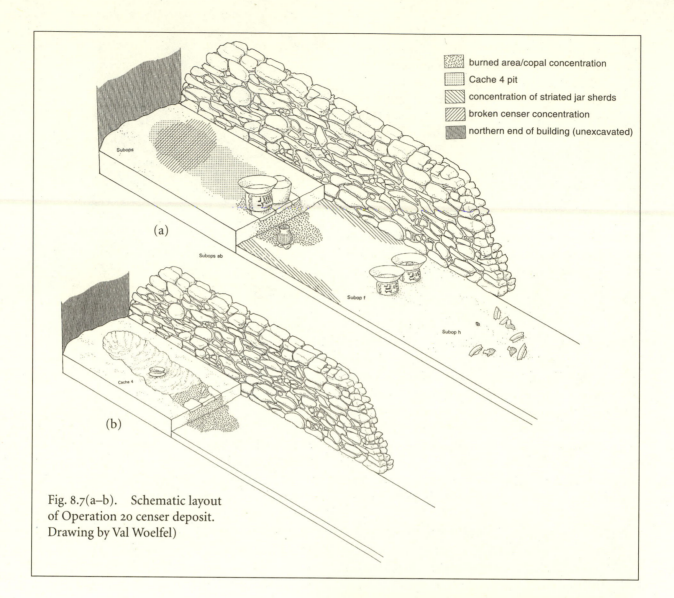

burned area/copal concentration
Cache 4 pit
concentration of striated jar sherds
broken censer concentration
northern end of building (unexcavated)

Subops

Subops ab

Subop f

Subop h

(a)

Cache 4

(b)

Fig. 8.7(a–b).　Schematic layout
of Operation 20 censer deposit.
Drawing by Val Woelfel)

Fig. 8.8.　Cache 4 in situ.

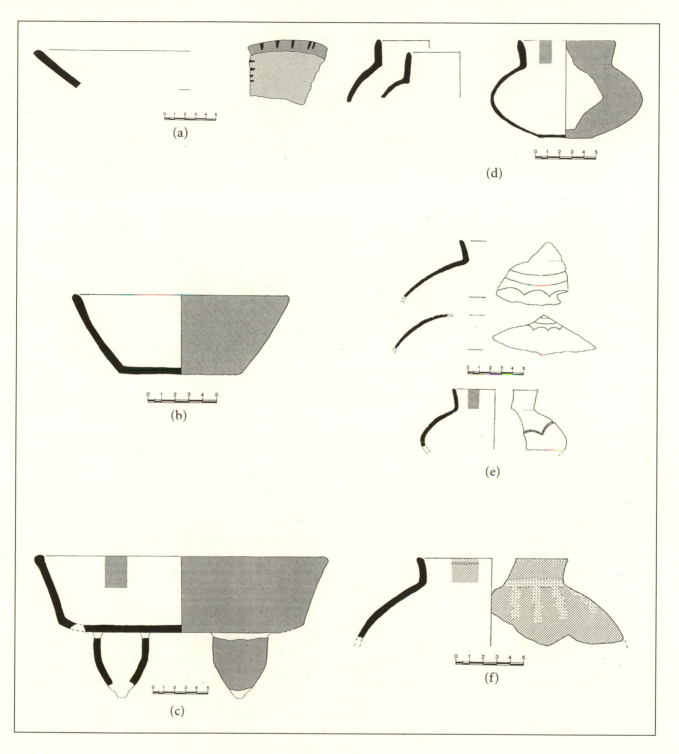

Fig. 8.9(a–f). Ceramic types from matrix around Cache 4.

Fig. 8.10.   Close-up of three censer stacks in schematic layout.

The matrix also contained additional jade fragments. Like its counterpart in Operation 25g, the cache matrix contained no censer sherds. Most vessels recovered from the matrix also seem to have been broken into halves or quarters before deposition, and the balance of these vessels was not present. Some sherds found in Operation 20 appeared to be fragments of pots deposited in Operation 25g, 13 m below at the base of the temple, although no fits were discovered. This surprising finding gave the first major analytical link between the two spatially distinct deposits, implying that a single ritual locus spanned the entire building.

After interring Cache 4, participants performed a series of rites in which up to six censer stacks were used. Three of these were left in situ in a triangular arrangement, providing vital clues for behavioral reconstruction (fig. 8.10). Broken bits of at least three other Botan Unslipped censer dishes and Peteltun Modeled censer stands were found atop the raised bench. A large Peteltun Modeled effigy censer stand was uncovered atop the severely burned edge of the raised bench (fig. 8.11). It was accompanied by a Pochkaak Red-on-Orange shallow bowl that had been used to burn incense. An unburned area where a copal ball once sat is clearly visible on the interior base of the vessel. Substantial quantities of copal were recovered from the surrounding matrix, and the entire area smelled strongly of copal, according to excavators. Shattered jade and *Spondylus sp.* shell fragments were also recovered at the locus. Immediately adjacent, excavators recovered a Botan Unslipped bucket, probably originally lidded, which may have held an unburnt offering (Freidel et al. 1988). Nearby, broken striated jar sherds were recovered banked against both walls of the chamber. Large jars such as these might have been used to contain a liquid during the rite. Perhaps a jar once rested atop the pot stand formed by a circle of five limestone balls discovered next to the censer stand.

Some 2 m south of the bench, excavators recovered two small Peteltun Modeled effigy censer stands, each associated with a Pochkaak Red-on-Orange censer dish (fig. 8.12). Contextual analysis revealed that each censer dish had been stacked atop its associated censer stand before the vault collapse. Photos and plan maps clearly document this. Because of the splayed distribution of effigy censer sherds, it is highly unlikely that they were broken before the vault collapse. In addition, despite the poor condition of the plaster floor, none of the censer sherds seemed particularly eroded: thus, the vault collapsed not long after the three censer stacks were set up inside Chamber 1. In sum, it is most likely that Chamber 1 collapsed shortly after the rites associated with censing were performed.

practice apparently continued into the Middle Classic, evidenced in excavations at Operation 20h.

Operation 20h

Sometime following the collapse of Chamber 1, a final deposit was left at the southern edge of the building, beyond the vault collapse (fig. 8.7). This group of vessels dates to the Middle Classic, considerably later than pots found inside the building. Excavation revealed a V-shaped arrangement of vessel fragments that surrounded a single obsidian blade (fig. 8.13). Several shallow, medial-flanged bowl fragments and two deep bowl fragments were discovered in discrete concentrations. As in Operations 20 and 25g, the bowls had been broken into segments before deposition. Most showed traces of burning after breakage. No contemporary Middle Classic ceramics are known from Structure 4, and only traces have been recovered in other excavations at Cerros.

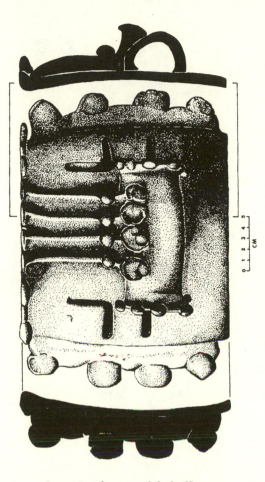

Fig. 8.11.   Large Peteltun modeled effigy censer stand. (Drawing by Kathy Roemer)

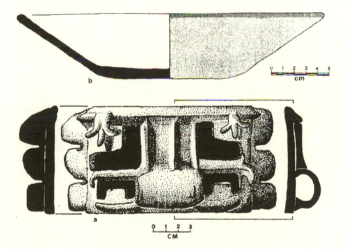

Fig. 8.12.   Small Peteltun modeled effigy censer stand and Pochkaak Red-on-Orange censer dish. (Censer stand drawn by Kathy Roemer)

PORTAL BUILDINGS AND THE TRADITION OF REMEMBRANCE

The Hubul Phase censer complex shows a clear developmental relationship with earlier Tulix censers, indicative of a tradition of censer use at Cerros (Walker 1990). Since censer stacks are classificatory portals to the Otherworld, their presence in archaeological deposits, given primary context, identifies ancient portal locales. In this view, Cerros Structure 4B-1st constituted a portal building during Hubul Phase, making it a conduit for supernatural power for the site. That Early Classic residents continued to use censer stacks at 4B-1st, even after the site was no longer a provincial central place, implies a tradition of remembrance revealed in its sacred geography. This

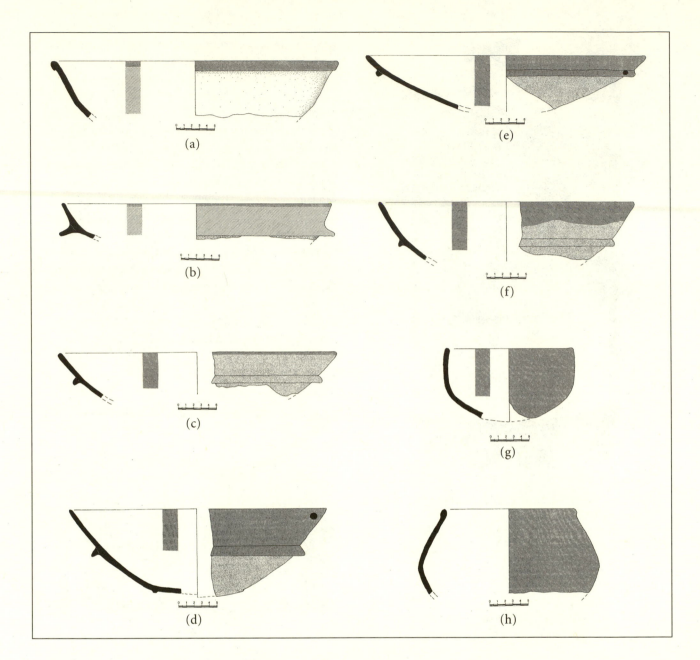

Fig. 8.13(a–h).   Operation 2oh vessel fragments.

Because these vessel fragments do not seem related temporally or spatially to the balance of the Operation 20 ritual, they probably constitute the remains of a later event, performed long after the Chamber 1 vault collapsed, when 4B-1st was in ruins. Most logically, these vessel fragments were brought from an unknown location already broken, functioning as temporary offering containers in which incense was burned. The secondary use of vessel fragments as temporary censers has been reported in contemporary Highland Maya cultures (see Vogt 1976), especially in the context of processional ritual. For these reasons, Operation 20h remains may be interpreted as a votive act of remembrance made by Middle Classic visitors at an ancient sacred spot on the Maya landscape. Whether participants lived in an as yet untested area of the site or brought their offerings to Cerros from elsewhere cannot be determined on the basis of present evidence.

Smashed Pots: Interpreting the Operation 20 Remains

During Tulix Phase, dedication and termination events occurred at various buildings in the site center. Accumulated evidence supports the hypothesis that each event was building-specific—that is, each enactment focused on construction or termination at an individual structure. Although precessional rites probably did take place, no specific evidence exists for this behavior for Tulix Phase, although it is present in later periods (Walker 1990). In contrast, the Hubul Phase ritual context at Structure 4B-1st constitutes a site-focused rather than building-focused rite. Although based on a long tradition of building dedications and terminations, this special deposit seems to have involved more people and more resources in a greater range of activities. Participants performed rites associated with the deposition of Cache 4, the offering of incense, and the systematic breakage of special-occasion pottery vessels. Based on Tulix Phase practices, they were sending mixed messages to the Otherworld by combining dedicatory acts (setting up the portal) with terminating behaviors (collapsing the vault, quartering and scattering vessels). Rather than confusing the issue, however, it appears that they had something else in mind. Worried about the future, Cerros residents took a set of orthodox symbols and reconfigured them for a new purpose. Most likely, the

rites performed inside Chamber 1 and in front of 4B-1st constituted a special category of rededication event, using ancient symbols in slightly different ways.

Interpretation of Cache 4 is illustrative of this point. The cache vessel, a polychrome basal-flange bowl, contained three jade fragments that were found situated in a triangular arrangement. This in itself is unique. Garber (1983) has documented that whole jade objects, such as beads and earflares, generally occurred in cache contexts at Cerros, while smashed jade fragments were restricted to termination deposits. He further suggested that the smashing and scattering of jade was one of the steps performed in a termination event. Evidence that bolsters his argument includes jade fragments collected from some termination deposits that can be refitted.

The cache vessel alone might be viewed simply as a Hubul era dedication event, but the use of jade fragments rather than whole jade beads makes the interpretation more complex. In fact, Cache 4 recalls the three-stone hearth, site of creation in Maya myth. These fragments might have been meant to reseed the locus with small objects that contained k'ulel. By replicating the arrangement of stones in the hearth, Cache 4 mimicked the ol of creation.

Jade fragments were recovered from the matrix surrounding the cache vessel and in association with the large censer stand nearby. Jade fragments were also collected from Operation 25g, at the base of 4B-1st. Thus, the deliberate arrangement of jade and scattering of jade both occurred in the same context. Perhaps the objects shattered to use in Chamber 1 were heirlooms from more prosperous Tulix times. Alternatively, they may have been the curated remains of jades smashed by warring invaders at Cerros. In any case, they were used and deposited as symbols of renewal, a new meaning drawn from the unique use of a traditional symbol set.

The symbolic triangular arrangement of Cache 4 is reiterated at a larger scale in the three censer stacks excavated in situ. Because they were situated along the medial axis of Structure 4B-1st, these three stacks likely outlined the literal perimeter of the portal at Chamber 1. Thus, the act of stepping within the triangle formed by the censer stacks put an individual in liminal space. When smoke rose from all three stacks, the original hearth from the Maya creation story was regenerated. With the portal open, individuals could then interact directly with the Otherworld and ask the lords of Xibalba to regenerate their community.

Freidel has argued (personal communication 1996) that the semi-subterranean vaulted room added another layer of meaning to the portal place: Entering there was entering the Otherworld. Because the chamber was subterranean, rites enacted within it literally happened in the Otherworld. Cache 4, then, was deposited underground within an Otherworld context, and the regenerated *ol* existed in Otherworld space. Hubul residents, it seems, required a highly orthodox set of conditions to open a portal and maintain communication with the supernatural forces of their world.

One might ask what scale of event demanded such orthodox action from a relatively impoverished community. A likely explanation is that the rite may have occurred in A.D. 435, in association with the completion of the eighth *baktun*, at 9.0.0.0.0. Although no radiocarbon date exists for the deposit, most of the pottery recovered from Operation 20 can be dated stylistically to c. A.D.400. While so specific a date is conjectural at best, it fits well with what we know about Maya period-ending rites. During the unlucky year-end *Wayeb* ceremonies, for example, Tozzer (1941) reports that residents broke pots and made new ones. The pottery dump at the base of 4B-1st could reflect such a behavior. Surely the Maya viewed the completion of a millennium as a critical juncture in time. A sitewide rite intended to draw on supernatural power might well have been performed on 9.0.0.0.0 to take full advantage of the period ending. As corroborating evidence, the use of effigy censer stacks portraying First Father *Hun-Nal-Ye* to create the new millennium echoes his original actsin the *Popol Vuh*, when he first laid the three stones in the hearth and created the *ol*, nine *baktunob* earlier at the beginning of time. Perhaps Hubul residents chose this most orthodox of Maya symbolism to regenerate Cerros from ten *katunob* of decline.

RESEEDING HUBUL PHASE CERROS

In support of the case for a sitewide rite, ceramic analysis has revealed very tenuous evidence linking those who participated in the Chamber 1 rituals with the establishment of new residences in the settlement. New Hubul residences are rare at Cerros, but a few houses first built in Hubul Phase have been identified through construction style and ceramic association (Structures 2B, 32A, 34A, 46B, 102A: Reese-Taylor et al. 1996; Scarborough 1991; Scarborough and Robertson 1986; Walker 1990,

1996). Rather than renovating Tulix structures, Hubul residents constructed these buildings anew, atop the original ground surface. In each case, a layer of white earth or *saskab* was laid over sterile paleosol before building construction. While the *saskab* was nearly void of archaeological remains, in all cases a few small sherds were retrieved from the white earth stratum. In each case, several pottery types were represented, none by more than a few sherds. These sherds appeared freshly broken and newly deposited, not typical of eroded construction admix. More surprisingly, types identified in these small samples were identical to rare Hubul types found in quantity only in ritual deposits at Structure 4B-1st. For example, sherds from Botan Unslipped censer dishes and Manfredi Incised jars were recovered. Since vault collapse sealed the censer sherds beneath it, handfuls of sherds seem to have been collected from the vicinity of Chamber 1 before its collapse.

Conceivably, a handful of sherds was intentionally placed in the *saskab* preparatory surface during a dedicatory rite for each building. As remnants of the ritual invocation of supernatural power at 4B-1st, the sherds could have seeded the locus with similar *k'ulel*, just as *Hun-Nal-Ye* provided seed for the first creation. Perhaps residents hoped to share personally in the dedication event by using ritual remains. Viewed in this context, the site-centric 4B-1st ritual becomes sitewide in scope. In this scenario, the dedication event was intended to rejuvenate the entire settlement, not just the portal locus. Assuming that the Maya were anxious about rekindling prosperity at Cerros through supernatural mediation, evidence for planting new buildings with seeds from the portal bolsters the argument for a 9.0.0.0.0 date.

SHATTERED DREAMS:
THE ABANDONMENT OF CERROS

Although the original purpose of the rites performed in Chamber 1 seems to have been rededication, the ritual had an unsuccessful outcome. The rite failed to revive an ancient seat of power, and Cerros was ultimately abandoned for the duration of the ninth *baktun*. According to Maya custom, it must have been important to close the portal at 4B-1st before abandoning the dying community. Following the Mesoamerican pattern, Hubul residents terminated the site before they left by intentionally collapsing the portal building, defusing the supernatural

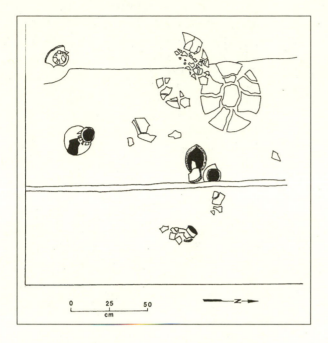

Fig. 8.14. Cache 2.

power of the ancient locus. Evidence collected at Hubul residences in the settlement implies that the residents simply walked away from their wattle-and-daub houses without cleaning the floors of debris. Perhaps they were chased away by intensified warfare or a forceful *huracán*. Perhaps they left when they could no longer maintain a drained field system on the swampy peninsula.

Where they went is the subject of ongoing research in the vicinity of Cerros (Walker 1994, 1995). Substantive Classic occupation elsewhere on Lowry's Point (the name of the point of land on which Cerros sits; see map 8.1) has not yet been documented. Although Santa Rita Corozal seems to have dominated Corozal Bay during the ensuing era (Chase and Chase 1988), San Estevan (Levi 1994) and Caledonia on the New River (Sidrys 1983) also gained population. Not far away, however, Ramonal in the interior (Scarborough 1991) and Xaman K'iwik on the Rio Hondo (Mitchum and King n.d.) exhibit substantial Classic era occupation. There were apparently many options for Hubul Phase Cerros emigrants.

Not until much later, in the tenth *baktun,* did colonists return to the site, and when they did, one of their first ritual actions was to lay Cache 2 at the summit of 4B-1st (fig. 8.14; Walker 1990:332). Sihnal Phase Terminal Classic residents seeded their offering with objects imbued with *k'ulel,* this time contained in ancient pots retrieved

from the eroding sea wall. Later Postclassic inhabitants and visitors continued the tradition of laying offerings atop the same building, even after the site was abandoned another, final time. Like other hallowed portal places in Maya sacred geography, Structure 4B-1st was remembered across the *katunob* and was treated with reverence long after its abandonment.

REFERENCES CITED

Chase, Diane Z.

1985   "Ganned But Not Forgotten: Late Postclassic Archaeology and Ritual at Santa Rita Corozal." In *The Lowland Maya Postclassic,* edited by A. Chase and P. Rice, 104–25. Austin: University of Texas Press.

Chase, Diane Z., and Arlen F. Chase

1988   *A Postclassic Perspective: Excavations at the Maya Site of Santa Rita Corozal, Belize.* Precolumbian Art Research Institute Monograph 4. San Francisco: Precolumbian Art Research Institute.

Cliff, Maynard B., and Cathy J. Crane

1989   "Changing Subsistence Economy at a Late Preclassic Maya Community." *Research in Economic Anthropology* suppl. 4:295–324.

Coe, William R.

1959   *Piedras Negras Archaeology: Artifacts, Caches and Burials.* University Museum Monographs. Philadelphia: University of Pennsylvania.

Freidel, David A.

1978   "Maritime Adaptations and the Rise of Maya Civilization: The View from Belize." In *Prehistoric Coastal Adaptations,* edited by B. Stark and B. Voorhies, 239–65. New York: Academic Press.

1985   "Polychrome Façades of the Lowland Maya Preclassic." In *Painted Architecture and Polychrome Monumental Sculpture in Mesoamerica,* edited by E. Boone, 5–30. Washington, D.C.: Dumbarton Oaks.

1986   "The Monumental Architecture." In *Archaeology at Cerros Belize, Central America, Volume 1: An Interim Report,* edited by R. Robertson and D. Freidel, 1–22. Dallas: Southern Methodist University Press.

Freidel, David A., Maria Masucci, Susan Jaeger, and Robin Robertson

1988   "The Bearer, the Burden and the Burnt: The Stacking Principle in the Iconography of the

Late Preclassic Maya Lowlands." In *Sixth Palenque Round Table*, edited by M. Robertson and Virginia M. Fields, 175–83. Norman: University of Oklahoma Press.

Freidel, David A., and Linda Schele
1989 "Dead Kings and Living Temples: Dedication and Termination Rituals among the Ancient Maya." In *Word and Image in Maya Culture*, edited by W. Hanks and D. Rice, 233–43. Salt Lake City: University of Utah Press.

Freidel, David, Linda Schele, and Joy Parker
1993 *Maya Cosmos: Three Thousand Years on the Shaman's Path.* New York William Morrow.

Gann, Thomas
1918 *The Maya Indians of Southern Yucatan and Northern British Honduras.* Bureau of American Ethnology Bulletin 64. Washington, D.C.: Smithsonian Institution.

Garber, James F.
1983 "Patterns of Jade Consumption and Disposal at Cerros, Northern Belize." *American Antiquity* 48(4): 800–7.
1989 *Archaeology at Cerros, Belize, Central America, Volume 2: The Artifacts.* Dallas: Southern Methodist University Press.

Houston, Stephen, and David Stuart
1989 "The *Wayglyph*: Evidence for "Co-essences" among the Classic Maya." *Research Reports on Ancient Maya Writing 30.* Washington, D.C.: Center for Maya Research.

Levi, Laura J.
1994 "Settlement Patterns at San Estevan." Ph.D. diss., University of Arizona.

Masucci, Maria
1983 "Beyond the Assemble-it-yourself Censer." MS on file at Southern Methodist University.

Mitchum, Beverly, and Eleanor King
n.d. "Preliminary Report on Investigations at Xaman K'iwik." MS.

Reese-Taylor, Kathryn, Debra S. Walker, and Beverly A. Mitchum
1996 "Interpolity Dynamics and the Demise of Cerros." Paper presented at the 61st Annual Meeting, Society for American Archaeology, New Orleans.

Rich, Michelle E.
1995 "Op 9305: Excavation at 4B-1st." In *Research at Cerros, Belize: Results of the 1994 Excavation Season,* edited by D. Walker. Miami: By the editor.

Robertson, Robin A.
1983 "Functional Analysis and Social Process in Ceramics: The Pottery from Cerros, Belize."

In *Civilization in the Ancient Americas: Essays in Honor of Gordon R. Willey,* edited by R. Leventhal and A. Kolata, 105–42. Albuquerque: University of New Mexico Press.

Robertson, Robin A., and David A. Freidel
1986 *Archaeology at Cerros, Belize, Central America, Volume 1: An Interim Report.* Dallas: Southern Methodist University Press.

Robertson-Freidel, Robin A.
1980 "The Ceramics from Cerros: A Late Preclassic Site in Northern Belize." Ph.D. diss., Harvard University.

Scarborough, Vernon
1991 *Archaeology at Cerros, Belize, Central America, Volume 3: The Settlement System in a Late Preclassic Maya Community.* Dallas: Southern Methodist University Press.

Scarborough, Vernon, and Robin Robertson
1986 "Civic and Residential Settlement at a Late Preclassic Maya Center." *Journal of Field Archaeology* 13:155–75.

Schele, Linda
1989 *Notebook for the 13th Maya Hieroglyphic Workshop at Texas.* Austin: University of Texas.

Schele, Linda, and David A. Freidel
1990 *A Forest of Kings: The Untold Story of the Ancient Maya.* New York: William Morrow.

Sidrys, Raymond V.
1983 *Archaeological Investigations in Northern Belize, Central America.* Institute of Archaeology Monograph 17. Los Angeles: University of California, Los Angeles.

Sullivan, Paul
1989 *Unfinished Conversations: Mayas and Foreigners between Two Wars.* New York: Alfred A. Knopf.

Tedlock, Dennis
1986 *Popol Vuh: The Definitive Edition of the Mayan Book of the Dawn of Life and the Glories of Gods and Kings.* New York: Simon and Schuster.

Tozzer, A. M.
1941 *Landa's Relación de las cosas de Yucatán.* Papers of the Peabody Museum of Archaeology and Ethnology 18. Cambridge, Mass.: Peabody Museum, Harvard University.

Vogt, Evon
1976 *Tortillas for the Gods: A Symbolic Analysis of Zinacanteco Rituals.* Cambridge, Mass.: Harvard University Press.

Walker, Debra S.
1990 "Cerros Revisited: Ceramic Indicators of Terminal Classic and Postclassic Settlement and Pilgrimage in Northern Belize." Ph.D. diss., Southern Methodist University.

1996   "Religion and Trade in Postclassic Yukatan: The Material Evidence from Chetumal Province." Paper presented at the 61st Annual Meeting, Society for American Archaeology, New Orleans.

Walker, Debra S., ed.

1994   *Research at Cerros, Belize: Results of the 1993 Excavation Season.* Miami: By the editor.

1995   *Research at Cerros, Belize: Results of the 1994 Excavation Season.* Miami: By the editor.

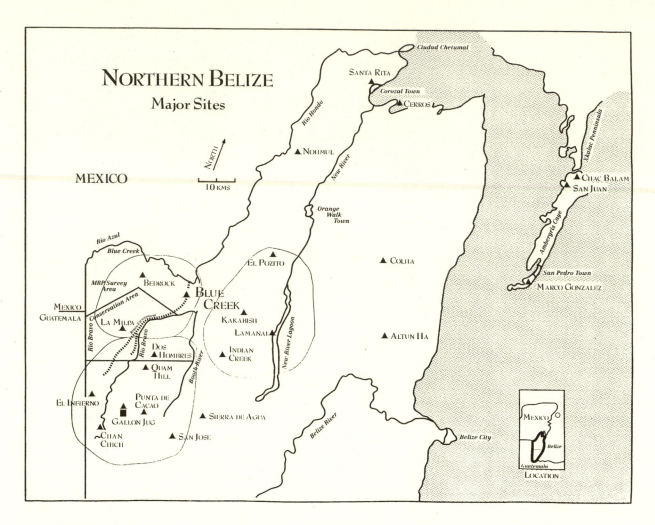

Map 9.1. Northern Belize, showing the location of Blue Creek.

CHAPTER NINE

The Blue Creek Jade Cache
Early Classic Ritual in Northwestern Belize

Thomas H. Guderjan
St. Mary's University

T HE BLUE CREEK RUIN IS A MEDIUM-SIZED CENTER in northwestern Belize (map 9.1), located on top of the 100 m high Bravo Escarpment near the confluence of the Rio Hondo and Rio Bravo. The site was first documented by Mary Neivens in 1976 (Neivens 1991) and since 1992 has been the focal point of a concerted and comprehensive research project by the Maya Research Program and St. Mary's University. Four annual field seasons have yielded enormous quantities of information (Guderjan et al. 1993; Guderjan et al. 1994; Guderjan and Driver 1995, 1996). While the original approach of this research was to deal with economic and political interaction between the Peten and coastal Belize regions, the project has been greatly expanded to become a comprehensive study of the dynamics of population demography, social structure, and agricultural technology, as well as regional interaction.

We have now documented much of the early history of Blue Creek: its founding in the Middle Preclassic, its growth in the Late Preclassic and Early Classic, the abrupt cessation of monumental construction at the end of the Early Classic, the construction of elite residences in the Late Classic, and, finally, its abandonment in the Terminal Classic/Early Postclassic. This history provides a context for interpreting events at Blue Creek. In this chapter, I discuss the events leading to, surrounding, and following the deposition of a major cache at Structure 4, a central build-

ing on the Main Plaza (map 9.2). I argue that this event was a pivotal point in the history of Blue Creek, marking a complete restructuring of political and civic affairs. Further, the events at Blue Creek may not have been an isolated phenomenon and may represent broad regional restructuring.

The complex ritual event, which included placement of several caches, occurred in about A.D. 500. The nearly one thousand jade artifacts included in the cache constitute the second largest collection of Maya jade originating from a single event ever found by archaeologists. This ritual act not only displayed the wealth and importance of Blue Creek, it also occurred at a critical juncture in the life of the community. Before the event, Blue Creek was a thriving independent Early Classic center. Afterward, monumental public construction at Blue Creek practically ceased, and for the most part only minor remodelings of public architecture took place thereafter. We see this event as a ritual act that terminated the sacred space inStructure 4. In addition, the event may have marked the termination of a royal bloodline and even of the independence of the community, while rededicating the site as a member of a larger polity.

THE BLUE CREEK RUIN

The site is strategically situated to take advantage of natural, economic, and political factors. Both above and below the escarpment, but especially below, Blue Creek has immediate access to very high-quality soils for agriculture. Water was also immediately accessible from spring-fed ponds and lakes above and below the escarpment. The placement of the site at the top of the escarpment enabled its leaders to oversee activities in the settlement zone and agricultural areas below.

One of the activities they oversaw was certainly the arrival and departure of trade canoes. Blue Creek is at the terminus of the complex riverine and coastal trade system that linked the diverse sectors of the Maya world. Only a few kilometers from the Blue Creek Ruin, and well within easy view, is the Rio Hondo, which now forms Belize's northern border with Mexico. More important, the Rio Hondo is the northernmost of the many Central American rivers that drain into the Caribbean, making it a very important route for riverine canoe trade. The headwaters of the Rio Hondo are formed at the confluence of the Rio Bravo and Blue Creek (Rio Azul). Blue Creek forms the continuation of the border, and the Rio Bravo flows from the southwest. Blue Creek is navigable for only a short distance past the confluence, since much of its flow originates from springs in the Bravo Escarpment. Although trade canoes could not proceed much farther westward on Blue Creek, they could do so on the Rio Bravo. In both cases, the canoes would be fully within view of the Blue Creek Ruin.

Blue Creek is also the westernmost Peten-style site. A series of coastal Belize sites is within view, including Kakabish, Indian Creek, and El Pozito (Guderjan 1995). The site of Lamanai is blocked from view by its location on the other side of Kakabish. Distinctly different patterns of settlement, architecture, and ceramic traditions are seen in the coastal northern Belize sphere and the Peten sphere. Therefore, Blue Creek is located where it could certainly have benefited from political and economic interaction between the two.

The Blue Creek Ruin is a medium-sized Maya center (map 9.2). Although smaller than the very large Maya centers, it exhibits many of the same characteristics. The site includes three buildings taller than 10 m, a ball court, two plazas, and ten to twelve elite courtyards near the site core, as well as two or perhaps three stelae. Surrounding the Main Plaza are six structures (Structures 1–6). Structure 1 is the largest, standing 12.7 m tall, and it dominates the plaza. Across the plaza to the south is Structure 4, the unpretentious, 6.4 m tall temple where the shaft caches were discovered. Just north of Structure 1 is the ball court.

Farther north is the Plaza B Complex, a linear arrangement of temples and elite residences centered on Plaza B. Defining the south end of the complex is Structure 9, the Temple of the Masks. This is a structure 11 m in height that underwent multiple construction phases. The north end is defined by Structure 25, Neiven's Temple of the Obsidian Warrior (1991). Immediately south of Plaza B is the Structure 13 Courtyard, which consists of two temples (Structures 10 and 14), a temple-palace (Structure 13), and two residential buildings (Structures 11 and 12). Immediately north of Plaza B is the Structure 19 Courtyard, a complex compound of elite residences.

ARCHITECTURE AND RITUAL AT BLUE CREEK

The earliest deposits so far discovered at Blue Creek come from a complex midden in front of and beneath the Temple of the Masks (Haines 1996). This deposit has since become the focus of intensive excavations aimed at understanding the origins of the Blue Creek community. By the Middle Preclassic period, Blue Creek was apparently a nucleated village engaged in complex communal ritual. We have not found any structural remains from this period. Interestingly, the closest ceramic affinities exhibited by Blue Creek at this time appear to be with coastal Belize.

The midden deposits at the Temple of the Masks include a rich record of Late Preclassic activity (Haines 1996). Moreover, it appears that by no later than the end of the Late Preclassic, the fundamental form of the Main Plaza was in place. Early phases of Structures 1, 4, and 6 were erected. An early phase of Structure 5 also probably existed (Pastrana 1995). However, we believe this building was razed at a later date. Although most of these buildings were unimposing at this time, Structure 1 probably rose 10 m or more above the plaza. As was the case at many sites, such as Cerros (Schele and Freidel 1990), this period saw the instatement of a royal lineage at Blue Creek. Overt indications of complex society include the creation of public and sacred space at Blue Creek.

Once established, the centralized authority at Blue Creek grew rapidly and became wealthy. Buildings on the Main Plaza were greatly expanded. Structure 4, for example, was remodeled in a form much larger than its Late Preclassic counterpart (Weiss 1995). The final version of Structure 5 was built. This range building, 50 m long and 6 m tall, defined the west side of the Main Plaza

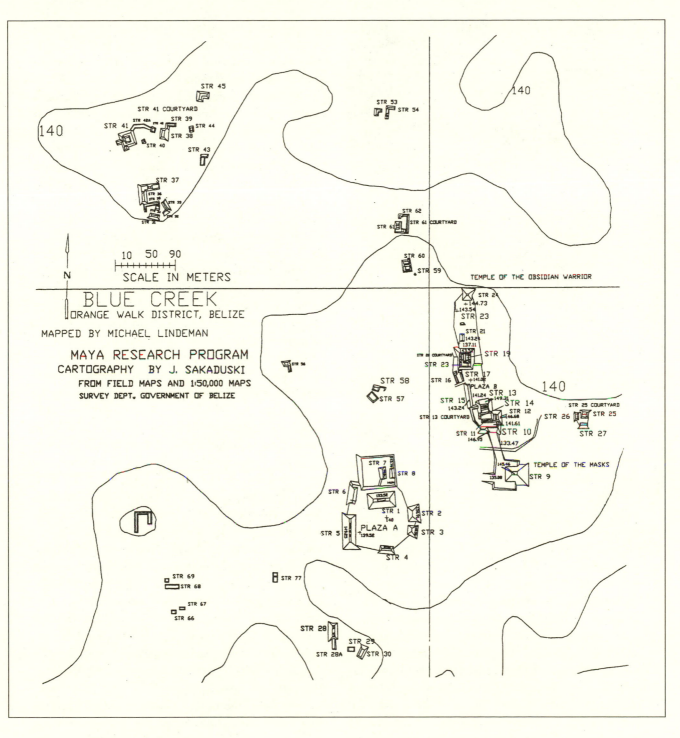

Map 9.2.   Blue Creek site core.

Fig. 9.1.   Structure 9 outset with stucco masks.

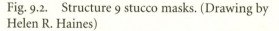

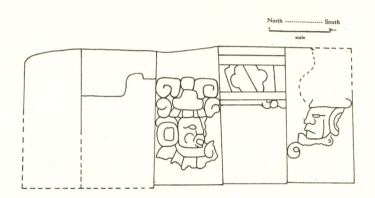

Fig. 9.2.   Structure 9 stucco masks. (Drawing by
Helen R. Haines)

(Pastrana 1995). Structure 6 was converted from a low
platform to a small but significant range building, immediately west of the towering Structure 1 (Pastrana 1996).

The special nature of Structure 1 is clear not only from
its Early Classic scale but also from the nature of its superstructure. On top of this tall temple was not a typical
southern Lowlands temple, but an open colonnaded
building (Driver 1995, 1996). The façade consisted of
eight round marl-and-masonrycolumns, and each end
of the building was open. Excavations have not yet defined the nature of the back wall, but we believe the
building had a perishable roof. The only similar structure in the region that may date from this period is
Structure V at Kohunlich (Andrews 1987). The existence
of these structures indicates that columned buildings

may be a southern Lowlands innovation that was incorporated into later northern Lowlands architecture,
rather than an indicator of Terminal Classic/Early Postclassic interaction, as some have argued.

At the southern end of Area B is the Temple of the
Masks (Structure 9), another dramatic statement as to
the nature of Blue Creek in the Early Classic period
(Haines 1995). The earliest phase of the building (Structure 9-I) dates to the Late Preclassic and is built on top
of Middle and Late Preclassic midden deposits. However,
by the middle of the Early Classic period, architecture of
the temple is typical of Peten temples, with a single-room
superstructure on top of a steeply inclined substructure.
Access to the superstructure was gained by a broad central staircase. Unlike most such buildings in the Peten,
though, the Temple of the Masks has a large staircase outset, near the top of the stairs. Similar outsets are seen are
Altun Ha (Pendergast 1979, 1982) and Kakabish (Guderjan 1996).

The façade of the outset is adorned with a complex
five-paneled stucco frieze in deep relief, which included
at least two and probably three anthropomorphic masks.
Two are in excellent condition, while the third (lefthand)
face has been destroyed (figs. 9.1, 9.2). Despite their Early
Classic style, we originally dated these to the Late Classic, based on confusing ceramics from an associated
cache, and argued that this was an archaizing trait
(Grube et al. 1995). After the 1995 season, however, we
recognized our error: These masks actually date to the
Early Classic.

Both faces have chin straps or bib motifs. The center
image has closed eyes, hollowed cheeks, a slack jaw, and
a protruding tongue. The face is wearing an elaborate
headdress decorated with volutes shaped like an *Ahaw*
glyph. The volutes represent smoke or foliation and may
be the Early Classic form of the phonetic symbol *ya*
(Thompson's T126). Grube (1990) has shown that the
Ahaw sign, when not used as a day sign, is a logogram for
the word *nik,* "flower." Thus we can interpret this as
marking the building as a *nikteil na,* "flower house"
(Grube et al. 1995). These are specific houses for dancing
and councils (Freidel et al. 1993:257–263), which may also
have served as accession houses for rulers.

Another element of the stucco façade further supports
this interpretation. A single glyph is located above the
recessed panel between the two masks. This is interpreted as representinga sky or earth band with the phonetic value *ki,* "heart" or "center" (Grube et al. 1995). This

glyph may represent the *axis mundi* (Grube et al. 1995), which can be associated with *Ahaw* (kingship) and political authority (Freidel 1992:127).

The presence of a *nikteil na* at Blue Creek is strong evidence that the community was ruled by an independent, local royal lineage. This is distinctly contrary to Adams's interpretation that the region was subsumed under a macro-state based at Tikal at the time (Adams 1995). Instead, we must see Blue Creek—and probably other medium-sized sites—as independent and self-governing. At Blue Creek, an independent royal lineage seems to have been established in the latter part of the Late Preclassic period; it then flourished economically and politically in the Early Classic. This era of independence and prosperity came to an abrupt end sometime during the first half of the fifth century.

The Ritual Event at Structure 4

In about A.D. 500, a major ritual act took place at Structure 4 on the south end of the Main Plaza. Although this act showed the wealth of Blue Creek, it also seems to have marked a turning point in the history of the community. Much of the specific data regarding this event comes from the work of Pamela Weiss, who excavated the material (Guderjan and Weiss 1995; Weiss 1995).

In preparation for the ritual, a large part of the center of the penultimate stage of Structure 4 was removed to accommodate the construction of a masonry-lined shaft. Later the sacrificial deposits were made in this shaft. Since the construction fill of Structure 4 is composed of loose-laid, large boulders, a sizeable excavation was necessary to safely construct the shaft. This preparatory excavation was dug immediately outside the superstructural building of Structure 4-2nd and reached a depth of 4.3 m with a north-south dimension of 4.6 m. On the eastern side a retaining wall was built to secure the excavation from wall collapse. The western limit of the prehistoric excavation is still being investigated.

After the initial excavation, the shaft was constructed, probably a few courses at a time, and the excavation refilled around the shaft. The shaft was stone-lined, with a diameter of approximately 50 cm and a depth of more than 3 m. During the refilling around the shaft, numerous caches of pottery vessels were placed around the shaft. In total, more than a hundred vessels were cached. Nearly all of them were of the type we have termed Blue Creek Orange, which is similar to yet distinct from types such as Garbut Creek Red. The caches were placed in nested arrangements of three inverted vessels or laid down as rim-to-rim caches. All the caches from this area were surrounded with small, irregular disks of burned limestone, often called "hamburger stones." Interestingly, these are mainly associated with Late Preclassic termination rituals at Cerros (Garber 1989:34). In addition to the pottery, fractured and complete jade beads, a stingray spine, and a bird leg bone were recovered from these caches (Guderjan and Weiss 1995).

The majority of the pottery vessels are low, outflaring-sided vessels with a matte orange slipped surface (Blue Creek Orange). Some darkening from firing is evident. Also, a blotchy postfire darkening is apparent on some of the vessels. It appears that artifacts were placed in the bottom of the vessels. The vessels placed in rather than around the shaft were covered with incense, which was burned long enough to darken the vessels before they were placed in the shaft. Also, several cylindrical censers were recovered that are similar to those later placed in the shaft.

After the shaft construction was completed, its dramatic filling occurred. This included a complex placement of individual caches in the shaft. However, we are certain that the shaft was filled in a single event. The sherds from partially reconstructable vessels were scattered throughout the fill of the shaft.

Three distinct ritual deposits were sequentially placed in the shaft during the ritual event. The lower portion of the shaft contained the bulk of the artifacts in Caches 9A–C, 10, and 11. Included in this area were worked jades, ceramics, shells, a chert eccentric, and human finger bone. The second segment was separated from the first by a marl "cap" and contained ceramic sherds from partially reconstructable vessels. The upper segment of the shaft contained only burned organic material.

The first cache placed in the lowest portion of the shaft was Cache 12. This consisted of a large, cruciform chert eccentric (fig. 9.3) and a small, unslipped pinch pot. The chert eccentric was oriented to the cardinal directions, and its north and south tips were broken off. The chert eccentric would normally be considered to be a symbol of creation and the World Tree or *axis mundi*. The relationship between the *axis mundi* and kingship has been established by Freidel (1992:127). However, the broken tips may negate the life-giving aspect (Weiss 1995). The complexity of the entire process, and the planning in-

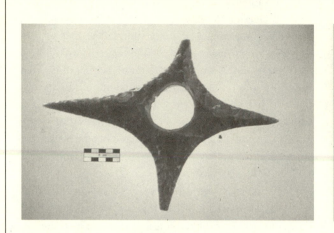

Fig. 9.3. Cache 12, cruciform eccentric with two tips intentionally broken.

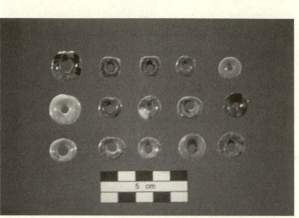

Fig. 9.6. Caches 9A and 9B, subspherical jade beads.

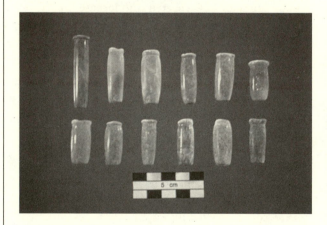

Fig. 9.4. Caches 9A and 9B, tubular jade beads.

Fig. 9.7. Caches 9A and 9B, jade earflares.

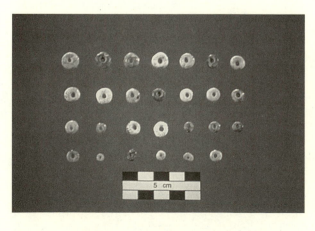

Fig. 9.5. Caches 9A and 9B, sperical jade beads.

Fig. 9.8. Cache 9C, jade artifacts.

volved, is seen in the placement of two other caches immediately outside the shaft at this level. Each consisted of two Blue Creek Orange vessels placed rim to rim. One was placed to the north and one to the south of the shaft, so that the broken tips of the eccentric were pointing to these caches. One cache contained an offering of mollusks, and the other contained a residue, presumably also of food.

About 1 m above Cache 12 was Cache 11, which held an organic offering with multiple vessels of Blue Creek Orange. While the precise number of vessels included has not been determined, theminimum number is twenty-one. Cache 10 was another rim-to-rim placement, containing forty-six shells of three freshwater and terrestrial species. It was placed only a few centimeters above Cache 11.

About 1 m above Cache 10, the shaft fill was capped with marl. The shaft fill in this area included diverse ceramic sherds, partially burned wood, and the remains of what was probably burning incense. Although no intact vessels were present, multiple sherds from several vessels were recovered. Cache 9B, placed on top of this marl surface, was the most dramatic of the individual caches found. It consisted of a rim-to-rim placement of two pottery vessels containing 356 artifacts, mostly jade beads (figs. 9.4–9.7, tables 9.1–9.3). Cache 9C was another rim-to-rim placement containing four artifacts: an anthropomorphic, tubular bead 10 x 4 cm in size, an anthropomorphic head pendant with an extended tongue, and two other beads (fig. 9.8). This was placed directly south of Cache 9B on the same surface.

The climax of the ritual event was to cap the entire deposit with a massive limestone bannerstone, 74 cm in diameter, with a central opening fashioned by grinding and exhibiting polish from use, and an uncarved stela, 1.48 m in length, that was laid flat over the northern portion of the bannerstone. The only other such buried stela that we know of was found at Cahal Pech and is believed to have been associated with the death of a king (Cheatham 1994). The bannerstone is unusual, but not unique. A similar artifact was found at Copan (Fash et al. 1992). The smoke of the burning incense wafted out of the deposit and around the prone stela. The ritual event was ended by the snuffing of the incense when additional construction material was used to bury the shaft opening.

We envision this ritual as a processional of nobles from Blue Creek as well as surrounding communities, who ascended the staircase of Structure 4 and removed personal adornments from their bodies (Guderjan and Weiss 1995;

Table 9.1. Shaft Cache Contents: Carved Jade Beads

Form	Cache 9A	Cache 9B	Cache 9C
Barrel	26	28	
Collared	24	17	
Disk	35	12	
Disk-wedge			1
Everted	2	19	
Flared	2	6	
Rectangular	6	7	
Spherical	9	32	
Spherical-petal		1	
Subspherical	40	90	2
Subspherical-flared	10	28	
Tubular	20	44	
Tubular-anthropomorphic	1		1
Wedge	1	4	

Table 9.2. Shaft Cache Contents: Carved Jades

Form	Cache 9A	Cache 9B	Cache 9C
		Earflares	
Petal	1	1	
Round	6	22	
Square		4	
		Head pendants:	
Bib	3	1	1
Olmecoid		1	
Zoomorphic		6	
		Pendants	
Anthropomorphic		1	
Disk		6	
Geometric		3	
Wedge		1	
Zoomorphic		1	
		Pebbles	
		2	
		Plaques	
	1	5	

Table 9.3. Shaft Cache Contents: Nonjade Artifacts

Form	Cache 9A	Cache 9B	Cache 9C
Beads			
Barrel			
Stone	1		
Disk			
Bone	1		
Coral	1		
Stone	4		
Rectangular			
Coral	1		
Spherical			
Coral	1		
Stone	1		
Subspherical			
Bone	1		
Stone	5	6	
Tubular			
Coral	1		
Stone	1		
Wedge			
Coral	1		
Faunal			
Labret	1		
Shell	1		
Snail	3		
Lithics			
Obsidian	4		
Chert			
Biface fragment	1		
Core	1		
Uniface tool	1		
Limestone votive	1		
Quartzite crystal	1	1	
Polishing stone	2		
Metate fragment	2		

Weiss 1995). These were then either carefully placed or broken and cast into the shaft. At the same time, those who were conducting and orchestrating the ceremony repeatedly cast burning *incensarios* into the hole as well.

DATING THE EVENT

The dating of this ritual event is based upon ceramic comparative analysis, two radiocarbon samples from within the shaft, and two radiocarbon samples from the area around the shaft, which was excavated to accommodate the shaft and then refilled. Dos Arroyos Orange-Polychromes associated with the building and Manik Phase ceramic complex material (Tikal) fix a date of approximately A.D. 250–550. In addition, a few Teotihuacan sherds were included in the shaft.

Radiocarbon dates from within the shaft were selected from quite different elevations. One was retrieved from the uppermost carbonized organic deposit and was separated from the rest of the ritual by a marl cap. The other sample came from the lowest level of the shaft. The corrected dates are ten years apart: 1440 +/− 110 B.P. (Beta-75432) and 1450 +/− 100 B.P. (Beta-76278). When the samples were cleaned in preparation for analysis, a large amount of wood was extracted from the completely organic sample, suggesting that the fire had been quickly extinguished.

The radiocarbon dates from caches in the fill around the shaft generally corroborate this date. One corrected date from Cache 21 was 1870 +/− 50 B.P. (Beta-82949) and a corrected accelerator mass spectrometry (AMS) date from Cache 14 was 1950 +/− 50 B.P. These Late Preclassic dates are clearly much too early, as the building itself is definitively Early Classic in style, with supporting ceramic evidence. Nevertheless, the question is open as to how long the shaft was in existence before the ritual event that filled it.

Consequently, we interpret the information as indicating that the ritual filling of the shaft occurred at about 1450 B.P. (A.D. 500). However, we must leave open the possibility that the shaft was in place somewhat earlier. One piece of information that casts doubt on this is the relative placement of Cache 12 and the two caches immediately outside the shaft, Caches 13 and 14. The chert eccentric in Cache 12 was clearly placed with full knowledge of the precise location (outside the shaft) of Caches 13 and 14. It seems unlikely that their locations could be known so precisely if so much time had elapsed since their placement.

Events after the Ritual

Across the Main Plaza at the same time or shortly after the Structure 4 ritual occurred, the magnificent columned superstructure of Structure 1 was razed, and a flat, apparently open-topped superstructural platform was built to accommodate the tomb of an important member of the Blue Creek community. This was the tomb of a young adult male interred with three ceramic vessels, a marine shell, two obsidian blades, a stingray spine, a worked shell plaque, two bone skewers, and two jade beads (Driver 1995). While this person was auspiciously interred, the destruction of the columned superstructure to accommodate the rather crudely built platform that replaced it is important. The replacement structure was not nearly so grand or well built as its earlier version.

This is essentially the situation across the entire site. Structures 1, 4, 5, 6, 9, 12, and 13—seven of the ten major temples—have been thoroughly investigated. We have found that almost no renovations of major buildings took place in the Late Classic period. No more large buildings were constructed, and public architectural activity virtually halted. The only known exception to this is a final construction phase built onto the façade of Structure 9, very late in the Late Classic. This construction episode buried the Peten-style temple with a coastal Belize–style, platform-topped pyramid (Haines 1995).

However, the Blue Creek community apparently continued to grow in the Late Classic. All the major elite residential courtyards near the site core were expanded or built during the Late Classic. Although our excavations have been limited to three such courtyards, more than six others have been surface-collected. Surface collections from these peripheral courtyards have proven very efficient, given the high degree of archaeological visibility provided by the clearing of land by the owners. Not only did courtyard use and construction increase, but some public space became secularized for elite residential space. The Structure 10 Courtyard was made by enclosing a small Early Classic plaza with residential structures.

Finally, with the Terminal Classic period came the end of Blue Creek. Elite residences were abandoned and used for disposal of garbage. Only a few sherds exist to hint at any activity whatsoever in the Early Postclassic period.

The Meaning of the Ritual

The Early Classic at Blue Creek is identified with political independence, dynamic construction of monumental architecture, individuality expressed in the ceramic record with influence from the Peten, and the display of wealth and power in the ability to accumulate elite goods. The Late Classic, however, is quite different. After A.D. 500, construction of monumental architecture virtually ceases. Architectural expression during the later occupation of the site becomes focused on elite residences and multiple, rather minor, remodelings rather than the large-scale buildings of the earlier period. Further, the individuality seen in ceramics gives way to more consistently northern Belize ceramic styles. These factors suggest that before the end of the Early Classic, something pivotal occurred in the political and economic life of Blue Creek.

We believe that the ritual event was related to the termination of a royal bloodline, perhaps with the death of a king. The many jade artifacts—virtually all of them personal adornments—deposited at Structure 4 were probably not solely from Blue Creek. We believe that rulers and elites from neighboring communities made a pilgrimage to Blue Creek to participate in this communal rite of passage (Guderjan and Weiss 1995). Some of the larger offerings may have been from the deceased king's own wealth. However, many artifacts are halves of paired sets, such as earspools (fig. 9.7). This leads us to believe that individuals, dressed in the finery of Maya high ritual, stepped up to the smoking opening of the shaft to personally cast a sacrifice into it.

Other aspects of the deposit suggest the act of termination as well as death. The shaft and its contents are structurally similar to rulers' tomb shafts in the eastern Peten, at sites such as Rio Azul (Hall 1987) and La Milpa. In these places, a shaft was dug to provide access to the tomb. After interment, the shaft was sequentially filled with layers of stone and specially produced chert flakes, not apparently used for any other purpose or in any other context. Further, as Weiss has noted (1995), many of the jade artifacts found in the shaft caches were ritually killed. In most cases, this amounted to intentional breakage. Further, in one case, a death mask was crudely inscribed on the face of a large anthropomorphic jade bead (Weiss 1995).

Regional patterning at this period is still very difficult to understand. An unprovenienced Early Classic jade plaque, which was ritually broken and burned, was recently unearthed by looters (David Freidel, personal communication 1995; Linda Schele, personal communication 1995; Herman Smith, personal communication

1995). The source of the plaque seems to have been one of the coastal Belize sites immediately east of Blue Creek. Robichaux (1995) has documented some increase in population from the Late Preclassic to the Early Classic at the centers of La Milpa and Dos Hombres to the southwest and south of Blue Creek. However, La Milpa seems to lack Early Classic monumental construction. Only one stela was erected, then intentionally broken during the Early Classic at La Milpa (Guderjan and Yaeger 1991). In fact, the entire region south and west of Blue Creek seems to have experienced minimal Early Classic monumental construction, or at least we do not yet have information about the Early Classic in these areas.

Consequently, our view of this time period remains on very shaky ground. Nevertheless, we know that the Early Classic saw highly variable dynamics of growth and apparently dramatic rises and falls of independent kingdoms, despite Adams's assertion that the "Tikal regional state" controlled the area (1995). Whatever the details of the Blue Creek event, the site had concluded its reign as an independent community and may have rededicated itself under the control of a larger polity within the northern Belize cultural sphere. Blue Creek would never again be the same.

ACKNOWLEDGMENTS

My great thanks go to the senior staff of the Blue Creek project, David Driver, Helen Haines, and especially Pam Weiss. This paper is an amalgam of their work, their ideas, and their support over the past years.

REFERENCES CITED

Adams, Richard E. W.
1995   "Introduction." In *The Programme for Belize Regional Archaeological Project: 1994 Interim Report,* edited by R. E. W. Adams and Fred Valdez, Jr., 1–14. San Antonio: Center for Archaeology and Tropical Studies and the University of Texas at San Antonio.

Adams, R. E. W., and Fred Valdez, Jr., eds.
1995   *The Programme for Belize Regional Archaeological Project: 1994 Interim Report.* San Antonio: Center for Archaeology and Tropical Studies and the University of Texas at San Antonio.

Andrews, George F.
1987   *Architecture at Kohunlich, Quintana Roo: A Preliminary Report.* Cuadernos de Arquitectura Mesoamerica 10. Mexico City: Universidad Nacional Autonoma de Mexico.

Cheatham, David
1994   "The Buried Stela of Zapilote, Cahal Pech." Paper presented at the Meeting of the Society for American Archaeology, Anaheim, California.

Driver, W. David
1995   "Architecture and Ritual at Structure 1." In *Archaeological Research at Blue Creek, Belize: Progress Report of the Third (1994) Field Season,* edited by Thomas H. Guderjan and W. David Driver, 27–45. San Antonio: Maya Research Program and Department of Sociology, St. Mary's University.

1996   "Continuing Excavations at Structure 1." In *Archaeological Research at Blue Creek, Belize: The 1995 Season,* edited by Thomas H. Guderjan and W. David Driver, 27–36. San Antonio: Maya Research Program and Department of Sociology, St. Mary's University.

Fash, Barbara, William Fash, Sheree Lane, Rudy Larios, Linda Schele, Jeffrey Stomper, and David Stuart
1992   "Investigations of a Classic Maya Council House at Copán." *Journal of Field Archaeology* 19:419–42.

Freidel, David A.
1992   "The Trees of Life: Ahua as Idea and Artifact in Classic Lowland Maya Civilization." In *Ideology and Pre-Columbian Civilization,* edited by Arthur Demarest, 115–34. Santa Fe, N.M.: School of American Research Press.

Freidel, David A., Linda Schele, and Joy Parker.
1993   *Maya Cosmos.* New York: William Morrow.

Garber, James F.
1989   *Archaeology at Cerros, Belize, Central America, Volume 2: The Artifacts.* Dallas: Southern Methodist University Press.

Garber, James F., David C. Grove, Kenneth G. Hirth, and John W. Hoopes
1993   "The Context of Jade Usage in Portions of Mexico and Central America: Olmec, Maya, Costa Rica and Honduras." In *Precolumbian Jade: New Geological And Cultural Interpretations,* edited by Fred Lange, 166–72. Salt Lake City: University of Utah Press.

Grube, Nikolai
1990   "The *Ahaw* Sign as *Nik,* 'Flower.'" MS on file, University of Bonn.

Grube, Nikolai, Thomas H. Guderjan, and Helen R. Haines
1995   "Late Classic Architecture and Iconography at the BlueCreek Ruin, Belize." *Mexicon* 17:3:51–56.

Guderjan, Thomas H.

1995 "Aspects of Maya Settlement in Northwestern Belize: The View from Blue Creek." In *Archaeological Research at Blue Creek, Belize: Progress Report of the Third (1994) Field Season*, edited by Thomas H. Guderjan and W. David Driver, 13–27. San Antonio: Maya Research Program and Department of Sociology, St. Mary's University.

1996 "Kakabish: Mapping a Maya Center." In *Archaeological Research at Blue Creek, Belize: The 1995 Season*, edited by Thomas H. Guderjan and W. David Driver, 117–20. San Antonio: Maya Research Program and Department of Sociology, St. Mary's University.

Guderjan, Thomas H., and W. David Driver, eds.

1995 *Archaeological Research at Blue Creek, Belize: Progress Report of the Third (1994) Field Season*. San Antonio: Maya Research Program and Department of Sociology, St. Mary's University.

1996 *Archaeological Research at Blue Creek, Belize: The 1995 Season*. San Antonio: Maya Research Program and Department of Sociology, St. Mary's University.

Guderjan, Thomas H., Helen R. Haines, Michael Lindeman, Shirley Mock, Ellen Ruble, Froyla Salam, and Lea Worchester

1993 *Excavations at the Blue Creek Ruin, Northwestern Belize: The 1992 Interim Report*. San Antonio, Texas: Maya Research Program.

Guderjan, Thomas H., Helen R. Haines, Michael Lindeman, Dale Pastrana, Ellen Ruble, and Pam Weiss

1994 *Excavations at Blue Creek: The 1992 and 1993 Field Seasons*. San Antonio: Maya Research Program and Department of Sociology, St. Mary's University.

Guderjan, Thomas H., and Pamela J. Weiss

1995 *The Blue Creek Jade Cache*. Final Report to the Foundation for the Advancement of Mesoamerican Studies, Clearlake, Florida.

Haines, Helen R.

1995 "Summary of Excavations at the Temple of the Masks." In *Archaeological Research at Blue Creek, Belize: Progress Report of the Third (1994) Field Season*, edited by Thomas H. Guderjan and W. David Driver, 73–99. San Antonio: Maya Research Program and Department of Sociology, St. Mary's University.

1996 "A Preliminary Discussion of Preclassic Midden Deposits at Blue Creek." In *Archaeo-logical Research at Blue Creek, Belize: The 1995 Season*, edited by Thomas H. Guderjan and W. David Driver, 85–108. San Antonio: Maya Research Program and Department of Sociology, St. Mary's University.

Hall, Grant D.

1987 "The Discovery of Tomb 23 and Results of Other Tomb Investigations at Rio Azul, Season of 1985." In *Rio Azul Reports, Number 3: The 1985 Season*, edited by R. E. W. Adams, 107–52. San Antonio: University of Texas at San Antonio.

Neivens, Mary

1991 "Operations at the Site of Blue Creek." In *Maya Settlement in Northwestern Belize: The 1988 and 1990 Seasons of the Rio Bravo Archaeological Project*, edited by Thomas H. Guderjan, 51–54. Culver City, Calif.: Labyrinthos.

Pastrana, Dale

1995 "Excavations at Structures 5 and 6." In *Archaeological Research at Blue Creek, Belize: Progress Report of the Third (1994) Field Season*, edited by Thomas H. Guderjan and W. David Driver, 63–73. San Antonio: Maya Research Program and Department of Sociology, St. Mary's University.

1996 "Excavations at Structure 5 and 6." In *Archaeological Research at Blue Creek, Belize: The 1995 Season*, edited by Thomas H. Guderjan and W. David Driver, 43–58. San Antonio: Maya Research Program and Department of Sociology, St. Mary's University.

Pendergast, David A.

1979 *Excavations at Altun Ha, Volume 1*. Toronto: Royal Ontario Museum.

1982 *Excavations at Altun Ha, Volume 2*. Toronto: Royal Ontario Museum.

Robichaux, Hubert Ray

1995 "Ancient Maya Community Patterns in Northwestern Belize: Peripheral Zone Survey at La Milpa and Dos Hombres." Ph.D. diss., University of Texas.

Schele, Linda, and David A. Freidel

1990 *A Forest of Kings*. New York: William Morrow.

Weiss, Pamela J.

1995 "Architecture and Ritual at Structure 4." In *Archaeological Research at Blue Creek, Belize: Progress Report of the Third (1994) Field Season*, edited by Thomas H. Guderjan and W. David Driver, 45–63. San Antonio: Maya Research Program and Department of Sociology, St. Mary's University.

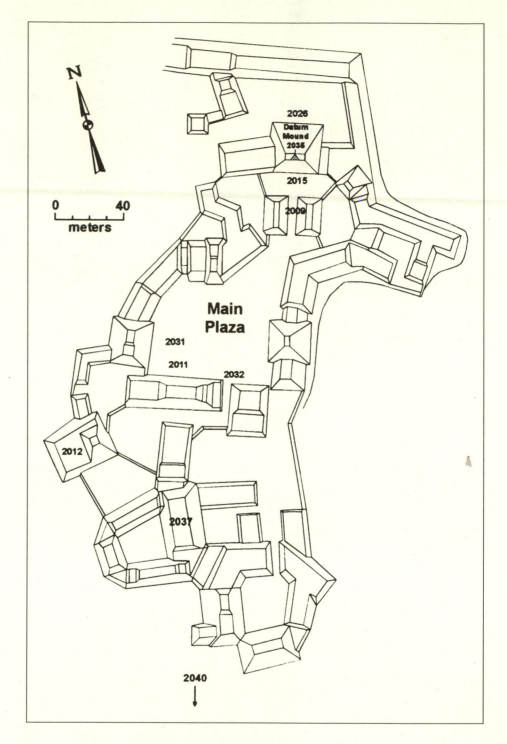

Map 10.1.   Monumental center, Colha, Belize.
(Map drawn by Jack Eaton, from Eaton 1979)

CHAPTER TEN

The Defaced and the Forgotten

Decapitation and Flaying/Mutilation as a Termination Event at Colha, Belize

Shirley Boteler Mock
University of Texas, San Antonio
and the Institute of Texan Cultures at San Antonio

In 1980 archaeologists uncovered evidence of a remarkable event at the site of Colha in northern Belize, which took place during the declining years of the Maya Late Classic period (c. A.D. 800–850; map 10.1). The evidence consisted of the flayed and mutilated skulls of twenty adults and ten children interred in a shallow pit adjacent to the stairway of an elite structure of the ceremonial center (Massey 1989; Steele et al. 1980). Archaeological evidence further suggests that widespread destruction, possibly contemporaneous with this event, also occurred at the site of Colha.

In this chapter I examine the event at Colha within the broader context of actions such as decapitation, flaying, mutilation, and selected placement of sacrificial victims, as recovered in the archaeological record of Mesoamerica. Evidence drawn from iconography, ethnohistorical documents, and comparative archaeological data suggests that this sacrificial event was a more than a simple execution of the elite rulers of Colha. From the perspective of the Mesomerican world view, I argue that it was not only an execution but also a ritual termination of their elite power and identity, and a rebirth through reenactment of mythic events from the first creation (Mock 1994).

THE COLHA SKULL PIT

The placement of human skulls within a culturally prescribed schema has great antiquity in Mesoamerica (Agrinier 1978; Fowler 1984; Robbin 1989; Sharer 1978; Smith 1950; Willey 1973). There is, however, significant variation and diversity from site to site in the type of human sacrifices, and also in their placement, a fact that underscores the structural transformations of this practice in both time and place. A survey of the archaeological evidence reveals the prominence of skulls in retainer burials, in mass graves or dedicatory sacrifices (e.g., Gann 1900, 1918; Robbin 1989), and in single interments in building or stela dedications (e.g., Smith and Kidder 1951:29–31; Thompson 1939; Willey 1973). The remarkable feature uncovered at Colha, a large lithic manufacturing site in northern Belize, is one of the best documented mass skull burials (Massey 1989, 1994; Steele et al. 1980:91; see also Hester et al. 1982, 1983; Hester and Shafer 1991; Mock 1994; Shafer and Hester 1983, 1986). Thirty individuals (twenty adults of both sexes and ten children ranging in age from infants to seven years) were beheaded and their skulls deposited in a shallow pit dug into the west side of the stairway of an elite structure

Fig. 10.1. The skull pit feature soon after discovery. View of initial exposure and cleaning of the upper portion of the feature. (From Massey 1989)

Fig. 10.2. The Colha Skull Pit at Operation 2011 after removal of ceramic fragments covering and surrounding skulls. (Drawing by Kathy Roemer, from Hester et al. 1980)

(Operation 2011; map 10.1).[1] There was no obvious pattern in the placement of the skulls except age: The skulls of older adults were found in the top layer of skulls (figs. 10.1, 10.2). Presumably these victims were the Colha elite, based on the evidence of distinctive cranial deformation of the skulls and tooth modification in the majority of the population (Massey 1989).

The Colha interment is also distinguished by the presence of cut marks on twenty of the thirty skulls, representing either removal of soft tissue, such as the eyes, nose, or mouth, or flaying (Massey 1994:218). In addition, one skull was burned and two others partially burned before deposition (Massey 1989:44–45). The absence of burning below the skull pit and the placement of the skulls in the lower level of the feature precludes postdeposition burning. Portions of worn, large, Late to Terminal Classic, Palmar Orange polychrome plates, Tinaja and Subin Red bowls and jars, striated jars, and a chalice vessel fragment, intentionally broken and placed around, under, and on top of the skulls in the pit, constituted the final act of the event. No matching sherds were recovered, which suggests either purposeful scattering or the use of portions of worn, discarded ceramics and other "garbage" to emphasize the final debasement of the victims. After the interment of the human victims, the elite structure above was burned, as indicated by the presence of fire-fractured stones (Eaton 1980; Hester et al. 1982; Mock 1994; Steele et al. 1980). Additional excavations at the inside corner of the east side of the stairway of the structure uncovered a dense concentration of *Pomacea* shells (60 cm x 36 cm) and scattered artifacts, such as chert flakes, tools, and broken ceramics. This concentration was covered by fall from the top of the structure. *Pomacea*, a species of freshwater mollusk, were used at Colha in other instances to cap Early Postclassic burials (Jack Eaton, personal communication 1992), and it is possible that their location on the eastern side of the stairway is conceptually related to the interment of human skulls on the western side (Mock 1994).

The skull pit feature, based on the associated ceramics, dates to c. A.D. 800–850, the Late to Terminal Classic—a period of considerable unrest and decline in the Maya Lowlands (Culbert 1973). Attendant problems at Colha are indicated by the discontinuation of construction activities, crowding in of inhabitants in the *plazuela* groups, and drawing in of settlement toward the center of the site possibly for defensive reasons (Hester 1985:12). Analysis of the children's skulls also suggests the presence of disease and malnutrition among the elite population

(Massey 1989, 1994). Colha was abandoned around this time and, after a brief hiatus, was reoccupied during the Early Postclassic by people bearing totally new traditions in ceramics, lithics, subsistence regimes, and settlement patterns (Adams and Valdez 1980; Hester et al. 1983; Valdez 1987). An overthrow of the ruling elite by internal rebellion or invasion by non-Colha people has been proposed (Hester 1985; Valdez 1987; Valdez and Adams 1982), either of which could account for the considerable evidence of dismantling and destruction of buildings before abandonment (Eaton 1979:88, 1982:138). Alternatively, the site could have been ritually terminated by the inhabitants as a form of desacralization.

Additional termination activity was suggested by the excavations at Operation 2012, an elite structure in the ceremonial center southwest of the skull pit feature (map 10.1), where a deposition of numerous, large stacks of Palmar Orange polychrome plate sherds was recovered on the west side of the structure (Conger 1986).[2] Additional evidence of scattered human remains, jade (including a small broken jade face ornament; Potter 1982:fig. 3, 102, 104), and chert and obsidian artifacts was noted in fill overlaying the structure. Similar termination activities involving burning, destruction, and deposition of polychrome sherds appear to have been a pattern at other elite structures at Colha at this time.

The sacrifice of the unfortunate victims interred in the skull pit, possibly the Colha elite, may have been part of this extensive termination activity at the site. It seems likely that the victims were selectively chosen for this particular event, considering the burning of specific skulls, the representation of children, and a possible equal distribution of adult males and females in the feature (Massey 1989). In addition, the location of the skull feature, on the west side of the interior corner of a stairway of the elite structure, follows patterns seen elsewhere in the placement of human skulls or dedicatory offerings. Such offerings were often deposited at liminal[3] interstices or places of transition, such as stairways, doorways, axial centers or lines, or the corners of structures. Arguments that this was an orchestrated ritual execution are based on the evidence of flaying and the removal of fleshy parts of the skulls. Such acts would require considerable expenditure of time and energy, and more effort by the perpetrators of the deed than the digging of the shallow pit to contain the skulls.

The skulls of decapitated victims reported in the archaeological literature for the most part are interpreted as dedicatory (Ricketson and Ricketson 1937; Thompson 1939)—that is, they were interred with the specific intent to open communication to the Otherworld. Such dedicatory offerings gave life to a structure through an offering of the most powerful part of the human body, the skull (e.g., Freidel et al. 1993). The symbolism underlying the treatment and placement of skeletal material in the archaeological record is not completely understood; however, the meaning of such ritual events can be illuminated by examining the ethnohistoric data of Mesoamerica concerning the ideology of the human body.

CAPTIVES AND FLAYED FACES

A consistent theme chronicled in the documents pertaining to Mesoamerican beliefs through time and space is the human body as a central organizing principle. Human bones—in particular, the human skull—were imbued with power (Furst 1978:26) and were believed to produce semen (López Austin 1988:176). In Nahuatl thought, *tonalli,* which originated in the crown of the head, was connected to the soul and spirit or the destiny of a person and to "protect one's head was to protect one's reputation, name, and fate" (López Austin 1988:218). At death *tonalli* escaped through the top of the head to be deposited elsewhere, and thus could enter into or revitalize another person, possession, or object (López Austin 1988:220).

A similar vital force, *ch'ulel* (Freidel et al. 1993:244–246; Schele 1989), meaning "inner spirit or soul" (derived from ancient Tzotzil *ch'ul* or *k'ul;* see Freidel et al. 1993:11; also Freidel, this volume; Walker, this volume), was an ideological ordering principle among the Tzotzil of Chiapas. Vogt (1976:18–19) notes that the Zinacantecos believed that not only deities and humans possessed *ch'ulel,* but also inanimate items, such as maize, household fires, crosses, and houses.

The skull, as we know from the *Popol Vuh* of the Highland Maya (Edmonson 1971; Tedlock 1985:5), was a primary source of regenerative power.[4] A human skull, therefore, whether taken from an ancestor or a prestigious enemy, when interred in a structure could literally ensoul it through the animating essence of *ch'ulel* (Schele 1989), like a seed planted in the ground (Carlsen and Prechtel 1991).

Despite the presence of so many skulls in the Colha feature and their auspicious placement in a liminal inner corner of the structure, it is doubtful that dedication was the objective of the event. On the contrary, the subse-

Fig. 10.3. Anthropomorphic censer displaying a flayed mask from the Late to Terminal Classic site of Northern River Lagoon, Belize.

quent destruction of the building above and abandonment of Colha shortly thereafter argue for a termination rather than an attempted ensouling of the structure. While evidence of smashed censers proves that an adjacent elite structure (Operation 2012; map 10.1) was ritually revisited during the Late Postclassic, the structure (Operation 2011) containing the skull pit feature shows no material evidence of revisits or attempts to reopen communication with the ancestors (Mock 1994).

Another significant factor to be considered in interpreting the feature is the presence of flaying marks on twenty of the skulls (Massey 1989:32). Although mutilation of human skeletons has been reported in the archaeological literature (Piedras Negras: Coe 1959; Cuello: Robbin 1989), the skull sample from Colha is the first instance in which flaying has been documented (Massey 1989). Mutilation, although less frequently depicted than decapitation, is alluded to in Maya iconography: for example, human bones and disembodied eyes depicted on polychrome vessels of the Late Classic period (e.g., Kerr 1989b:200, 208; Schele and Miller 1986:pl. 109) and, more graphically, the mutilated captives (and one decapitated head) depicted in the Room 3 mural at Bonampak (Miller 1986:pl. 2).

Rituals of the Xipe Totec complex of Central Mexico, the flayed god of fertility and renewal, include similar programs of decapitation, and flaying/mutilation of captives (Sahagún 1950:74–80). During the great Aztec feast of *Tlacaxipehualiztli* dedicated to Xipe Totec, men, women, and children were killed and flayed (Broda 1970), some of the heads being displayed on the *tzompantli*, "skull-rack" (Seler 1963, 1:131–132). Typically, the impersonator of Xipe Totec is depicted wearing a flayed human skin with dangling hands or holding a human skull. Landa also describes the practice of flaying the body of a victim of heart sacrifice (Tozzer 1941:119) as a solemn occasion in Yucatan. In his accounts of Mexico, Motolinia (1950:76) notes another custom of skinning the heads of sacrificed prisoners of war. Particular attention was given to the heads of notable prisoners, which were dried and worn or displayed as trophies, presumably attaching the power *(tonalli)* of the prestigious victim to the captor.

In the Nahuatl belief system, the face itself was the source of vital breath (López Austin 1988:173), personality, and individual identity: "the very element that removed ... anonymity" (Leon-Portilla 1988:114). This association may explain the presence of human crania with removed facial portions recovered in burial contexts at Maya sites such as Uaxactún (Ricketson and Ricketson 1937:145, pl. 48a–b) and Copan (Rebecca Storey, personal communication 1991). Special significance attached to the face is similarly reflected in Classic Maya iconography showing the facial portion of altered crania or flayed faces used as masks (e.g., Kerr 1989a:39). Stela D at Copan has been interpreted by Benson (1987:191, fig. 1) as a ruler wearing a flayed mask, perhaps in imitation of the sun god. More convincing is the flayed mask displayed on the anthropomorphic censer shown in figure 10.3, recovered at Northern River Lagoon, a Late to Terminal Classic coastal site near Colha (Mock 1993, 1994).

The corpus of Maya iconography also provides evidence that the flayed face is an integral part of the Tlaloc-Venus war complex (Freidel et al. 1993:243:409; Schele and Freidel 1990). A quadripartite badge or shield made of a flayed face *(tok'-pakal)*, accompanied by a flint alluding to decapitation and war (fig. 10.4), is displayed prominently on lintels commemorating accession ceremonies of the nobility of Palenque and other Maya kingdoms (Schele and Freidel 1990:243; Schele and Miller 1986:115, figs. 7, 11). The *tok'-pakal*, a symbol of royal kingship, was a material embodiment of power or life force appropriated from a captured, humiliated, and sacrificed elite ruler.

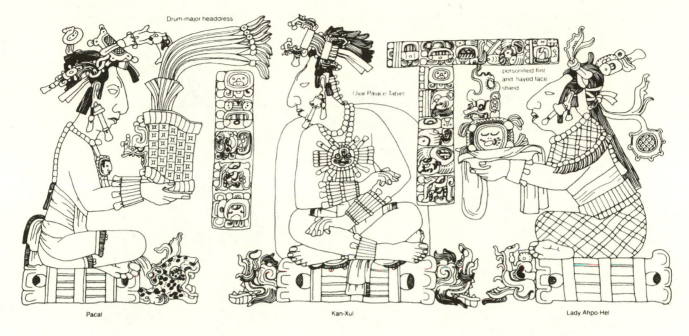

Drum-major headdress

Oval Palace Tablet

personified flint
and flayed face
shield

Pacal

Kan-Xul

Lady Ahpo-Hel

Fig. 10.4. Palenque Palace Tablet. Lady Ahpo-Hel hands the *tok'pakal*, "flayed shield," to Kan-Xul. (Drawing by Linda Schele. Copyright 1986, Kimbell Art Museum. Schele and Miller 1986:fig. II.7,115)

More explicit evidence of flayed faces and relationship to the Tlaloc war complex can be seen in a roll-out of a cylinder vessel (Kerr 1989b; fig. 10.5 here) from the site of Motul de San Jose (Justin Kerr, personal communication 1992). Among the figures depicted, three are distinguished by black- and red-spotted flayed masks, worn inside out, displaying the typical Xipe Totec–style mouths and slit eyes. One masked participant in this ritual scene wears the conical, clown like hat of Xipe Totec (e.g., Kubler and Gibson 1951:fig. 13d) and appears to be howling. He strikes a pose over the body of a contorted performer (who appears to mimic the throne of the deposed captive) wearing an identical flayed mask. A third figure wearing a flayed mask kneels in front of a mutilated and bound captive and holds a knife to his face. Central to the scene is the victorious royal captor wearing a profile mask who threatens the defiant captive with his spear—a captive forced to view his own *tonalli* in the mirror placed in front of him in a large footed ceramic vessel. The juxtaposition of cavorting figures wearing flayed masks and the mirror graphically symbolizes a rite of reversal (Turner 1969), in which the royal captive is not only humiliated, mocked, and tortured but also undergoes a reversal of status in which he loses his *tonalli* or *ch'ulel* to the victor, in this case the masked figure (Mock 1992, 1994).

THE LOSING OF FACE

Another dimension of termination ritual related to the Colha skull feature—given the association of human faces with social identity—is the termination of an individual's *chul'el* or *tonalli* through defacement by flaying and mutilation of facial features. Carrying this idea further, I contend that a metaphoric association between the human face, the social self, and human portraits is an essential component in the symbolic repertoire of Mesoamerican iconography. In fact, this association is more than an analogy; it assumes the dimensions of reality. The identification is supported by evidence such as the deliberate and systematic defacement of the eyes and muzzles of the monumental masks at Cerros (Freidel 1986; Freidel and Schele 1989) in northern Belize. Both the defacement of the masks and the well-known dedication-termination rituals accompanying the abandonment of the 5C-1st structure at Cerros (Garber 1989; Robertson-Freidel 1980) point to the complexities of this ideological complex. Chaos and disorder reign during these ritual events (see introduction, this volume), involving not only effacement but also layering, scattering, burning, and breaking of artifacts or stone monuments in acts of deliberate destruction. In post-Contact times the recursive relationship of destruction and chaos to

Fig. 10.5. Polychrome vase from San Jose de Motul. (Roll-out photograph courtesy of Justin Kerr, file no. 2025)

rebirth and renewal was re-created in the New Year Renewal described by Landa (Tozzer 1941:151–152), in which household goods, such as pottery, and even "idol wrappings" were burned or smashed and ceremonially cast away, to be replaced by new ones.

The antiquity of such ritual destruction is similarly indicated by the treatment of Olmec statues and monuments. Coe and Diehl (1980) describe the determination with which features of the colossal heads were mutilated by pitting, fracturing, slotting, or battering at the Olmec site of San Lorenzo. At Chalcatzingo, Grove (1981:61, 1984:158–59) notes the destruction focused on the heads and faces of portrait monuments and more specific defacement of many portrait monuments by grinding. Grove (1981, 1984:159–60) connects the mutilation to attempts to release supernatural power following the death of the ruler portrayed or the end of cycles, rather than attributing it to internal strife.

Similar defacements of other monuments in Meso-america emphasize the scope of this ideological program of termination. The destruction of facial features on the stelae at Copan, Honduras, is a notable example. Schele's (1991:4–5) interpretation of an inscription of Stela 11 as recounting the literal defacement (u lob, "he defaced him" or "he ruined him") of the founder Yax-K'uk-Mo' by Yax-Pax further supports the simultaneity of the de-

struction of face with the erasure of social identity and dispersal of ch'ulel. Schele (1991:5) observes that "the act of defacing as a part of ending the life of things like buildings and objects was so pervasive and fundamental to Maya thought, that it functioned as a metaphor for the ending of the Copán dynasty."

These episodes of destruction can be related to similar events of the third creation described in the *Popol Vuh*, following unsuccessful attempts by the gods to create a competent human race. The writers describe this failed attempt as a time of "humiliation, destruction, and demolition," in which wooden humans are "pounded down to the bones and tendons, smashed and pulverized even to the bones," because of their incompetence (Tedlock 1985:84). Significantly, their faces are burned, smashed, and abused by their dogs, their griddles, their cooking pots, their hearthstones, and all other creatures of the earth that rise up against these humans who have treated them badly (Edmonson 1971:29–30; Tedlock 1985:84–85). As if this humiliation is not enough, the *Popol Vuh* emphasizes the attempts made by these miserable, unworthy humans to escape the wrath of the gods (Tedlock 1985:85):

They want to climb up on the houses but they fall as the houses collapse.

They want to climb the trees; but they're thrown off by
the trees.
They want to get inside the caves, but the caves slam
shut in their faces.

The trees and caves represent the portals to the Otherworld that are effectively closed to these ungrateful humans of creation. Their ancestral houses or lineages are
also destroyed, so these ungrateful rulers cannot be reborn to rule again.

Edmonson's (1986:155) comments on rituals described
in the *Book of Chilam Balam,* marking the end of the
katun among Yucatecan Maya, also support this connection of flaying/mutilation and decapitation of humans
or anthropomorphic images to the dedication-termination complex. Speaking of the outgoing jaguar or sacrificial priests (and sacrificial victims), Edmonson observes
that "their heads were beaten, and then their faces were
flattened, and then they were forgotten." He further connects these acts to the defacement of the Classic Maya
katun monuments at the end of the *katun* cycle. I contend that "flattening" here again refers to the erasure of
the personhood through flaying/mutilation of the human face and head, not only the ultimate humiliation
but also the final destruction of an individual's identity
and *chul'el* or *tonalli.*

Allusions to the decapitation-flaying mutilation complex are a consistent theme in the *Ritual of the Bacobs* in
response to improper behavior (Roys 1965:61). This book
of shamanic incantations describes flaying as analogous
to the husking of an ear of maize; the speaker boasts of
being "the great loosener," "the great husker," when he
stands erect. Besides references to bruising, cutting, and
demolition of the offending party's face, the incantations
also include passages referring to the chopping of his
head and cutting off or scratching of his "cover" or face
(Roys 1965:44, 47). These incantations, like the creation
story of the *Popol Vuh,* lend support to the metaphoric
association of face with self-identity and *chul'el* and also
to decapitation and flaying/mutilation as a divinely or-
dained punishment for recalcitrant spirits and humans,
as well as elite offenders or unworthy or defeated kings.

DEFACEMENT AND DÉNOUEMENT

Considered together, the ethnohistoric and iconographical data presented above and the archaeological evidence
of the interment of skulls at Colha suggest some conclusions. Although the motivations of the perpetrators of
the deed or the transgressions of the sacrificial victims
interred in the skull pit cannot be known, these sources
of evidence offer a plausible scenario.

As noted above, termination events may be a pre-
condition for rebirth. Additional evidence from sites
such as Cerros (Freidel1986; Freidel and Schele 1989) also
supports the idea that the deliberate destruction of monumental portraiture may be a prelude to rebirth or revitalization attempts. A similar relationship of death to
rebirth explains the interment of many human skulls as
dedicatory sacrifices in the archaeological record.

The Colha elite, however, appear to have suffered an
ignominious fate not unlike that of the fallen rulers of
the great center of Copan. The interment of flayed skulls
near the stairway of an elite structure at Colha—the act
accompanied by burning, smashing, and placing of
broken polychrome plates and ceramics around the
skulls—perhaps synchronized with termination events
occurring in other areas of the ceremonial center. An additional component of the interment is the ignoble treatment of the dead: the presence of broken and worn-out
objects symbolizing chaos or abasement, and the ran-
dom placement of the skulls in the pit, representing the
loss of original order. Indeed, the evidence suggests that
these victims became "nonpersons," the potentially
dangerous forces of their *chul'el* or *tonalli* and identity
effectively terminated by both the act of mutilation and
debasement. Moreover, given the evidence, it is possible
that the victim's power was transferred to flayed masks
or *tok'-pacal* shields displayed by the new wielders of
power at Colha, whether disillusioned commoners, re-
bellious nobles, or ambitious outsiders.

I have argued that the decapitation and the flaying and
mutilation of the faces of the Colha victims are analogous to the effacement and destruction found on monumental art elsewhere in Mesoamerica. Not only were
these elite victims of Colha sacrificed, but also the potent
force of their self-identity was ritually terminated. The
event reenacted the original sacrifice of the third creation in the *Popol Vuh,* in which the incompetent humans (Edmonson 1971; Tedlock 1985) had their faces and
mouths destroyed and crushed, just as the offending
spirits in the *Ritual of the Bacabs* (Roys 1965) and the outgoing priests in the *Book of Chilam Balam* (Edmonson
1986) were mutilated and defaced. These elite individuals of Colha, possibly because of their inability to influ-

ence the gods and turn the tides of fate during the Maya Late to Terminal Classic period, were defaced and forgotten, their identity lost, their communication to the Otherworld closed forever.

ACKNOWLEDGMENTS

I wish to express my appreciation to Thomas R. Hester, of the University of Texas at Austin, for his encouragement and comments in regard to the interpretation of this paper. I also gratefully acknowledge the collaborating institutions of the Colha projects. These institutions include the University of Texas at San Antonio, the Centro Studi Ricerche Ligabue (Venice, Italy), Texas A&M University, and the University of Texas at Austin.

I want to thank Shirley McGinnis and Michael Haynes for their constructive criticism and comments. In particular, Shirley generously made time in her busy schedule to edit my revisions. I am grateful to Anna J. Taylor for her impeccable field notes and Jack Eaton, former acting director of the Center for Archaeological Research of the University of Texas at Austin, for his insightful observations on Terminal Classic settlement and architecture at Colha.

To Linda Schele of the University of Texas at Austin and her "Warfare in Mesoamerican Art" seminar, 1991, I owe the impetus for this endeavor and journey into "meaning." Finally, I thank Robert Hill of the University of Texas at San Antonio, who not only gave generously of his time to listen to my ideas but also provided invaluable insight into the ethnohistoric documents of Mesoamerica.

NOTES

1. All crania were found with associated mandibles and vertebrae (Massey 1989:3).

2. One additional lens of sherds stacked on edge was found on the north side of the structure. The excavator also notes the presence of flat lenses of ceramics and suggests that they were ritually broken.

3. *Liminal* (from Latin *limen*, "threshold"), as explained by Turner (1969), is a "betwixt and between" state of ambiguity. In this context, liminality is applied to points of architectural structures that show change, such as intersections or openings.

4. The twins Hun-Hunahpu and Vucub-Hunahpu, after losing the ball game with the Lords of Xibalba, are sacrificed. The head of Hun-Hunahpu becomes a gourd in a tree and magically impregnates the maiden Xquic by spitting into her hand. She subsequently gives birth to the hero twins, Hunahpu and Xbalanqueh, whose adventures are chronicled in the *Popol Vuh*.

REFERENCES CITED

Adams, Richard E. W., and Fred Valdez, Jr.
1980   "The Ceramic Sequence at Colha, Belize: 1979 and 1980 Seasons." In *The Colha Project, Second Season, 1980 Interim Report*, edited by T. R. Hester, J. D. Eaton, and H. J. Shafer, 15–40. San Antonio: University of Texas at San Antonio and Centro Studi e Richerche Ligabue, Venice.

Agrinier, Pierre
1978   *A Sacrificial Mass Burial at Miramar, Chiapas, Mexico.* Papers of the New World Archaeological Foundation 42. Provo, Utah: Brigham Young University.

Benson, Elizabeth P.
1987   "Uses of Symbol and Style on Copan Stelae." In *The Periphery of the Southeastern Classic Maya Realm*, edited by Gary W. Pahl, 189–208. Los Angeles: Latin American Center Publications, University of California, Los Angeles.

Broda, Johanna
1970   "Tlacaxipehualiztli: A Reconstruction of an Aztec Calendar Festival from Sixteenth Century Sources." *Revista española de antropologia americana* 5:197–274.

Carlsen, Robert, and Martin Prechtel
1991   "The Flowering of the Dead: An Interpretation of Highland Maya Culture." *Man* 26:23–42.

Coe, Michael D., and Richard A. Diehl
1980   *In the Land of the Olmec: The Archaeology of San Lorenzo Tenochtitlan.* Austin: University of Texas Press.

Coe, William R.
1959   *Piedras Negras Archaeology: Artifacts, Caches, and Burials.* Philadelphia: University of Pennsylvania Museum.

Conger, Buryl
1986   "Colha Operation 2012: Goals for Thesis and Continuing Research." MS on file at Texas Archeology Research Lab, University of Texas at Austin.

Culbert, T. Patrick, ed.
1973   *The Classic Maya Collapse.* Albuquerque: University of New Mexico Press.

Eaton, Jack D.

1979   "Preliminary Observations of the Architecture of Colha, Belize." In *The Colha Project 1979: A Collection of Interim Papers,* edited by Thomas R. Hester, 77–98. San Antonio: Center for Archaeological Research of the University of Texas at San Antonio.

1980   "Operation 2011: Investigations within the Main Plaza of the Monumental Center at Colha." In *The Colha Project: Second Season, 1980 Interim Report,* edited by T. R. Hester, J. D. Eaton, and H. J. Shafer, 145–162. San Antonio: Center for Archaeological Research of the University of Texas at San Antonio and Centro Studi e Ricerche Ligabue, Venice.

1982   "Colha: An Overview of Architecture and Settlement." In *Archaeology at Colha, Belize: The 1981 Interim Report,* edited by Thomas R. Hester, Harry J. Shafer, and Jack D. Eaton, 123–40. San Antonio: Center for Archaeological Research of the University of Texas of San Antonio and Centro Studi e Ricerche Ligabue, Venice.

1994   "Archaeological Investigations at the Main Datum Mound, Colha, Belize." *Continuing Archeology at Colha, Belize,* edited by Thomas R. Hester, Harry J. Shafer, and Jack D. Eaton, 99–108. Studies in Archeology 16. Austin: Texas Archeological Research Laboratory of the University of Texas at Austin.

Edmonson, Munroe

1971   *The Book of Counsel: The Popol Vuh of the Quiche Maya of Guatemala.* Middle American Research InstitutePublication 35. New Orleans: Middle American Research Institute.

1986   *Heaven Born Merida and Its Destiny: The Book of Chilam Balam of Chumayel.* Translated and annotated by Munro S. Edmonson. Austin: University of Texas Press.

Fowler, William R., Jr.

1984   "Late Preclassic Mortuary Patterns and Evidence for Human Sacrifice at Chalchuapa, El Salvador." *American Antiquity* 49(3):603–8.

Freidel, David A.

1986   "The Monumental Architecture." In *Archaeology at Cerros Belize, Central America, Volume 1: An Interim Report,* edited by Robin A. Robertson and David A. Freidel, 1–22. Dallas: Southern Methodist University Press.

Freidel, David A. and Linda Schele

1989   "Dead Kings and Living Temples: Dedication and Termination Rituals among the Ancient Maya." In *Word and Image in Maya Culture: Explanations in Language, Writing, and Representation,* edited by William F. Hanks and Don S. Rice, 233–43. Salt Lake City: University of Utah Press.

Freidel, David A., Linda Schele, and Joy Parker

1993   *Maya Cosmos: Three Thousand Years on the Shaman's Path.* New York: William Morrow.

Furst, Jill L.

1978   "Veracruz: Skeletonized Mother Goddess of Earth and Fertility." In *The Ninth Level: Funerary Art from Ancient Mesoamerica,* 104. Ames: University of Iowa Museum of Art.

Gann, Thomas W. F.

1900   "Mounds in Northern Honduras." In *The Bureau of American Ethnology Annual Report 19, Part 2,* 665–92. Washington, D.C.: Smithsonian Institution.

1918   *The Maya Indians of Southern Yucatan and Northern British Honduras.* Bureau of American Ethnology Bulletin 64. Washington, D.C.: Smithsonian Institution.

Garber, James F.

1989   *Archaeology at Cerros, Belize, Central America, Volume 2: The Artifacts.* Dallas: Southern Methodist University Press.

Gossen, Gary H.

1986   "Mesoamerican Ideas as a Foundation for Regional Synthesis." In *Symbol and Meaning beyond the Closed Community: Essays in Mesoamerican Ideas,* edited by Gary H. Gossen, 1–8. Albany: Institute for Mesoamerican Studies, State University of New York, Albany.

Grove, David C.

1981   "Olmec Monuments: Mutilation as a Clue to Meaning." In *The Olmec and Their Neighbors; Essays In Memory of Matthew W. Stirling,* edited by Elizabeth P. Benson, 49–68. Washington, D.C.: Dumbarton Oaks.

1984   *Chalcatzingo: Excavations on the Olmec Frontier,* edited by Colin Renfrew and Jeremy A. Sabloff. London: Thames and Hudson.

Hester, Thomas R.

1985   *The Classic–Early Postclassic Archaeological Investigations at Colha, Belize.* San Antonio: Center for Archaeological Research of the University of Texas at San Antonio.

Hester, Thomas R., G. Ligabue, Jack D. Eaton, Harry J. Shafer, and R. E. W. Adams

1982   "Archaeology at Colha, Belize: The 1981 Season." In *Archaeology at Colha, Belize: The 1981 Interim Report,* edited by Thomas R. Hester,

Harry J. Shafer, and Jack D. Eaton, 1–10. San
Antonio: Center for Archaeological Research
of the University of Texas at San Antonio,
and Centro Studi e Ricerche Ligabue, Venice.

Hester, Thomas R., Harry J. Shafer, and Jack D. Eaton, eds.
1980   *The Colha Project: Second Season, the 1980
        Interim Report,* San Antonio: Center for
        ·Archaeological Research of the University of
        Texas at San Antonio, Centro Studi e
        Ricerche Ligabue, Venice.

Hester, Thomas R., Harry J. Shafer, Jack D. Eaton,
Richard E. W. Adams, and Giancarlo Ligabue.
1983   "Colha's Stone Tool Industry." *Archaeology*
        36(6):4652.

Hester, Thomas R. and Harry J. Shafer, eds.
1991   *Maya Stone Tools: Selected Papers from the
        Second Maya Lithic Conference.* Monographs
        in World Archaeology 1. Madison, Wis.: Pre-
        history Press.

Kerr, Justin
1989a   *The Maya Vase Book, Volume 1.* New York:
        Kerr Associates.
1989b   *The Maya Vase Book, Volume 2.* New York:
        Kerr Associates.

Kubler, George, and Charles Gibson
1951   *The Tovar Calendar: An Illustrated Mexica
        Manuscript, Reproduced with Commentary.*
        Memoirs of the Connecticut Academy of Arts
        and Sciences 11. New Haven: Yale University
        Press.

Leon-Portilla, Miguel
1988   *Time and Reality in the Thought of the Maya.*
        Norman: University of Oklahoma Press.

López Austin, Alfredo
1988   *The Human Body and Ideology: Concepts of
        the Ancient Nahuas.* Translated by Thelma
        Ortiz de Montellano and Bernard Ortiz de
        Montellano. Salt Lake City: University of
        Utah Press.

Massey, Virginia
1989   *The Human Skeletal Remains from a Terminal
        Classic Skull Pit at Colha, Belize.* Papers of the
        Colha Project3. Austin: Texas Archeological
        Research Laboratory of the University of
        Texas at Austin and Texas A&M University.
1994   "Osteological Analysis of the Skull Pit Chil-
        dren." In *Continuing Archeology at Colha,
        Belize,* edited by Thomas R. Hester, Harry J.
        Shafer, and Jack D. Eaton, 209–20. Austin:
        Texas Archeological Research Laboratory of
        the University of Texas at Austin.

Miller, Mary Ellen
1986   *The Murals of Bonampak.* Princeton, N.J.:
        Princeton University Press.

Millon, Rene
1991   "The Last Years of Teotihuacán Dominance."
        In *The Collapse of Ancient States and Civiliza-
        tions,* edited by Norman Yoffee and George L.
        Cowgill, 102–64. Tucson: University of Ari-
        zona Press.

Mock, Shirley B.
1992   "Xipe Totec Images on Classic Maya Poly-
        chromes." MS on file with author.
1993   "The Northern River Lagoon Site (NRL):
        Late to Terminal Classic Maya Settlement,
        Saltmaking, and Survival on the Northern
        Belize Coast." Ph.D. diss., University of Texas
        at Austin.
1994   "Destruction and Dénouement during the
        Late-Terminal Classic: The Colha Skull Pit."
        In *Continuing Archeology at Colha, Belize,*
        edited by Thomas R. Hester, Harry J. Shafer,
        and Jack D. Eaton, 221–232. Austin: Texas
        Archeological Research Laboratory of the
        University of Texas at Austin.

Motolinia, Fray Toribio
1950   *Motolinia's History of the Indians of New
        Spain.* Translated and edited by Elizabeth
        Andros Foster. Westport, Conn.: Greenwood
        Press.

Potter, Daniel R.
1982   "Some Results of the Second Year of Investi-
        gation at Operation 2012." In *Archaeology at
        Colha, Belize: The 1981 Interim Report,* edited
        by Thomas R. Hester, Harry J. Shafer, and
        Jack D. Eaton, 123–40. San Antonio: Center
        for Archaeological Research of the University
        of Texas at San Antonio and Centro Studi e
        Ricerche Ligabue, Venice.

Ricketson, Oliver G., Jr., and Edith B. Ricketson
1937   *Uaxactun, Guatemala Group E: 1926–1931.*
        Carnegie Institution of Washington Publica-
        tion 433. Washington, D.C.: Carnegie Institu-
        tion of Washington.

Robbin, Cynthia
1989   *Preclassic Maya Burials at Cuello, Belize.* BAR
        International Series 480. Oxford, England:
        BAR.

Robertson-Freidel, Robin A.
1980   "The Ceramics from Cerros: A Late Preclassic
        Site inNorthern Belize." Ph.D. diss., Harvard
        University.

Roys, Ralph
1965 *Ritual of the Bacabs.* Translated and edited by Ralph L. Roys. Norman: University of Oklahoma Press.

Sahagún, B. de
1950 *General History of the Things of New Spain, Florentine Codex.* Translated by Charles E. Dibble and Arthur J. O. Anderson. Santa Fe, N.M.: The School of American Research and the University of Utah.

Schele, Linda
1989 *Notebook for the 13th Maya Hieroglyphic Workshop at Texas.* Austin: University of Texas at Austin.

1991 *Another Look at Stela 11.* Copan Mosaic's Project Note 103. Austin, Texas: Copan Acropolis Archaeological Project and the Instituto Hondureno de Antropologia e Historia.

Schele, Linda, and David R. Freidel
1990 *A Forest of Kings: The Untold Story of the Ancient Maya.* New York: William Morrow.

Schele, Linda, and Mary Miller
1986 *The Blood of Kings: Dynasty and Ritual in Maya Art.* Fort Worth: Kimbell Art Museum.

Seler, Eduard
1963 *Commentaries al Codice Borgia.* Translated by Mariana Frenk. 3 vols. Mexico City: Fondo de Cultura Economica.

Shafer, Harry J., and Thomas R. Hester
1983 "Ancient Maya Chert Workshops in Northern Belize, Central America." *American Antiquity* 48(3):519–43.

1986 "Maya Tool Craft Specialization and Production at Colha, Belize: A Reply to Mallory." *American Antiquity* 51(1):158–66.

Sharer, Robert, ed.
1978 *The Prehistory of Chalchuapa, El Salvador, Volume 1.* Philadelphia: University of Pennsylvania Press.

Smith, A. Ledyard
1950 *Uaxactun, Guatemala: Excavations of 1931–1937.* Carnegie Institution of Washington Publication 568. Washington, D.C.: Carnegie Institution.

Smith, A. Ledyard, and Alfred V. Kidder
1951 *Excavations at Nebaj, Guatemala.* Carnegie Institution of Washington Publication 594. Washington, D.C.: Carnegie Institution of Washington.

Steele, D. Gentry, Jack D. Eaton, and Anna J. Taylor
1980 "The Skulls from Operation 2011 at Colha: A Preliminary Investigation." In *The Colha Project, Second Season, 1980 Interim Report,* edited by Thomas R. Hester, Jack D. Eaton, and Harry J. Shafer, 163–72. San Antonio: Center for Archaeological Research of the University of Texas at San Antonio, and Centro Studi e Richerche Liguabue, Venice.

Taylor, Anna J.
1980 MS of excavation notes on file at Center for Archaeological Research, University of Texas at San Antonio.

Tedlock, Dennis
1985 *Popol Vuh: The Mayan Book of the Dawn of Life.* New York: Simon and Schuster.

Thompson, J. Eric S.
1939 *Excavations at San Jose, British Honduras.* Carnegie Institution of Washington Publication 506. Washington, D.C.: Carnegie Institution of Washington.

Tozzer, Alfred M.
1941 Landa's Relación de las cosas de Yucatán. Papers of the Peabody Museum of American Archaeology and Ethnology 18. Cambridge, Mass.: Peabody Museum, Harvard University.

Turner, Victor
1969 *The Ritual Process: Structure and Anti-Structure.* Ithaca, N.Y.: Cornell University Press.

Valdez, Fred, Jr.
1987 "The Prehistoric Ceramics of Colha, Northern Belize." Ph.D. diss., Harvard University.

Valdez, Fred, Jr., and Richard E. W. Adams
1982 "The Ceramics of Colha after Three Field Seasons:1979–1981." In *Archaeology at Colha, Belize: The 1981 Interim Report, Volume 1,* edited by T. R. Hester, H. J. Shafer, and J. D. Eaton, 21–30. San Antonio: Center for Archaeological Research of the University of Texas at San Antonio and Centro Studi e Richerche Liguabue, Venice.

Vogt, Evon Z.
1976 *Tortillas for the Gods: A Symbolic Analysis of Zinacanteco Rituals.* Cambridge, Mass.: Harvard University Press.

Willey, Gordon R.
1973 *The Altar de Sacrificios Excavations, General Summary and Conclusions.* Peabody Museum of Archaeology and Ethnology Papers 64(3). Cambridge, Mass.: Peabody Museum, Harvard University.

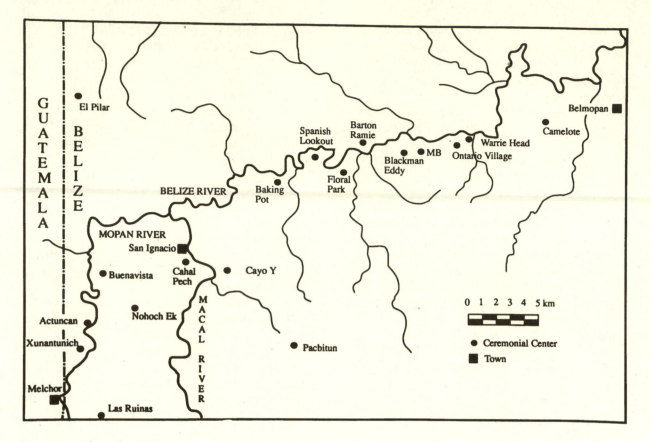

Map 11.1.   The Belize Valley.

CHAPTER ELEVEN

Bloody Bowls and Broken Pots
The Life, Death, and Rebirth of a Maya House

James F. Garber
Southwest Texas State University

W. David Driver
University of Southern Illinois
Maya Research Program

Lauren A. Sullivan
University of Texas, Austin/
University of Massachusetts at Boston

David M. Glassman
Southwest Texas State University

ARCHAEOLOGICAL EVIDENCE FOR THE CREATION, USE, and deactivation of sacred space is widespread throughout Mesoamerica. At the site of Blackman Eddy, in western Belize, excavations conducted in a small house-mound complex demonstrate a diachronic pattern of ritual that represents a wide range of dedication, termination, and rebirth or renewal activity. This structure was a relatively simple component of a nonelite residential complex.

A few deeply seated structural principles unify the Mesoamerican world view, past and present (Freidel et al. 1993; Mock, introduction, this volume). The vast majority of data concerning this prehistoric world view have come from elite contexts, in the form of dedication and termination rituals associated with monumental architecture. The data from Structure 1C at Blackman Eddy clearly show that these organizing structural principles of life, death, and rebirth were an important part of the religious lives of both commoners and the elite.

Several of the essays in this volume document elaborate examples of dedication or termination activities and illustrate the extravagance and complexity of these events. They demonstrate components of the life, death, and rebirth continuum. The Blackman Eddy examples, although relatively simple in form and content, come from a single structure and thus illustrate the sequential nature and interrelated character of dedication, termina-

tion, and rebirth. These events are parts of a process that marked the transitional stages in the life of a structure, and therein lies their significance. By examining these events in a diachronic manner, we can gain a greater understanding of each event and the concepts it represented. Dedication and termination rituals illustrate the notion that households, and also monumental architecture, can function as animated entities that pass through stages of life, death, and rebirth.

BLACKMAN EDDY

Blackman Eddy is in the Belize River Valley, approximately 18 km northeast of the town of San Ignacio in Cayo District, Belize. Its position, on top of a first terrace ridge of the Maya Mountains, gives it a commanding view of the Belize River and its alluvial plain (map 11.1). Construction in the site core began during the Middle Preclassic and continued through the Late Preclassic, Early Classic, and Late Classic periods. The Late Classic period witnessed an expansion of the site core and accelerated building activity. All monumental construction ended by the close of the Late Classic, and the site core and its immediate settlement zone were abandoned.

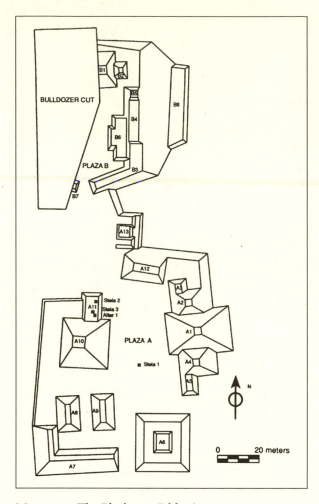

Map 11.2.   The Blackman Eddy site core.

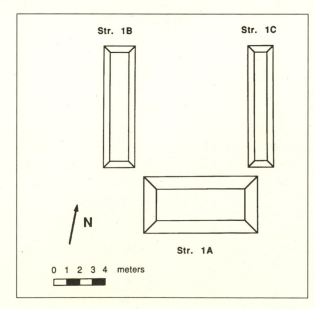

Fig. 11.1.   Group 1 at Blackman Eddy.

The central core of Blackman Eddy consists of two plazas enclosed by several medium-sized mounds (map 11.2). These include temples, a ball court, several range structures, and a *sacbe.* Investigations revealed five stone monuments, including an early-style stela inscribed with a Cycle 8 Long Count date (Garber 1992).

Located approximately 150 m to the west of the site core is a *plazuela* group designated as Group 1 (fig. 11.1). It consists of three long, low mounds surrounding a rectangular courtyard measuring 18 x 20 m. Excavation units, positioned to straddle the primary axes of each mound, revealed that each represented a simple low platform composed of two construction phases. For each, the earliest construction phase occurred during the Early Classic and the final phase in the Late Classic. Excavations and surface collections at Group 1 produced a high density of domestic debris, including manos, metates, large bifaces, and utilitarian pottery, and revealed a series of deposits that illustrate the concepts of life, death, and rebirth.

GROUP 1 RITUAL ACTIVITY

The eastern mound of Group 1, Structure 1C, contained several deposits suggesting its prominence as the focus of ritual activity in the *plazuela* group. Investigations did not reveal ritual deposits in either of the other two mounds of the group. The focusing of ritual activity in eastern mounds occurred at other sites in the Belize Valley: Floral Park (Glassman et al. 1995), Cahal Pech (Awe et al. 1992; Goldsmith 1993), and Baking Pot (Powis 1993). Chase (1993) reported an eastern focus for plaza groups in the Caracol settlement zone and cited this characteristic as evidence for affiliations between Caracol and the Ixtun and Ixtutz regions of the southeast Petén (LaPorte 1991, 1994; LaPorte et al. 1989). Eastern-focus mound groups appear to be a distinctive ceremonial tradition that encompassed the Caracol area, southeast Petén, and the Upper Belize Valley. Excavations at Structure 1C revealed two distinct construction phases and a series of ritual deposits extending from bedrock to its uppermost surface (Garber et al. 1992). These features chronicled the creation, use, destruction, and renewal of sacred space at this location. From earliest to latest these were:

- Ritual Event 1, an initial Early Classic dedicatory cache associated with the initial construction
- Ritual Event 2, a Late Classic dedicatory cache associated with the final construction

-Ritual Event 3, a Late Classic human burial
-Ritual Event 4, a Late Classic combination termination/
dedication cache

Ritual Event 1

The earliest phase of Structure 1C consisted of a low plat-form bounded by a vertical retaining wall of uncut lime-stone blocks. A dedicatory cache placed on the surface of the underlying bedrock initiated the construction of the platform.

Although this bedrock cache was the earliest artifac-tual evidence of ritual activity at this location, it was not the first ritual action. The lowermost construction fill did not overlie an old land surface, but rather was placed upon leveled, clean bedrock that did not exhibit weath-ering. The construction of a simple low platform of un-trimmed limestone blocks did not structurally require a prepared foundation and probably represented a ritual cleansing before construction. The practice of preparing a "cleansed" ground surface before construction oc-curred at other locations at Blackman Eddy and at other sites in the Belize Valley.

This initial cache, BE Cache 7, was on the primary east-west axis of the mound and consisted of two lip-to-lip Early Classic bowls (Hewlett Bank). The lower bowl contained a layer of white marl, nine large, crude brown chert flakes, burned twigs, and a rodent skeleton (fig. 11.2). The flakes are roughly oval in shape with large, irregular flaking scars on their dorsal surfaces. They range in size from 4.4 to 4.9 cm long and from 2.0 to 4.0 cm wide. On the basis of their uniformity of color and texture, the flakes appear to be from the same core. Visual examination did not reveal evidence of edge wear or residue.

This cache is consistent with the standard depositional pattern characteristic of dedicatory offerings. Maya schol-ars recognize dedicatory offerings as an important source of chronological information on the construction history of sites and structures (Coe 1959; Kidder et al. 1946; Ricketson and Ricketson 1937; Smith 1950, 1972; Smith and Kidder 1951; Thompson 1931, 1939; Willey et al. 1965). These studies em-phasize the deliberate spatial grouping of the deposited artifacts within completed structures.

More recent studies propose that cached offerings re-flect Maya concepts of world creation and the role of dedication in the animation or activation of sacred space (Freidel 1989; Freidel et al. 1993; Schele and Freidel 1990), and serve as symbolic models of the cosmos (Chase 1988; Joyce 1992). The artifacts represent sacred symbols in

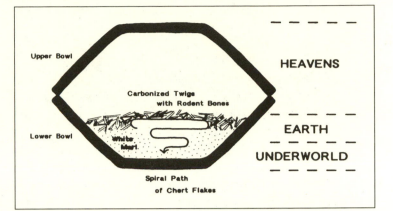

Fig. 11.2.   Blackman Eddy, section view of BE Cache 7, Structure 1C.

which supernatural powers reside and evoke the pres-ence of those spirits through creation reenactment or cosmological modeling. Such offerings were vital in the establishment and maintenance of a structure's connec-tion to ancestral spirits and supernatural forces.

The overlapping arrangement of the nine flakes formed a downward spiral, and the flakes were partially embedded in the layer of white marl. The innermost flakes of the spiral were deeper in the layer than the out-ermost ones. The layer of carbonized sticks and the skel-etal remains of a small rodent covered the spiral of flakes.

The patterned position of the cache contents demon-strates intentional placement. Layered caches are sym-bolic representations of the layered cosmos (Chase 1988; Joyce 1992). The nine flakes of BE Cache 7 represent a recurring spiritual theme associated with Maya ideology involving the number nine. This sacred number appears repeatedly in Maya architecture, caches, art, and calend-rics, and frequently represents the nine Lords of the Night or Underworld. Caches containing nine chert or obsidian flakes occur in sites throughout the Lowlands (Coe 1959; Smith 1950, 1972; Willey et al. 1965). Although the materials within this cache represent the low end of the quality continuum, they are the functional equiva-lents of more sumptuous examples, such as the nine elaborately chipped stone eccentrics recovered within a dedicatory cache at Copan (Fash 1991) or the nine imitation stingray spines found in a dedicatory cache at Tikal (Harrison 1970).

Placed on a specially prepared surface, BE Cache 7 represented the initial ensouling of what was to become the focal point of ritual for this residential *plazuela* group. The creation of a portal to the Underworld ensouled the structure. Symbolic cosmological layering is evident within the cache. The marl layer represents the clean bedrock base beneath the structure. The nine flakes represent the nine Lords of the Night or Underworld. The spiral pattern indicates downward movement, resulting in a portal to the supernatural world. Small rodents play a role in Maya mythology as beings of the Underworld (Pohl 1983), life forms of prior creations, and middle world beings that can descend below the surface of the earth (Thompson 1970). The symbolism indicated by the contents of the cache shows that it functioned as a portal to the Underworld. The nine chert flakes, like the nine imitation stingray spine bloodletters from the Tikal cache, were the instruments that activated the portal and allowed supernatural power to flow into the structure. Once activated, this portal spiritually ensouled the building. In the Maya world view, just as a person must receive a soul, so must a building, whether a temple, palace, or common house.

Cached offerings, when found in association with elite monumental architecture, are usually items of rare or exotic materials elaborately fashioned by master craftsmen (Coe 1959; Fash 1991; Garber et al. 1993). Their placement within a new building was a sacred and costly expenditure made by the contributing individual or lineage (Garber 1983, 1989). The materials within dedicatory offerings of the nonelite were typically more mundane. Commoners' buildings contained items that held importance in their lives, such as utilitarian pottery, grinding stones, and sometimes small jade or shell beads. Although these items were not as exotic as those of the elite, they probably represented an equivalent sacrificial contribution. The significance of a dedicatory cache is not the value of its containers or contents, but rather the idea of birth or ensouling that the symbolic act of dedication represents.

Utilitarian objects, such as manos and metates from construction fill of monumental architecture at Cerros, served as possible votive offerings from the laborers who constructed the mounds (Garber 1989). Deliberately selected for their symbolic significance, they are the physical instruments employed by humans to transform corn,

the essence of life. The value of the cache and its associated sacrifice was secondary to the ritual's crucial function of animating the structure.

Ritual Event 2

The final construction phase of the Structure 1C platform consisted of a retaining wall of uncut limestone completed during the Late Classic period. BE Cache 6 was a dedicatory cache associated with this construction and was just beneath the surface of the platform on the primary east-west axis of the mound. It consisted of two poorly preserved, unidentified plain vessels placed lip to lip. No associated artifacts were present. Empty lip-to-lip caches are common in the Lowlands and may have originally contained perishable offerings (see Pendergast, this volume). Landa in Tozzer (1941) mentioned lip-to-lip offering plates in the context of *Uayeb* rituals, and Freidel and colleagues (1993) noted that present-day Yucatecan Maya use lip-to-lip vessels as *pib*, "earth ovens," to prepare special foods for a variety of rituals. Like offerings of manos and metates, they are instruments of transformation and thus serve as links to the supernatural world.

Ritual Event 3

This event was the interment of a single adult. The burial, BE Burial 5, was approximately 75 cm below the surface of Structure 1C. It was poorly preserved due to its proximity to the surface and the high soil acidity. Skeletal remains included rib fragments, a few cranium fragments, and teeth. The burial orientation was north-south with head to the north. Analysis of the teeth indicated that the individual was an adult, although the incomplete nature of the skeletal remains prohibited a determination of sex. The burial was intrusive into the final Late Classic construction phase.

Burial goods consisted of a small oblong jade bead, four drilled univalve shells, and three ceramic vessels. The jade bead and drilled shells were immediately next to the cranium and teeth, and were probably once strung together as a necklace. The ceramic vessels, all heavily weathered and poorly preserved, were at the mid-torso of the body. The fragmented plate was upside down on one of the bowls (Dolphin Head Red). Neither bowl contained artifacts.

Maya burials occurred frequently under house floors, a practice that continued into the historic era. Within the previously noted zone of eastern-focus mound groups, burials are frequently, and sometimes exclusively, located

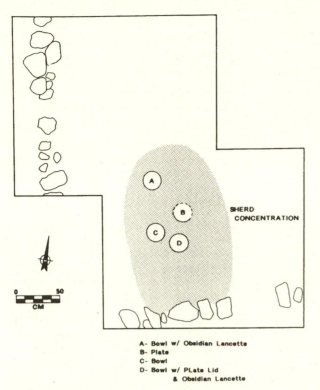

A- Bowl w/ Obsidian Lancette
B- Plate
C- Bowl
D- Bowl w/ PLate Lid
   & Obsidian Lancette

Fig. 11.3. Blackman Eddy, plan view of BE Cache 8, Structure 1C: (a) Dolphin Head Red bowl; (b) Mountain Pine Red plate; (c) Dolphin Head Red bowl; (d) Dolphin Head Red bowl with Mountain Pine Red plate inverted over it.

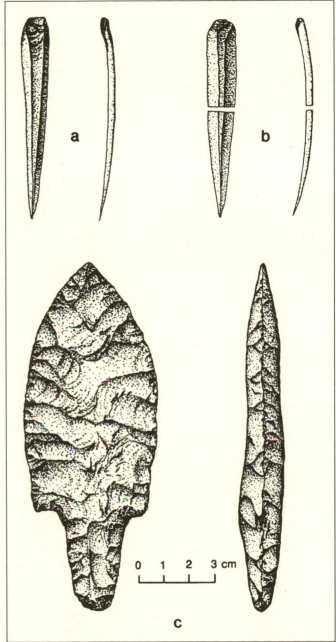

Fig. 11.4. Blackman Eddy artifacts from BE Cache 8: (a) obsidian lancet; (b) broken obsidian lancet; (c) stemmed biface.

in the eastern structure. Interment in eastern structures cumulatively added to the power of these locations.

Ritual Event 4

The final construction phase of Structure 1C contained the most complex feature of the *plazuela* group (fig. 11.3). The co-occurrence of termination and dedication elements of BE Cache 8 prohibits its classification as either. The combination of the two forms suggests a special relationship between the two. We interpret this as a ritual of renewal or rebirth, possibly a New Year ceremony, that contained destructive and subsequent regenerative components. The feature consisted of five whole vessels within a matrix of densely packed, heavily burned sherds. The volume of sherds could represent more than

Fig. 11.5.   Blackman Eddy notched sherds from BE Cache 7.

a hundred vessels, although there was no evidence of in situ vessel breakage. Associated artifacts included a whole stemmed chert biface (fig. 11.4c); a broken oval biface; nine used obsidian blade fragments; three mano fragments; one metate fragment; a broken oblong, shaped slate pendant; and four ground and notched sherds of unknown function, all broken on one end (fig. 11.5).

At the base of the deposit was a carbon lens 2–3 cm thick. The area of the concentrated sherd matrix was approximately 1.5 m in diameter and varied in thickness from 35 to 40 cm. The upper limit of the feature was approximately 50 cm below the ground surface. Carbon and ash were present throughout the sherd matrix. The concentration of sherds was very dense, with only small amounts of carbon-laden dirt and small burned limestone chunks intermixed within the matrix. The entire deposit was intrusive into the surrounding construction fill and dated to the Late Classic.

All sherds within the matrix showed evidence of heavy burning and subsequent weathering. The whole vessels, while also heavily weathered, were unburned. Proximity to the surface and high soil acidity accounted for the extensive in situ weathering. Only minute portions of slip remained on the whole vessels and slipped sherds. Surfaces of the exposed paste showed pitting. Extensive sherd damage prohibited the reconstruction of vessels.

Because there were no concentrations of similarly colored sherds, the matrix appeared to be a secondary deposit, although the burning could have taken place in situ, as evidenced by the carbon lens at the base of the feature and within the matrix. Similar deposits, of the same period, were encountered at the nearby sites of Floral Park (Glassman et al. 1995) and Ontario Village (Garber et al. 1994). The Floral Park deposit was considerably more extensive and may have represented more than a thousand vessels. Burning and heavy weathering characterized the sherd concentrations at both these sites, and no in situ breakage of vessels was evident. In both cases, these deposits directly overlaid the final phase of architectural construction.

We believe that these sherd concentrations are not transposed domestic middens, for two reasons: First, sherd density is considerably higher than in domestic middens; second, the deposits are almost exclusively sherds that lacked the other typical domestic components, such as lithic debris, bone, and shell. However, they are clearly secondary deposits, and we interpret them as transposed ritual middens.

The ethnohistoric and ethnographic literature provide clues to the meaning of these deposits. In his *Relación,* Landa described the rituals and activities associated with the first day of *Pop,* the initiation of the New Year in the 365-day year (Tozzer 1941). The New Year followed the *Uayeb* (five days of bad luck and apprehension following the *Haab* of 360 days). Landa described the New Year preparation and celebration as one in which the entire community participated. This was a ritual of destruction and renewal or rebirth. Destructive actions preceded the establishment of order in the New Year. "To celebrate it with more solemnity, they renewed on this day all the objects which they made use of, such as plates, vessels, stools, mats and old clothes and the stuffs with which they wrapped up their idols. They swept out their houses, and the sweepings and the old utensils they threw out on the waste heap outside the town; and no one, even he in need of it, touched it" (Landa, translated by Tozzer 1941:151–52). This ritual destruction involved ordinary mundane items analogous to those seen in the Belize Valley sherd concentrations. The great majority were utilitarian wares.

Sahagún (1946) described the New Fire ceremony among the Aztecs that took place at the end of the fifty-two-year cycle. The smashing of pottery and the extinguishing of fires occurred during this ritual. The passage of the Pleiades through the zenith signaled the start of a new cycle. A fire kindled in the splayed chest cavity of a sacrificial victim was used to relight the fires throughout the Valley of Mexico. It was a ritual of destruction and renewal or rebirth, a symbolic reestablishment of order out of chaos.

In the New Year ceremony with a *Cauac* Year Bearer, Landa described the lighting of a large fire (Tozzer 1941). After the fire had died down, men would walk on its coals as a sacrificial act. Similarly, in the *Popol Vuh,* the Hero Twins sacrificed themselves in fire—a necessary action for rebirth and creation of the next world.

The theme of rebirth was evident within BE Cache 8. The unburned whole vessels formed a quadripartite pattern oriented to the cardinal directions (fig. 11.3). Bowls (Dolphin Head Red) were in the north, south, and west positions. A plate (Mountain Pine Red) was in the eastern position, and an inverted plate (Mountain Pine Red) was over the southern bowl.

An unbroken obsidian lancet measuring 7.9 cm long was in the southernmost bowl (fig. 11.4a). The northernmost bowl contained an identical lancet, although broken (fig. 11.4b). It could not be determined whether this lancet was intentionally broken at the time of its deposition or later by natural agents. The obsidian lancets are thin, fragile, and have delicate slender points. Sharply pointed blades such as these were common items used in bloodletting ritual. Blood sacrifice and its symbolism was, and still is, an important aspect of Maya religion and was the means of activating portals to the Underworld (Chase 1985; McGee 1990, this volume; Schele and Freidel 1990; Schele and Miller 1986; Tozzer 1941). Landa (Tozzer 1941) described bloodletting rites associated with New Year ceremonies among the Yucatec Maya. Iconographic representations of bloodletting and associated events often portray the sacred World Tree. Bloodletting paraphernalia are depicted at the base of the tree, which is the portal to the Underworld. The sacred tree in Maya mythology supported the heavens and was an important element in the Maya creation story. Raising the World Tree separated earth and sky. Partitioning the world into its four sides and four corners created the form of the world. Creation of humans occurred next. The quadripartite positioning of the whole vessels was a symbolic reenactment of the creation partitioning.

Partitioning was a common feature of New Year rituals during the ethnohistoric period, as it is of renewal or rebirth ceremonies of the ethnographic present. In his accounts of Yucatec New Year ceremonies, Landa described ritual processions associated with shrines at the cardinal directions and ritual assistants that occupied the four corners of the central plaza (Tozzer 1941). The BE Cache 8 contents, configuration, and orientation represent important components of destruction, creation, and rebirth. The inclusion of a symbolic representation of creation, in conjunction with characteristics of termination, indicates that it was a ritual of ending and one of beginning. In Momostenango, Guatemala, ritual leaders make a four-part ritual circuit to the positions that define the four corners of their world (Tedlock 1982). At the center of their world is a *waqibal,* "Six-Place," that has pits containing ritual fires and hundreds of broken ceramic vessels (Tedlock 1982).

Most of the available information on prehistoric dedication and termination has come from elite contexts. In contrast, the Blackman Eddy example demonstrates the importance of structure dedication, termination, and rebirth among nonelites. Additionally, households could serve as spiritually charged loci. The significance of any cache lies not in the material nature of its contents, but rather in the symbolic nature of the act. This has important ramifications for our understanding of Maya social structure. The ritual act of caching, and the concept it represents, was not one of the features that separated commoner from elite. For if the basic concepts of life, death, and rebirth permeated all levels of society, then the ritual and ideological differences between commoner and elite were not as great as some have suggested (Thompson 1970). The caches from Structure 1C indicate that bloodletting was not exclusively an elite activity. The king let blood for the polity, the sublords let blood for the polity subdivisions, and the commoner let blood for the well-being of his family. If this were not the case, bloodletting would have disappeared with the collapse of Maya society. These symbolic expressions of the concepts of life, death, and rebirth are deeply rooted in time throughout all levels of society. Like any renewal ritual that eases psychological fears and anxieties, the rebirth rite within Structure 1C at Blackman Eddy assured the continuance of life's cycles and prepared the group's residents for their journey into a new era.

ACKNOWLEDGMENTS

The data on which this chapter is based were collected during the 1991 and 1992 field seasons of the Belize Valley Archaeology Research Project, Department of Anthropology, Southwest Texas State University. Maps 11.1 and 11.2, and fig. 11.1 were drafted by James F. Garber; figs. 11.2 and 11.3 were drafted by W. David Driver; and fig. 11.4 was drafted by A. Sean Goldsmith. We are grateful to the Department of Archaeology, Belmopan, Belize, for its continued support of this project. We would also like to thank our student volunteers and the people of Blackman Eddy village and San Ignacio for their friendship and hospitality.

REFERENCES CITED

Awe, Jaime, Jim Aimers, and Catherine Blanchard

1992   "A Preclassic Round Structure from the Zotz Group at Cahal Pech, Belize." MS on file, Department of Anthropology, Trent University, Peterborough.

Chase, Arlen F.

1993   "Polities, Politics, and Social Dynamics: 'Contextualizing' the Archaeology of the Belize Valley and Caracol." Paper presented at the 58th annual meeting of the Society for American Archaeology, St. Louis.

Chase, Diane Z.

1985   "Lifeline to the Gods: Ritual Bloodletting at Santa Rita Corozal." In *Fourth Round Table of Palenque, Volume 6,* edited by Elizabeth Benson, 89–96. San Francisco: Pre-Columbian Art Research Institute, San Francisco.

1988   "Caches and Censerwares: Meaning from Maya Pottery." In *A Pot for all Reasons: Ceramic Ecology Revisited,* edited by Charles C. Kolb and Louanna M. Lackey, 81–104. Philadelphia: Laboratory of Anthropology, Temple University.

Coe, William R.

1959   *Piedras Negras Archaeology: Artifacts, Caches, and Burials.* Museum Monographs. Philadelphia: University of Pennsylvania.

Fash, William L.

1991   *Scribes, Warriors, and Kings: The City of Copán and the Ancient Maya.* London: Thames and Hudson.

Freidel, David A.

1989   "Dead Kings and Living Temples." In *Word and Image in Maya Culture: Explorations in Language, Writing, and Representation,* edited by W. F. Hanks and D. S. Rice, 233–43. Salt Lake City: University of Utah Press.

Freidel, David A., Linda Schele, and Joy Parker

1993   *Maya Cosmos: Three Thousand Years of Shamanism.* New York: William Morrow.

Garber, James F.

1983   "Patterns of Jade Consumption and Disposal at Cerros, Northern Belize." *American Antiquity* 48(4): 800–7.

1989   *Archaeology at Cerros, Belize, Central America, Volume 2: The Artifacts.* Dallas: Southern Methodist University Press.

1992   "A Possible Cycle 8 Stela from the Lowland Maya Site of Blackman Eddy, Belize." Paper presented at the 57th annual meeting of the Society for American Archaeology, Pittsburgh.

Garber, James F., W. David Driver, Lauren S. Sullivan, and Sean Goldsmith

1992   "The Blackman Eddy Archaeological Project: Results of the 1991 Field Season." MS on file with Department of Archaeology, Belmopan, Belize.

Garber, James F., David M. Glassman, W. David Driver, and Pamela Weiss

1994   "The Blackman Eddy Archaeological Project: Results of the 1993 Field Season." MS on file with Department of Archaeology, Belmopan, Belize.

Garber, James F., David C. Grove, Kenneth G. Hirth, and John W. Hoopes

1993   "The Context of Jade Usage in Portions of Central America: Olmec, Maya, Costa Rica, and Honduras." In *Precolumbian Jade: New Geological and Cultural Interpretations,* edited by Fred W. Lange, 211–231. Salt Lake City: University of Utah Press.

Glassman, David M., James M. Conlon, and James F. Garber

1995   "Survey and Initial Excavations at Floral Park." In *The Belize Valley Archaeology Project: Results of the 1994 Field Season.* MS on file with Department of Archaeology, Belmopan, Belize.

Goldsmith, A. Sean

1993   "Household Archaeology in the Belize Valley." M.A. thesis, University of Calgary.

Harrison, Peter D.

1970   "The Central Acropolis, Tikal, Guatemala: A Preliminary Study of the Functions of Its Structural Components during the Late Classic Period." Ph.D. diss., University of Pennsylvania.

Joyce, Rosemary A.

1992   "Ideology in Action: Classic Maya Ritual Practice." In *Ancient Images, Ancient Thought: The Archaeology of Ideology, Proceedings of the 23rd Annual Chacmool Conference,* edited by

A. Sean Goldsmith, Sandra Garvie, David Selin, and Jeanette Smith, 497–505. Calgary: Department of Archaeology, University of Calgary.

Kidder, Alfred V., Jesse D. Jennings, and Edwin. M. Shook
1946   *Excavations at Kaminaljuyu, Guatemala.* Carnegie Institution of Washington Publication 561. Washington, D.C.: Carnegie Institution of Washington.

LaPorte, Juan P.
1991   "Reconocimiento regional en el noroeste de las Montanas Mayas, Guatemala: Segundo reporte." *Mexicon* 13(2):30–36.
1994   *Ixtonton, Dolores, Petén: Entidad politica del noroeste de las Montanas Mayas.* Atlas arqueologico de Guatemala 2. San Carlos, Guatemala: Escuela de Historia, Universidad de San Carlos.

LaPorte, Juan P., R. Torres, and B. Hermes
1989   "Ixtonton: Evolucion de un asentamiento en el Alta Mopan, Petén, Guatemala." *Mayab* 5:19–29.

McGee, R. Jon
1990   *Life, Ritual, and Religion among the Lacandón Maya.* Belmont, Calif.: Wadsworth.

Pohl, Mary
1983   "Maya Ritual Faunas: Vertebrate Remains from Burials, Caches, Caves, and Cenotes in the Maya Lowlands." In *Civilization in the Ancient Americas: Essays in Honor of Gordon R. Willey,* edited by Richard Levanthal and Alan Kolata, 55–103. Albuquerque: University of New Mexico Press.

Powis, Terry G.
1993   "Special Function Structures within Peripheral Groups in the Belize Valley: An Example from the Bedran Group at Baking Pot." In "Belize Valley Archaeological Reconnaissance Report: Progress of the 1992 Field Season." MS on file with Department of Archaeology, Belmopan, Belize.

Ricketson, Oliver G., and Edith B. Ricketson
1937   *Uaxactun, Guatemala: Group E 1926–1931.* Carnegie Institution of Washington Publication 477, Washington, D.C.: Carnegie Institution of Washington.

Sahagún, Fray Bernardino de
1946   *Historia general de las cosas de Nueva España.* 3 vols. Mexico City: Editorial Nueva España.

Schele, Linda, and David A. Freidel
1990   *A Forest of Kings: The Untold Story of the Ancient Maya.* New York: William Morrow.

Schele, Linda, and Mary Ellen Miller
1986   *The Blood of Kings: Dynasty and Ritual in Maya Art.* Fort Worth: Kimbell Art Museum.

Smith, A. Ledyard
1950   *Uaxactun, Guatemala: Excavation of 1931–1937.* Carnegie Institution of Washington Publication 588. Washington, D.C.: Carnegie Institution of Washington.
1972   *Excavations at Altar de Sacrificios: Architecture, Settlement, Burials, and Caches.* Cambridge, Mass.: Peabody Museum, Harvard University.

Smith, A. Ledyard., and A. V. Kidder
1951   *Excavations at Nebaj, Guatemala.* Carnegie Institution of Washington Publication 594. Washington, D.C.: Carnegie Institution of Washington.

Tedlock, Barbara
1982   *Time and the Highland Maya.* Albuquerque: University of New Mexico Press.

Thompson, J. Eric
1931   *Archaeological Investigations in the Southern Cayo District, British Honduras.* Field Museum of Natural History, Anthropology Series 17(3). Chicago: Field Museum.
1939   *Excavations at San Jose, British Honduras.* Carnegie Institution of Washington Publication 506. Washington, D.C.: Carnegie Institution of Washington.
1970   *Maya History and Religion.* Norman: University of Oklahoma Press.

Tozzer, Alfred M.
1941   *Landa's Relación de las cosas de Yucatán: A Translation.* Papers of the Peabody Museum of American Archaeology and Ethnology 18. Cambridge, Mass.: Harvard University.

Willey, Gordon R., William R. Bullard, Jr., John B. Glass, and James C. Gifford
1965   *Prehistoric Settlement in the Belize Valley.* Papers of the Peabody Museum of Archaeology and Ethnology 54. Cambridge, Mass.: Harvard University.

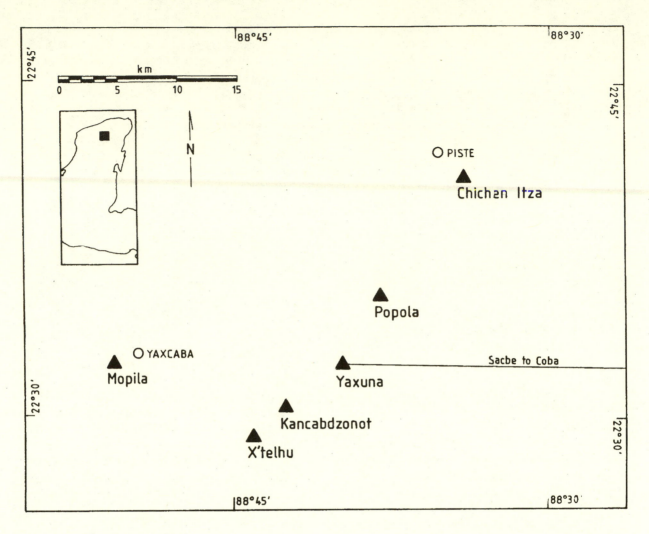

Map 12.1.　The Yaxuna region.

CHAPTER TWELVE

Termination Ritual Deposits at Yaxuna

Detecting the Historical in Archaeological Contexts

David A. Freidel
Southern Methodist University

Charles K. Suhler
Southern Methodist University

Rafael Cobos Palma
Tulane University and the University of Yucatan

ARCHAEOLOGISTS WORKING AT THE LATE PRECLASSIC site of Cerros in northern Belize formally identified and defined Maya termination ritual deposits as a type of context in the late 1970s and early 1980s (Freidel 1986; Garber 1983, 1989; Robertson 1983; Robertson-Freidel 1980). Continued analysis of and research on Cerros material by Debra Walker (1991, this volume) and Kathryn Reese-Taylor (1996) confirms the validity and usefulness of this concept for understanding culture history in Maya country. It is hardly surprising that the Cerros research raised this distinctive form of primary deposit. The ancient inhabitants, or their enemies, terminated virtually all of the civic-religious architecture of this center at the time of its collapse and abandonment in the Late Preclassic period. In the context of this pervasive termination of the final, ceramically coeval, construction episodes on many public buildings, we can speak of an archaeologically detectable historical event of major consequence.

Freidel (1992) and Reese-Taylor (in preparation) now believe that this Late Preclassic historical event at Cerros probably followed in the wake of a decisive military defeat of the Cerros king. This destruction may have been carried out by disenchanted members of the defeated community (Schele and Freidel 1990:127). Alternatively, extrapolation of the Classic period patterns of desecration of Maya centers by victors (Freidel et al. 1993:chap. 7; Schele and Freidel 1990:chap. 5; Suhler 1996) alerts us to the prospect that termination of civic centers, even in the Preclassic period, constituted an important act of war. Indeed, a careful reading of William Coe's (1990) monograph on the North Acropolis at Tikal reveals substantial evidence for burning and desecration of Preclassic buildings there.

Current work at the site of Yaxuna in northern Yucatan is generating the material basis for a pattern of destruction comparable in some respects to that found at Cerros, dated by preliminary ceramic evidence to the end of the Early Classic period or the beginning of the Late Classic period. We believe that as we proceed with the Yaxuna research, we will be able to effectively test our hypothesis: that at various points in time the government of this center suffered major defeats and the systematic termination of its ritual structures and principal residences. Because Maya archaeologists are still in the process of defining what termination rituals look like in the ground, we provide here a detailed description of test exposures in one Early Classic palace in an important elite residence complex in the southern part of the settlement. We now have substantial evidence for similar termination deposits from other building groups in the site, particularly in the northern acropolis.

YAXUNA: SOME BACKGROUND

Yaxuna is a second-rank center situated 20 km southwest of Chichén Itzá in Yucatan (map 12.1); it is designated site 16Qd(8):3 in the *Archaeological Atlas of Yucatán* (Garza T. and Kurjack 1980). The site is famous as the place where the longest intersite masonry causeway, or *sacbe*, ends its journey from the city of Coba near the east coast of the peninsula (map 12.2). Eight summer seasons of research (Ambrosino 1996; Ardren et al. 1994; Freidel 1987, 1989; Freidel et al. 1990; Freidel, Suhler, and Cobos P. 1992; Freidel and Suhler 1995) have recorded more than 650 structures in the central 1.5 sq km of the site, varying from major acropolises covering more than a hectare to small foundations of surface-level perishable buildings. The mounded features of the site continue unabated outward from the center for at least 1 km in all directions, and we have discovered no clear limit to the ancient community. At minimum, the formal community covered 4 sq km.

Our research generally shows that the Early Classic period witnessed the culmination of major construction stretching back to the Middle Preclassic. In the Early Classic, Yaxuna was a royal capital ruled by kings using mainstream Maya symbols of royal power (Freidel and Suhler 1995). During the Early Classic, a king of Yaxuna was decapitated, entombed with his entourage in Structure 6F-4 (a pyramid of the northern acropolis), and replaced by his conqueror. Forensic anthropologist Sharon Bennett (1994) documented this event. Stratigraphically and contextually, the tomb was part of broader desecration and dedication deposits in the pyramid and elsewhere in the northern acropolis (Suhler 1996). That conqueror evidently raised a stela portrait of himself in Mexican-style war regalia (Brainerd 1958). In the Late Classic period, the northern acropolis at Yaxuna was again attacked, and this Early Classic conqueror's victory monument was desecrated and dumped on the northern side of Structure 6F-4 (Ambrosino 1996; David Johnstone, personal communication 1996). Indeed, the northern acropolis remained a focus for repeated military activity in the later history of the community.

But with continued research, we hypothesize that other important building groups in the site center witnessed similar repeated attacks. We think that the Early Classic sacrificial event in the northern acropolis was part of a larger sacking of the city that included the destruction of the Structure 5E-50 Group and other buildings in the southern sector of the community. In the Late

Classic period the settlement evidently witnessed more modest activity in the main buildings, and there was a smaller community in the central zone (with the caveat that the ceramic diagnostics of the Late Classic period are only now being effectively defined and identified in stratigraphic contexts). The Terminal Classic period at Yaxuna (A.D. 800–1000), when the *sacbe* definitely joined it to Coba (Andrews and Robles 1985; Robles and Andrews 1986), saw a resurgence of occupation and public construction. The evidence for the end of the Early Classic community and the relatively more modest Late Classic occupation includes radical reorientation of buildings and groups of buildings during the Terminal Classic period and the direct stratigraphic superposition of some Terminal Classic construction on top of Early Classic and Preclassic building surfaces. Additionally—and despite a very impressive and extensive reoccupation of the settlement zone—the Terminal Classic people only selectively reused civic-religious buildings. The final construction phases of some buildings thus date to the Early Classic or Late Preclassic period.

THE STRUCTURE 5E-50 GROUP: A TERMINATED ELITE RESIDENCE

Our project concentrated great effort in the Structure 5E-50 Group during the 1991 field season, under the field supervision of Rafael Cobos Palma. In our field reports we have argued that evidence from settlement patterns shows that this large and complex group was significantly spatially integrated into the civic-ceremonial urban design of Yaxuna in its early phase of occupation. We think this group may have housed part of the ruling family of the community in the latter part of the Early Classic period, or Yaxuna IIb (roughly equivalent to Manik III at Tikal; Suhler, Ardren, and Johnstone n.d.). Our rationale for the royal residence here is based on the integration of this group into a remarkably clear spatial plan of building groups and intrasite *sacbeob* defining the public sectors of Yaxuna in the early phase of occupation (fig. 12.1). Kurjack and Garza T. (1976) have reviewed the extensive evidence for intrasite causeways in the northern Lowlands and their significance in linking major groups of buildings within them. Wendy Ashmore (1989) has proposed that some Maya centers were organized with royal public architecture in the northern sector linked to royal or high elite residential groups in the southern sector, as an expression of cosmological principles of spatial order.

Structure 5E-52, with a height of 3 m, is the principal building of the group (map 12.2). It falls into the lower end of the range of identifiable civic-religious buildings at Yaxuna, but it also has a relatively broad summit amenable to a superstructure with ample interior space. Moreover, it is not part of a formal triadic compound of structures, such as those that typify the larger acropolises at Yaxuna. Instead, Structure 5E-52 is flanked on both the east and west by extensive low substructures characteristic of residential compounds. The principal orientation of the building was to the east, but it likely had an access on the northwest as well.

This building and its group are connected to the formal plan of the center in several strategic ways. First, Structure 5E-52 is oriented to the civic cardinal axes (c. 20° east of north) and faces eastward toward the southern plaza, which anchors the central north-south axis of the community (linking the northern acropolis with the southern plaza by means of *Sacbe* 3). Second, the importance of this connection to the civic plan by means of the southern plaza (the plaza of Structures 5E-26 is through 5E-34) is emphasized by the presence of *Sacbe* 5, which

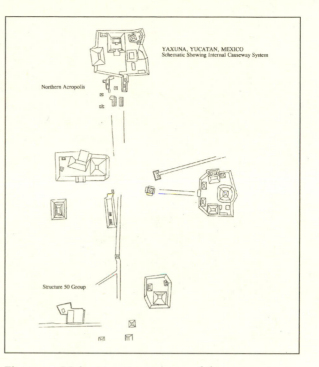

Fig. 12.1.   Major structure groups of the center at Yaxuna.

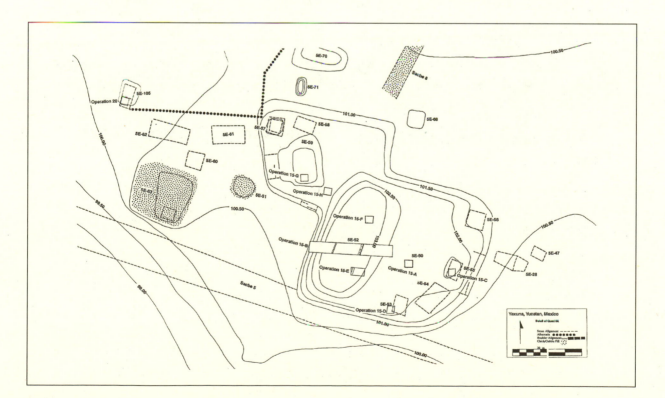

Map 12.2.   The 5E-50 Group and environs.

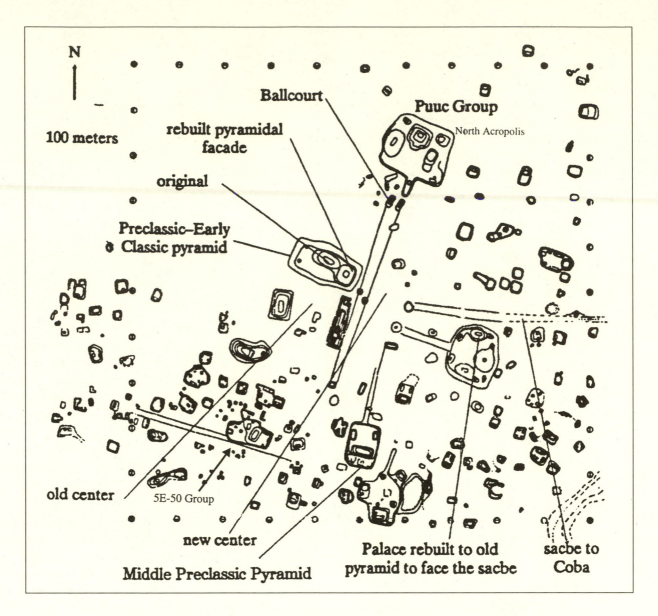

N

100 meters

Ballcourt

Puuc Group

North Acropolis

rebuilt pyramidal
facade

original

Preclassic–Early
Classic pyramid

5E-50 Group

old center

new center

Middle Preclassic Pyramid

Palace rebuilt to old
pyramid to face the sacbe

sacbe to
Coba

Map. 12.3.   Yaxuna site center and sacbes.

runs along the southern edge of the group housing 5E-52 and links it concretely to the southern plaza of the civic plan.

Excavation revealed that Structure 5E-52 was a masonry-walled superstructure situated on a low building platform and facing eastward onto the eastern plaza of the group. This is a large superstructure for Yaxuna, 7 m wide and at least 14 m long (at least 100 sq m of interior space). No doubt the building had a perishable roof, possibly of palm thatch. The walls of the eastern, plaza side were built of well-dressed masonry blocks. These walls carried a frieze of modeled and red-painted stucco. Our test excavations did not encounter interior walls or clear evidence of the eastern doorways. In part, this lack of plan details can be laid at the feet of the people who thoroughly and ritually destroyed this building in antiquity. The 1991 excavations in the Structure 5E-50 Group (map 12.3) not only document the ritual destruction of the main building, but also point to the termination of smaller buildings in the group. The precise timing of this major event in the Early Classic history of Yaxuna remains to be pinpointed through ceramic chronology and other means. We believe that the group functioned as a household for leaders in the community, that it was violently destroyed at the end of the Early Classic, and that its destruction marked the eclipse of early-phase Yaxuna as a political capital.

Structure 5E-52 is rather modest construction for a royal palace. But the lack of thick walls and a vaulted roof was offset by the masonry front wall, which carried a modeled and red-painted stucco frieze along the length of its surface. Only a few elements from this frieze, now completely shattered into small pieces, carry symbols we can now interpret; most of the pieces are fragments of scrolls. Scrolls in Classic Maya stucco friezes carry the general connotation of *ch'ul*, "holy spirit" (Freidel et al. 1993:182, also 244–246 *[ch'ulel]*; Walker, this volume *[k'ul]*), although lazy-s scrolls specifically can mean *muyil*, "clouds" or "atmospheres." A recently discovered royal lineage house at the city of Copan in Honduras carries on its frieze the lazy-s *muyil* scrolls between portraits of ancestors peering out of portals (Andrews and Fash 1992). One interpretable symbol in the Yaxuna case is the lower half of a face of a god with a t-shaped incisor and large corner scrolls in the mouth. This tau-shaped tooth is diagnostic of such gods as Hun-Nal-Ye, First Father, and the Ancestral Hero Twins, his children, and it constitutes a small but clear documentation of Yaxuna's participation in mainstream Classic period royal iconography. Human kings also wear the tau-tooth when they are portrayed masked as gods on early friezes, as in the case of the famous Early Classic building at Kohunlich. The presence of this stucco frieze on the Yaxuna building, combined with the ample interior space of the structure and its settlement context, provides encouraging support for the original hypothesis that this is a royal compound.

Our Suboperation 15-B resulted in a trench, 24 m long and 2 m wide, that ran east-west across the middle of Structure 5E-52, following compass orientation as laid out by the transit. In the course of excavation, archaeologists determined that the orientation of the building is actually east of north, like the general north-south axis of the causeways connecting the southern residential area to the northern acropolis. The original unit of Suboperation 15-B (3 × 2 m, long axis east-west) was the easternmost unit in the trench; the seven additional units were 3 × 2 m extensions appended onto the western edge of this first unit. Ambient ground surface elevations of the suboperation ranged from 100.67 m in the lower plaza on the western side of the structure to 103.41 m on top of the structure to 102.38 m in the raised plaza of 5E-50.

A postabandonment humus, dark dirt, and small rock mix covered the surface of the entire trench with a depth of 8–40 cm. Under this upper natural layer occurred a white marl layer. The upper 20–40 cm of this deposit was a darker gray in color than the lower parts of the deposit. We attribute this discoloration to mixing and downward seepage of the black humus-rich surface soil layer. The lower part of the white marl deposit was pure white in color and covered the north-south–oriented rectangular building platform and superstructure. This structure was 7 m wide with the north-south dimensions as yet not determined, but at least 14 m. The structure appears to have had a perishable superstructure, as the archaeologists did not encounter evidence of masonry vaulting or the characteristic concrete debris of beam and mortar roofing during the excavations.

The two outer walls of the structure were quite distinctive in their construction techniques. The western wall was preserved to a higher elevation than the eastern wall and was not quite as robust. The blocks used in construction of the western wall were less than half the size of those used in the eastern wall. It is possible, however, that the row of blocks at the outer base of the western wall constituted the foundation of a fallen second layer of masonry. This would have more than compensated for the smaller size of the building blocks in the wall. Additional excavation should clarify this issue.

To the west of the western wall of the superstructure, the excavators found two terraces leading down to the westernmost plaza in this group. These two terraces were around 2 m in width and 1 m in height. The floor of the western plaza was not found during these excavations. We presume that it was eroded away in antiquity. We regard this western side of 5E-52 as the back of the structure, and it is a fairly elaborate primary substructure for a residence group. The excavators found wall stones of the western wall fallen and embedded into the marl layer outside and downslope of the western wall of the superstructure, suggesting that this wall, like the eastern wall, was at least partially made of stone.

The interior floor of the superstructure on Structure 5E-52 occurred at about 102.61 m over the entire area. This floor was around 20 cm thick and was underlain by large cobble construction fill. Time did not permit further penetration of this area. The preserved eastern wall of the building platform was two courses high and footed on gravel and dirt. An uppermost exterior plaza floor abutted the eastern face of the wall at 102.15 m. The placement of this floor showed that it was associated with the construction of the building. However, there were two earlier floors underneath this one: one at 102.03 m and another at 101.81 m. We identify the lower of these two floor as an earlier general plaza level for the group, for we have evidence of this floor on the eastern side of the plaza in Suboperation 15-C.

From our limited probe of this stratigraphic sequence, it appears that the people who raised the building platform began by laying down a compact layer of gravel and dirt on the floor at 101.81 m, raising the level to about 102 m. They then established the retaining walls of the building platform and filled in behind them with cobbles to a thickness of about 40 cm, at which point they capped off the construction fill with an interior floor at 102.6 m and continued to raise the walls of the superstructure directly on top of the retaining walls of the building platform. We infer that the floor at 102.15 m represents some limited refurbishment of the plaza floor in the immediate vicinity of the eastern side of the building, perhaps placed to seal an offering piercing the 102 m floor somewhere in this zone. Only further excavation will reveal the complete sequence of construction events on this part of Structure 5E-50.

Extending out 3–4 m east of the face of the building platform, and continuing for 2–3 m west of the edge of the plat-

form into the interior of the superstructure, the excavators found a layer of pure white marl that rose to cover the building platform. This layer contained jumbled dressed masonry stones from the eastern superstructure wall and red-painted stucco fragments from the decorative frieze that adorned the wall. We believe that the stratigraphic facts of the context show conclusively that this was a primary and deliberately created deposit. The extensive deposition of the wall stones and shattered stucco frieze remains on both sides of the original eastern "front" wall, layered in a pure white marl lacking any evidence of humus accumulation from a long period of simple abandonment, could not be the product of natural wall collapse. This pattern of deposition, when coupled with the similar scattering of the western wall stones down over the western slope, shows that ritualists tore down the two walls of the superstructure. They then scattered and buried the wall stones and frieze fragments in white marl as part of a deliberate ceremony. The presence of painted stucco in the destruction zone of the eastern wall and the absence of painted stucco in the destruction zone down the slope of the western wall show that only the eastern wall of the building was decorated.

David Johnstone's preliminary analysis of the ceramic materials from the lower portion of the deposit in direct association with the building suggests that they are wholly Early Classic period in date. This indicates that the building itself dates to the early-phase occupation at Yaxuna.

The information gathered from Suboperation 15-B documents an early-phase superstructure, 7 m in width east-west and at least twice that long on its north-south axis (we exposed the east wall of the building platform in Suboperation 15-E; see discussion below). Based on the quantity of eastern wall stones, we estimate the original height of that front wall at 1–2 m. This wall was decorated with a red-painted stucco frieze. At some point, people deliberately pulled down the walls and scattered their fragments upon a prepared surface of white marl; they then covered the broken pieces of stucco frieze and the wall stones with another layer of white marl. Pending our ceramic analyses, we hypothesize that the event occurred at the end of the Early Classic period and at the end of the early-phase occupation at Yaxuna. After this termination ritual, there was no further occupation of this structure locality. We hope to investigate other important structures in the vicinity to see if this was an event of destruction and termination repeated in other areas in Yaxuna as part of some wider extinction of the center as a political capital.

SUBOPERATION 15-E

Four meters south of the Suboperation 15-B trench, on top of Structure 5E-52, archaeologists opened up Suboperation 15-E, a 2 × 2 m test unit. Average ground surface elevation was 103.27 m. The excavators hoped to determine the southern extent of the buried building platform inside Structure 5E-52. As it happened, they contacted the eastern retaining wall of the building platform in the initial 2 × 2 m unit; it ran north-south through the unit, continuing south for an undetermined distance. We hope eventually to clear and expand this unit and follow the wall to the corner.

The initial 30–46 cm of the suboperation was composed of humus and soil. Below this humus layer, the archaeologists uncovered a layer of marl and gravel that extended over the entire unit. This marl-and-gravel layer appears to be the same termination deposit that was found in Suboperation 15-B. In this stratum, the excavators discovered pieces of painted and modeled stucco mixed in with the other material of the deposit. They recovered the majority of the painted stucco pieces from the eastern portion of the unit, outside the building platform. As in Suboperation 15-B, they also found cut stones mixed with the stucco pieces, and this destruction layer appeared to be sandwiched between upper and lower layers of white marl. This entire termination deposit rested on a hard plaster floor at 101.98 m, the general elevation for the plaza floor associated with the building platform. In the western edge of the unit, the archaeologists cleared the upper course of the building platform. They then established a 2 × 2 m extension to the eastern edge of Suboperation 15-E to expose the deposit fronting this feature to the east.

The upper stratigraphy of this extension, Suboperation 15-E-1, was the same as that in the unit to the west. The humus layer was a little thicker, and the plaster layer seemed to slope to the east (as expected), because the unit was close to being off the top of the mound and on the slope. The broken modeled stucco was still present in the same manner as in the original unit and in Suboperation 15-B. Rafael Cobos Palma made an unexpected discovery of a large monolithic stone block dug out in the manner of a grinding stone. He found this stone resting on the plaza floor of Suboperation 15-E-1. The top of this monolith was at 102.36 m, the approximate level at which the painted stucco and cut stone became particularly concentrated in the white marl. This monolithic block, converted into a deep grinding surface or *pila,* was exactly like those we have found exposed on the surface of mounds at Yaxuna, but as might be expected, this one was much better preserved. The basin of the monolith was filled with the same white marl as surrounded it, and the base of the stone itself rested directly on the hard plaster floor at 101.94 m.

Given the context relative to Structure 5E-52, this grinding basin either was associated with the regular use of the building or was brought in for the specific act of termination. Since the structure appears to have been "swept clean" before being terminated, we think that this massive metate is associated with the termination ritual itself. Corroborating evidence for this interpretation may be found in the fact that monoliths converted to grinding stones in other mound groups at Yaxuna occur either on the surfaces and edges of the lower plazas or on the ground surface surrounding the mound groups—that is, at some distance from building platforms and foundation braces. Moreover, as Freidel notes in his concluding remarks to this volume, grinding stones are featured in termination rituals elsewhere in the Maya area, including Terminal Classic Chichen Itzá.

Suboperation 15-E exposed the eastern retaining wall of the building platform and the 5E-52 superstructure, which we documented in Suboperation 15-B. Moreover, we found substantive evidence of the same termination ritual: the presence of jumbled wall stones and stucco frieze fragments deposited between two layers of white marl.

We have detailed our preliminary excavations in Structure 5E-52 to give some idea of the kind of contextual documentation we can bring to bear on the recognition of termination rituals at Yaxuna. The test excavations elsewhere in the Structure 5E-50 Group corroborate those in the main palace (Freidel, Suhler, and Cobos P. 1992) and show that the entire group was destroyed, blanketed with white marl, and abandoned as a single event. The Structure 5E-50 Group illustrates both the prospects and the challenges of identifying large-scale, multi-feature primary deposits in Maya archaeological contexts. On the one hand, such deposits do not consistently occur in each plausible locality, both because of variable processes of erosion and preservation and because of variation in the intensity of spatial focus by the ritualists. On the other hand, the presence of the distinctive deposit in different parts of this group allows for an integrated stratigraphic interpretation of the whole on the basis of limited and selective exposures.

The characteristic white marl matrix of the termination deposits in the Structure 5E-50 Group is readily identifiable in other test excavations elsewhere at Yaxuna, especially in the same general southeastern zone of the settlement. In 1989 (Freidel et al. 1990), we dug a 26 m trench and exposed the south side of Structure 4E-5, a pyramidal secondary substructure on an extensive primary substructure that marked the end of the east-west *Sacbe* 5. This is the *sacbe* that runs along the southern edge of the Structure 5E-50 Group. Our original interpretation of the deposit posed that the white marl matrix was "stucco melt" and natural decay of a thickly plastered decorated terrace with cut-stone walls. In retrospect, we now think it more likely that this deposit represents a termination ritual, for the jumble of cut blocks we found there resembles the deliberately destroyed front wall of Structure 5E-52 more than any natural deterioration we have seen elsewhere at Yaxuna. The very small ceramic sample included three Cehpech diagnostics, four Early Classic Cochuah sherds, and two Tohosuco Late Preclassic sherds. Since the summit of this pyramid was reused for a substantial perishable superstructure in Terminal Classic times, we think the side deposit likely dates to the early phase of occupation at Yaxuna.

Similarly, a 2 × 2 m summit test on a small, 4 m high pyramid about 200 m northwest of Structure 4E-5 (Freidel, Suhler, and Cobos P. 1992) exposed the same characteristic white marl, laid directly on the surface of a two-step building platform. We anticipate that the ceramics sealed under the plaster floor of this platform will date to the Early Classic period and earlier.

White marl was a characteristic matrix of termination deposits at Cerros in Belize, so there may be some distinct quality to this material, which is nowadays prized for house floors and wall daub. Although marl can be quarried almost anywhere under the caprock, the pure white material is only available in some places. The color likely carried special connotations for the ancient Maya. The word *sak* in pre-Columbian Maya texts means "white, resplendent, human-made." *Sak-lak*, "white bowl," was a general name for dedicatory flaring-sided bowls and other vessels used in lip-to-lip caches in the Classic period. There are good reasons to believe that dedicatory and termination rituals involved many of the same materials, including white marl layers (Freidel and Schele 1989).

However, we should clearly expect to find differences among Maya termination ritual practices. At Cerros, termination rituals included a variety of broken and scattered artifacts, including pottery vessels and jades. So far, termination ritual deposits in this southern royal residential area of Yaxuna include only the broken stucco of façades and the cut stones of destroyed walls. In the northern acropolis, we have evidence that a thick white marl blanketing of the southeastern plaza area next to Structure 6F-4 included sherds from smashed Early Classic polychrome vessels and a restorable miniature "poison bottle" probably used to hold paint for writing.

Maya termination rituals show promise of providing an especially valuable form of primary deposit that can allow the documentation of extensive contemporaneous intentional actions in large and complex sites. These deposits, however, can also be especially vulnerable. Many termination deposits occur outside the final preserved architectural contexts, walls and floors. Traditionally, Maya archaeologists have searched for "sealed deposits" of artifacts inside such preserved buildings, to the detriment of their observations of "out of context" dirt and marl matrix blanketing the buildings. With care and caution, however, we may begin to find that the "out of context" overburden contains some of our most useful evidence of intentional behavior.

References Cited

Ambrosino, James
1996   "Excavations at Structure 6F-4, 6F-68, and 6F-72." In *The Selz Foundation Yaxuna Project, Final Report of the 1995 Field Season*. Dallas: Department of Anthropology, Southern Methodist University.

Andrews, A. P., and F. Robles C.
1985   "Chichén Itzá and Coba: An Itza-Maya Standoff in Early Postclassic Yucatán." In *The Lowland Maya Postclassic*, edited by A. F. Chase and P. M. Rice, 62–72. Austin: University of Texas Press.

Andrews, E. Wyllys, and Barbara W. Fash
1992   "Continuity and Change in a Royal Maya Residential Complex at Copán." *Ancient Mesoamerica* 3:63–88.

Ardren, Traci, David Johnstone, Sharon Bennett, Charles Suhler, and David Freidel
1994   *The Selz Foundation Yaxuna Project: Final Report of the 1993 Field Season*. Dallas: Department of Anthropology, Southern Methodist University.

Ashmore, Wendy
1989   "Construction and Cosmology: Politics and Ideology in Lowland Maya Settlement Patterns." In *Word and Image in Maya Culture: Explorations in Language, Writing, and Representation,* edited by William F. Hanks and Don S. Rice, 272–286. Salt Lake City: University of Utah Press.

Bennett, Sharon
1994   "The Burial Excavations at Yaxuna in 1993." In *The Selz Foundation Yaxuna Project Final Report of the 1993 Field Season,* 89–105. Dallas: Department of Anthropology, Southern Methodist University.

Brainerd, George W.
1958   *The Archaeological Ceramics of Yucatán.* University of California Anthropological Records 19. Berkeley: University of California Press.

Coe, William R.
1990   *Excavations in the Great Plaza, North Terrace, and North Acropolis of Tikal.* 5 vols. Tikal Report 14. University Museum Monograph 61. Philadelphia: University Museum.

Freidel, David A.
1986   "Introduction." In *Archaeology at Cerros, Belize, Central America, Volume 1: An Interim Report,* edited by R. A. Robertson and D. A. Freidel, xiii–xxiii. Dallas: Southern Methodist University Press.
1987   *Yaxuna Archaeological Survey: A Report of the 1986 Field Season.* Dallas: Department of Anthropology, Southern Methodist University.
1989   *Yaxuna Archaeological Survey: A Report of the 1988 Field Season.* Dallas: Department of Anthropology, Southern Methodist University
1992   "Krieg, Mythos und Realitat" (Maya Warfare, Myth and Reality). In *Die Welt der Maya* (The World of the Maya), 158–76. Mainz am Rhein: Verlag Phillip Von Zabern.

Freidel, David A., and Linda Schele
1989   "Dead Kings and Living Mountains: Dedication and Termination Rituals of the Lowland Maya." In *Word and Image in Mayan Culture: Explorations in Language, Writing, and Representation,* edited by William Hanks and Don Rice, 233–43. Salt Lake City: University of Utah Press.

Freidel, David A., Linda Schele, and Joy Parker
1993   *Maya Cosmos: Three Thousand Years on the Shaman's Path.* New York: William Morrow.

Freidel, David, and Charles K. Suhler
1995   "The Tikal Sky Seat: Maya Wars in Monu-

mental Architectural Context." Paper presented at the Second UCLA Maya Weekend, Los Angeles.

Freidel, David, Charles Suhler, and Rafael Cobos P.
1992   *The Selz Foundation Yaxuna Project: Final Report of the 1991 Field Season.* Dallas: Department of Anthropology, Southern Methodist University.

Freidel, David A., Charles Suhler, and Ruth Krochock
1990   *Yaxuna Archaeological Survey: A Report of the 1989 Field Season and Final Report of Phase One.* Dallas: Department of Anthropology, Southern Methodist University.

Garber, James F.
1983   "Patterns of Jade Consumption and Disposal at Cerros, Northern Belize." *American Antiquity* 48(4):800–7.
1989   *Archaeology at Cerros, Belize, Central America, Volume 2: The Artifacts.* Dallas: Southern Methodist University Press.

Garza Tarazona de Gonzalez, Silvia, and Edward B. Kurjack
1980   *Atlas arqueologico del estado de Yucatán, Tomo 1.* Mexico City: Instituto Nacional de Antropologia e Historia.

Kurjack, Edward B. and Silvia Garza Tarazona de Gonzalez
1976   "Pre-Columbian Community Form and Distribution in the Northern Maya Area." In *Lowland Maya Settlement Patterns,* edited by Wendy Ashmore, 287–309. Albuquerque: School of American Research and University of New Mexico Press.

Reese, Kathryn Victoria
1996   "Narratives of Power: Late Formative Public Architecture and Civic Center Design at Cerros, Belize." Ph.D. diss., University of Texas at Austin.

Robertson, Robin A.
1983   "Functional Analysis and Social Process in Ceramics: The Pottery from Cerros, Belize." In *Civilization in the Ancient Americas: Essays in Honor of Gordon R. Willey,* edited by Richard M. Leventhal and Alan L. Kolata, 105–42. Albuquerque: University of New Mexico Press.

Robertson-Freidel, Robin A.
1980   "The Ceramics from Cerros: A Late Preclassic Site in Northern Belize." Ph.D. diss., Harvard University.

Robles C., Fernando, and Anthony P. Andrews
1986   "A Review and Synthesis of Recent Postclassic Archaeology in Northern Yucatán." In *Late Lowland Maya Civilization,* edited by J. A. Sabloff and E. W. Andrews V, 53–98. Albu-

querque: School of American Research and University of New Mexico Press.

Schele, Linda, and David A. Freidel
1990   *A Forest of Kings: The Untold Story of the Ancient Maya.* New York: William Morrow.

Suhler, Charles
1996   "Excavations in the North Acropolis, Yaxuna, Yucatan, Mexico." Ph.D. diss., Southern Methodist University.

Suhler, Charles, Traci Ardren, and David Johnstone
n.d.   "The Northern Classic Period: Ceramic Evidence from Yaxuna." Submitted to *Ancient Mesoamerica.*

PART THREE

Archaeological Evidence from Mesoamerica

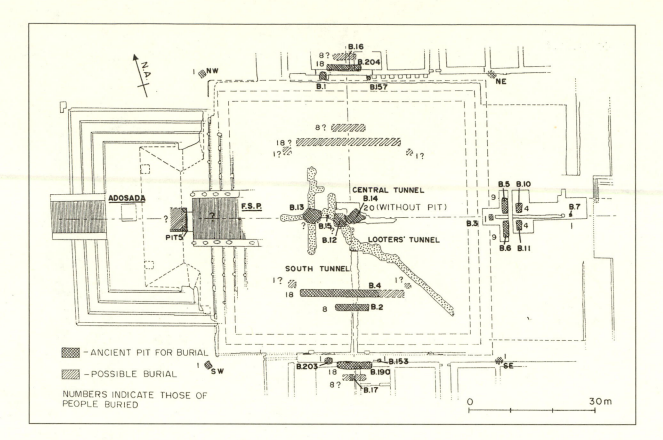

Map 13.1.   General plan of the FSP, showing areas excavated, locations of the burials found to date, and looters' tunnel.

CHAPTER THIRTEEN

Termination Programs and Prehispanic Looting at the Feathered Serpent Pyramid in Teotihuacan, Mexico

Saburo Sugiyama
Arizona State University

Recent excavations in the Ciudadela[1] at Teotihuacan have revealed that the Feathered Serpent Pyramid (FSP), the third largest pyramid in Teotihuacan, was erected with unusual sculptured façades sometime during the ascent of the city and that probably more than two hundred people were sacrificed and buried in the dedication of the pyramid (map 13.1; Cabrera et al. 1991; Sugiyama 1989). The archaeological records suggest that a complex of ritual meanings was involved in the dedication of the pyramid.[2] The front façade of this monument was later covered by a new construction, the Adosada platform, which bore typical Teotihuacan *tablero-talud* walls with stucco plaster and mural painting. This addition seems to have constituted a deliberate act of profanation, as already suggested by Marquina (1979 [1922]) about seventy-five years ago. The recent excavations provide substantial information on the Adosada construction and other acts of profanation that seem to have taken place while the city was functioning. This essay focuses on the prehispanic programs of termination and the subsequent exploitation of symbols at the FSP.

In reference to evidence of destruction in the city in general, it has been pointed out that some buildings, mainly in the central part of the metropolis, were intentionally burned. Two explanations have been proposed. Ignacio Bernal (1965) argued, on the basis of carbon 14 analysis of samples from the Avenue of the Dead, that the central part of the city was destroyed intentionally and abandoned around A.D. 300, while peripheral areas continued to function until A.D. 650. René Millon (1973) disagreed, proposing that the samples used for these dates were reused wood, which gave dates several centuries earlier than that of the actual abandonment of the city core. On the basis of Teotihuacan ceramic chronology,[3] Millon argued that the city flourished until the eighth century, at which time the core was burned and destroyed somewhat suddenly (Millon 1988). Millon's argument may be supported by the fact that strong Teotihuacan influence throughout Mesoamerica was mainly recorded after A.D. 400, although this is not entirely inconsistent with Bernal's hypothesis.

Concerning the collapse of the city in the eighth century, Millon (1988:149–56) argued that the principal targets of burning were temples, pyramids, and public buildings. He concluded that the destruction in Teotihuacan was so extensive, intense, and excessive that the city never again became a major center, and that the objective of this religious destruction should therefore be regarded as fundamentally political. Although Millon's interpretation has been generally accepted by other scholars, the question of the absolute date of the final destruction remained unresolved.

The Ciudadela is one of the places where destruction and looting are unquestionably manifested. The Mexican project of INAH (PAT80–82) in the early 1980s obtained data that indicate intentional destruction and burning in the residential compound located on the north side of the FSP (Jarquín and Martínez 1982). Millon (1988:151–55) described extensive damage within the Ciudadela, including burning, destruction of monuments, dismantling of sculptured façades, looting of burials, dismemberment of slaughtered individuals in the palaces, and the smashing of sculptures of gods. He argued that almost all these events took place for political reasons at the time of the collapse of the city in the eighth century.

The chronological data that Millon relied upon derived mainly from two test pits in the South Palace in the Ciudadela, where the latest construction level provided ceramics of the Metepec phase, the last in the city's history. Significant amounts of Metepec ceramics were also recorded in the surface collection taken from the Ciudadela by the Teotihuacan Mapping Project (table 13.1). Therefore, the association of the latest construction level with Metepec ceramics is evident at the Ciudadela, although the relation of the Metepec phase to absolute dates needs to be refined with more C14 dates (e.g., Rattray 1991). Recent excavations at the Ciudadela by PAT80–82 removed all post-Teotihuacan stratigraphy to uncover the Teotihuacan architecture and thus obtained a large amount of material, including ceramics and C14 samples. Unfortunately, comprehensive chronological information is not yet available from that project. Only archaeomagnetic dating by Wolfman (1990:297) of three samples obtained from the north residential compound (North Palace or 1-D: N1E1 in Millon et al. 1973) provides absolute dates. The dates are earlier than those Millon proposed for the last burning at the Ciudadela: A.D. 465–505, 475–495, and 480–510.[4] Based on these dates and others obtained with samples from different parts of the city, Wolfman (1990:301) proposed that the constructions along the Avenue of the Dead, including the Ciudadela, were destroyed probably in the late fifth century. Thus, absolute chronological assessment for the collapse of the city remains unclear. This question fundamentally affects the interpretation of termination events in Teotihuacan, discussed below.

In his explanation of the collapse of the city, Millon cautiously differentiated the burning and partial covering of the FSP by the Adosada from other acts of destruction,

and he interpreted the former as a ritual destruction. In this essay, the termination of the monument is reconsidered with new excavation data in order to reveal a more complex internal history and the sociopolitical implications of acts of the profanation. The results of C14 analysis are also presented, since the absolute chronology of termination events is critical, given the current state of our understanding of the city's collapse and the lack of precision in its dating. The information adds more specific features to the scheme described by Millon about the acts of destruction. I argue that the construction of the FSP was probably completed during the first half of the third century A.D. and that shortly after its completion the FSP suffered intensive and extensive destruction and looting that probably began about the time of the Adosada construction in the fourth century, if not earlier. I am inclined to think that this event reflects internal political conflicts, rather than simply a periodic ritual act. While the Ciudadela and some parts of the city were continuously in use after the Adosada construction and ritual termination of the FSP, the FSP seems to have become a target for the *official* looting or exploitation of symbols by newly raised ruling groups, until the end of the city's functioning.

CHRONOLOGICAL SEQUENCE OF THE EVENTS AT THE FEATHERED SERPENT PYRAMID

The acts of dedication and termination involving the FSP are manifest in several different stages (fig. 13.1). The first goes back to the period before its construction. Although the data on that period are very scarce, we know stratigraphically that there were at least two construction stages below that of the FSP. One of the excavations of PAT80–82 at the south side of the pyramid uncovered one small remnant of a plastered wall (within Burial 190: Sugiyama 1989:88–89, 1991:284–89). Later excavations by PTQ88–89 also uncovered remains of superimposed Teotihuacan concrete floors beneath the fill of the pyramid (Cabrera et al. 1991:83–84). The presence of several stone blocks in the fill of the pyramid suggests that earlier masonry construction existed in the near vicinity. Another block, sculptured with an unknown geometric motif on one side and a "petal" motif of the feathered serpent on the other, was discovered by PAT80–82 (Cabrera and Sugiyama 1982:photo 6). This suggests that an earlier structure had stone façades with iconographic

Table 13.1.   Counts of Ceramic Categories in Teotihuacan Mapping Project Surface Collections from the Ciudadela and 2:N1E1

Totals of Phased Ceramics and Others	Proveniences				
	Surrounding Platforms	Pyramids on Platforms	Palaces	All Ciudadela Collections	2:N1E1
Patlachique	171 (14%)	92 (5%)	3 (2%)	273 (8%)	21 (2%)
Zacualli	157 (13%)	247 (14%)	16 (13%)	460 (14%)	43 (3%)
Miccaotli	426 (36%)	482 (28%)	11 (9%)	1,000 (30%)	114 (9%)
Tlamimilolpa	193 (16%)	447 (26%)	37 (30%)	731 (22%)	287 (22%)
Xolalpan	71 (6%)	79 (5%)	11 (9%)	178 (5%)	334 (26%)
Metepec	20 (2%)	62 (4%)	12 (10%)	106 (3%)	67 (5%)
Regular Thin Orange	98 (8%)	196 (11%)	20 (16%)	337 (10%)	247 (19%)
Coarse Thin Orange	20 (2%)	22 (1%)	4 (3%)	48 (1%)	70 (5%)
All Post-Teotihuacan	40 (3%)	121 (7%)	9 (7%)	228 (7%)	110 (8%)
Totals	1,196	1,748	123	3,361	1,295

Source: After Cowgill 1983: table 11.1.
Note: Counts of ceramic categories in Teotihuacan Mapping Project surface collections from the Ciudadela, based on ceramic reanalyses supervised by Evelyn Rattray. Figures in parentheses are percentages of column totals. Thin Orange Ware is unphased. 2:N1E1 is located outside of the Ciudadela, although it seems to have functioned with close relation to the Ciudadela. The ceramic counts indicate that the Ciudadela seems to have been occupired mainly during the Miccaotli and Tlamimilolpa phases. Notice also the significant percentage of pre-Ciudadela sherds, Patlachique and Tzacualli. The percentages of Xolalpan or Metepec Phase sherds are smaller. This may indicate less activity in the Ciudadela during a later period of Teotihuacan than in the earlier phases.

elements. In addition, one incomplete burial suggesting human sacrifice by heart extraction was found beneath the pyramid in association with one of these substructures. The skeletal remains consisted of the pelvis, vertebral column, and right ribs found in anatomical relation, with the partial cranium of an animal occupying the position of the heart. The earlier structures were deliberately leveled, apparently when the FSP was built. Unfortunately, the destruction was so thorough that no detailed information on the act of destruction was recovered.

The construction of the FSP was probably completed early in the third century, as shown in Figure 13.1 and discussed below in the section on C14 analyses. The stratigraphic data indicate that the sacrificial burial complex associated with the FSP was undertaken at an early stage of the construction work, although sacrifices found outside the pyramid could have taken place at a later stage of construction. After the completion of the construction, the monument was presumably used for a certain period for ceremonial activities, although archaeological evidence does not give any information about them. In contrast, evidence of later acts of destruction at the pyramid are unusually visible in the material remains.

One such action in an early period can be seen on the main west façade of the FSP (fig. 13.2). The upper part of the staircase and its lateral walls appear to have been damaged by the extraction of stone blocks, damages that were later repaired with small lava stones and typical Teotihuacan concrete. These traces of repairs also can be observed on one large, enigmatic sculptured block dis-

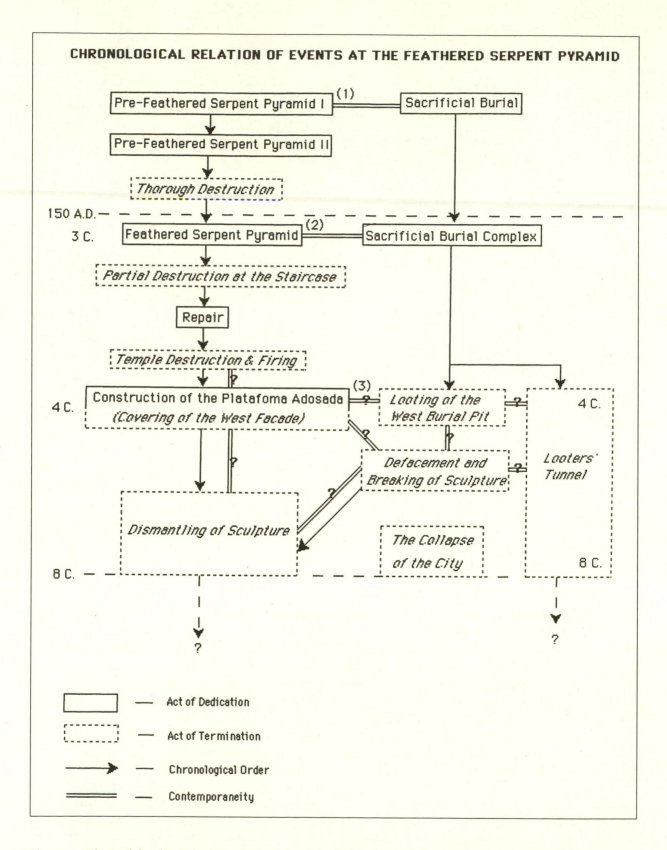

Fig. 13.1.   Chart of the chronological relationship of the dedication and termination events at the FSP.

covered beneath the original north balustrade of the staircase. It appears that this stone block originally had been fitted in around one of the feathered serpent heads, but was extracted, damaged, and finally concealed by the balustrade when the repair was made. After this happened, the pyramid probably continued to be used, since the repair would not otherwise have been necessary.

The west façade suffered burning (Millon 1988:154). Since the evidence of stone cracking and charcoal remains were found on the west façade and the floor of the same side, this should have happened sometime after the completion of the pyramid but before the construction of the Adosada, which covered this side. However, the firing and the extraction of stone blocks and repair at the staircase might have taken place just before the covering of the façade.

The covering of sacred images (the Feathered Serpent and another unidentified entity carved on the façade) by the Adosada appears to have been in itself an act of profanation. This probably took place along with other acts of desecration. Excavation by PTQ88–89 found an ancient large rectangular pit in front of the staircase of the pyramid. The pit seems to have been part of the burial complex associated with the FSP, although no skeletal remains were found in it. Only bone fragments and artifacts of high quality found near the pit suggest its function as a grave (Pit 5 in map 13.1). Excavation by Cowgill and Oralia Cabrera (1991) revealed that the pit was emptied and sealed with the construction fill of the Adosada. The excavation was not extended to the west to uncover the whole pit, but the looting seems to have taken place at the time of the Adosada construction and was so thorough as to leave virtually nothing of the original contents.

When the Adosada was built, another act of profanation appears to have taken place at the top of the pyramid. Excavation of a pit atop the Adosada by PTQ88–89 uncovered many fragments of intricately modeled fired-clay walls (Cabrera et al. 1991:87). Stratigraphic data suggest that they were from walls of the temple that had once stood on top of the FSP. When the Adosada was built over the façade of the original pyramid, the temple itself may have been razed, and fragments of the temple were apparently incorporated in the construction fill of the Adosada.

On the other three façades of the pyramid, there is further evidence of profanation that may also have taken place when the Adosada was built (Sugiyama 1995). One hundred fifty-four fallen sculptural blocks were discov-

Fig. 13.2. South lateral wall of the staircase at the FSP, suggesting that the staircase was partially repaired. Upper portion of balustrade made with stone blocks was apparently replaced by unworked small rocks and Teotihuacan concrete, remains of which were still visible currently. (See also Lámina VI in Gamio 1922.)

ered around the north and south sides of the FSP, where entire post-Teotihuacan layers were removed. Many of these were incomplete blocks that had already been fragmented. On the basis of the data available from the principal façade of the pyramid, I calculate that approximately 11,500 small and large stone blocks were necessary to cover the north and south façades of the pyramid. That only 1.3% of them were recovered from the excavations means that the pyramid has been a target of intense looting of stone blocks, probably for centuries for new construction in nearby sites. No evidence to date the acts of destruction was available. However, careful observation suggests that acts of profanation may have begun at a time when the sculptural blocks were still on the façades. Some of the large head blocks have cut marks on

Fig. 13.3. Defaced sculptured head found near the north side of the FSP. This large block had originally been a complete head sculptured in the form of the feathered serpent. The face was later cut off, and the surface of the cut mark was covered with stucco that was finally painted with red paint.

Fig. 13.4. Another defaced sculptural head, representing unidentified entity in the form of headdress, found at its original place on the south side of the FSP. The surface of the cut mark has remains of stucco.

the surface, mainly on the parts of faces of mythological animals, and they occasionally have a layer of white stucco on the cut area (figs. 13.3, 13.4). Finally, the surfaces of stucco were often painted with red. Although the time of the profanation is uncertain, the fact that the cut marks and remains of stucco can be observed only on the parts of animal heads that were originally visible on the façade indicates that it probably happened while the stone blocks were still in place on the walls, sometime before the dismantling of the façades.

The date of the final abandonment of the FSP-Adosada complex is also uncertain. Millon (1988:152) believes that it happened at the time of the city's collapse and involved the dismantling of the façades of the FSP. Although no stratigraphic or chronological data were available concerning the removal of blocks, other information indicates that it began while the city, or at least a part of the city, was functioning (Sugiyama 1989:104). The Teotihuacan Mapping Project directed by Millon (1973:41) excavated in the so-called Barrio Oaxaqueño, a Oaxaca-type tomb with a doorjamb that had a Oaxaca glyph. This jamb originally seems to have been a block forming the lower molding of a *tablero* at the FSP, according to a comparison of the form and measurements of the jamb with those of the molding stones at the pyramid. Since there was no other known *tablero-talud* structure in Teotihuacan whose molding was made with stone blocks of the same sizes and forms, it is likely that the destruction of the pyramid took place no later than the construction of the tomb in the Barrio Oaxaqueño. According to Millon (1973:42), this dates to the seventh century A.D.

One of the most striking indications of termination of the consecrated monument may be the looters' tunnel that I found inside the FSP (Cabrera et al. 1991:82–84). It seems to have started at the southeast corner of the monument and continued diagonally toward the central part, destroying the internal structure of the original construction fill of the pyramid (map 13.1). Since the entrance to the tunnel had been sealed by later collapses, its existence was previously unknown, and neither surface observation nor collection in the tunnel gave any indication about when and why the tunnel was originally made. Therefore, we excavated a series of pits on the floor of the tunnel to obtain continuous stratigraphic data along the tunnel, as well as to recover associated archaeological materials. This revealed that two multiple burials near the center of the pyramid had been looted;

the looters apparently scattered parts of offerings and human bones on the tunnel floors mainly near these looted burials. They apparently did not leave behind any of their own artifacts. However, we collected in the looters' layers a large amount of burned wood fragments that may directly date the event by C14 analysis, since many of them were probably remains of combustible materials used by looters to provide illumination in the tunnel.

CHRONOLOGICAL DATA FROM THE LOOTERS' TUNNEL

Although many of the aforementioned acts of termination cannot be dated precisely, the absolute chronology of the looters' tunnel may be inferred by the C14 analysis of these wood samples. Table 13.2 shows the results of recent C14 analysis of thirty-six samples collected at the FSP that may date the pyramid itself as well as the looters' tunnel.[5] The box-and-whisker plots (fig. 13.5) show, in chronological order, ranges of calibrated dates given by Beta Analytic in Miami, the Subdirección de Servicios

Académicos del Instituto Nacional de Antropología e Historia, Mexico City, Isotrace Laboratory at the University of Toronto, and Krueger Enterprises in Cambridge, Massachusetts. The boxes show 1 sigma ranges (68% interval of probability), and the whiskers show 2 sigma (95% interval of probability). Krueger Enterprises calibrated 1 sigma, and INAH did not calibrate. Therefore, Cowgill calibrated these on the basis of the calibration curve used by Beta Analytic. A small sample (0.3 g) was taken from the wooden baton discovered in one of the looted pits and sent to the Eidgenössische Technische Hochschule in Zurich (ETH-6749/6750) for dating by the accelerator mass spectrometry (AMS) technique. These technical details, as well as condition and type of samples (table 13.2), should be kept in mind when the results are interpreted.

The first eleven samples should refer to the time of the construction of the FSP or earlier, since they were found in undisturbed layers within the pyramid or in graves prepared during the pyramid construction. Eight samples were taken from charcoal, wood, shell offerings, and human bones in the multiple graves discovered at the

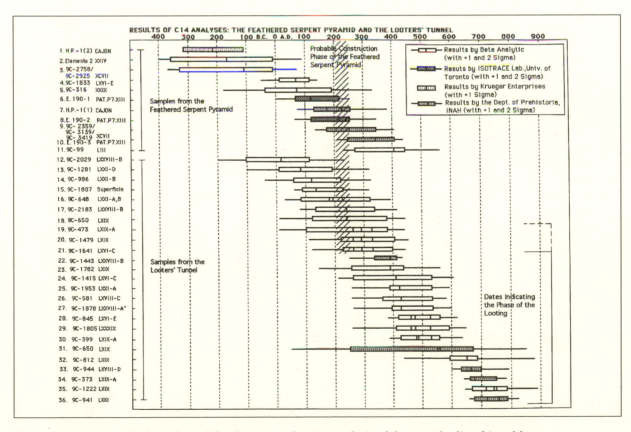

Fig. 13.5. Box-and-whisker plots of the dates given by C14 analysis of the samples listed in table 13.2.

Table 13.2.   Results of C^{14} Analyses: Feathered Serpent Pyramid & Looters' Tunnel

	BAG # *	LAB #	DATE(B.P.)	-2 SIGMA	-1 SIGMA	MEANS
1	PAT.H.P.1(2)	GX-10268	2165±105		320 B.C.	215 B.C.
2	ELE.-2	49414	2120±110	400 B.C.	366 B.C.	168 B.C.
3	9C-2758/2925	49423	2090±80	370 B.C.	331 B.C.	110 B.C.
4	9C-1833	37833/ ETH6749	1935±50	50 B.C.	11	69
5	9C-316	49412	1930±100	180 B.C.	40 B.C.	72
6	PAT.E.190-1	TO 887	1880±60	1 B.C.	66	119
7	PAT.H.P.1(1)	INAH327	1802±58	75	(90) 130	(148) 175-225
8	PAT.E.190-2	TO 888	1820±60	65	119	215
9	9C-2359/ 3139/3419	INAH1068	1750±50	135	(150) 175	(200) 250
10	PAT.E.190-3	INAH394	1702±55	210	(193) 245	(248) 342
11	9C-99	49427	1650±70	230	264	405
12	9C-2029	49422	1980±90	200 B.C.	101 B.C.	15
13	9C-1281	49405	1910±80	100 B.C.	7	82
14	9C-986	49408	1880±70	40 B.C.	57	118
15	9C-1807	49421	1850±50	60	87	134
16	9C-648	32611	1810±70	29	82	180, 194, 225
17	9C-2183	49426	1780±70	80	134	239
18	9C-650	49410	1780±100	10	120	239
19	9C-473	49409	1730±80	10	100	261,288,327
20	9C-1479	49415	1730+-80	110	220	261, 288, 327
21	9C-1641	49417	1730±70	120	227	261, 288, 327
22	9C-1443	INAH1067	1675±35	250	(240) 335	(275) 390
23	9C-1782	49413	1670+-80	145	253	391
24	9C-1415	49403	1640±90	210	261	411
25	9C-1953	49404	1610±60	260	390	425
26	9C-581	32610	1610±60	259	362	426
27	9C-1878	49424	1600±60	264	397	429
28	9C-845	49420	1560±60	380	420	463, 478, 530
29	9C-1805	49418	1560±80	264	411	463, 478, 530
30	9C-399	32609	1550±50	390	427	482, 488,534
31	9C-650	INAH1064	1534±211	50	(205) 250	(416) 550-560
32	9C-812	49419	1380±100	440	595	654
33	9C-944	INAH1066	1350±65	600	(535) 630	(600) 665
34	9C-373	INAH1063	1320±45	640	(585) 660	(630) 675
35	9C-1222	49416	1270±60	650	669	716, 743, 757
36	9C-941	INAH1065	1265±45	660	(640) 675	(685) 720-760
37	9C-249	49425	MODERN±100	1850	1950	2050

*9C & ELE- Project Templo de Quetzalcoatl 88-89; PAT-Proyecto Arqueológico Teotihuacan 80-82 INAH

Note: The results of C14 analysis of the samples taken from the FSP and the Looters' Tunnel. Stratigraphic data indicate that Samples 1–11 relate to the date of the construction of the pyramid, while 12–36 may refer to those of the looting activities. However, as discussed in the text, samples 12–21 more likely date the FSP, and 22–35 indicate the phase of looting activities.

+1 SIGMA	+2 SIGMA	ZONE/PIT	LAYER	FOSA/BURIAL	DESCRIPTION
110 B.C.	-	South Side	"Cajón"	Trench 1	Wood/Charcoal Piece
10 B.C.	90	South Tunnel	XXIV	F.1/B.2	Charcoal Fragments
9 B.C.	70	Central Tunnel	XCVII	B.14	Charcoal Fragments
116	140	Z.8/P.23	LXVI-E	F.4(B.13)	Baton Fragment, AMS***
193	328	South Tunnel	XXIX	F.2/B.4	Charcoal Fragments
216	250	South Side	PAT.P7.XIII	B.190	Complete Cuneiform
(206) 255	385	South Side	"Cajón"	Trench 1	Wood/Charcoal Piece
250	343	South Side	PAT.P.7.XIII	B.190	Complete Cuneiform
(250) 345	405	Central Tunnel	XCVII	B.14	Wood/Charcoal Fragments
(303) 410	435	South Side	PAT.P.7.XIII	B.190	Worked Shells
442	560	South Tunnel	LIII	P.H.#3	17 Wood Fragments
113	230	Z.8/P.31	LXXVIII-B	F.4(B.13)	3 Wood Fragments
194	316	Z.6/P.7	LXXI-D	F.3(B.12)	Charcoal Fragments
221	322	Z.6/P.9	LXXI-B	F.3(B.12)	Wood Piece
228	316	Z.10/P.41	Surface		Charcoal Piece
323	390	Z.6/P.6	LXXI-A/B	F.3(B.12)	Charcoal Piece
338	410	Z.8/P.23	LXXVIII-B	F.4(B.13)	Wood/Charcoal Piece
380	440	Z.7/P.15	LXIX	-	Wood Piece
380	440	Z.6/P.9	LXIX-A	F.3(B.12)	Charcoal Piece
406	450	Z.10/P.36	LXIX	-	Wood Piece
399	440	Z.11/P.39	LXVI-C	-	Wood/Charcoal Piece
(310) 415	430	Z.8/P.23	LXXVIII-B	F.4(B.13)	Wood/Charcoal Fragments
435	560	Z.12/P.45	LXIX	-	Wood Piece
535	610	Z.8/P.24	LXVI-C	-	Wood/Charcoal Piece
535	593	Z.6/P.7	LXXI-A	F.3(B.12)	Wood/Charcoal Piece
535	580	Z.5/P.3	LXVIII-C	-	Charcoal Piece
540	600	Z.8/P.23	LXXVIII-A"	F.4(B.13)	Wood Piece
562	620	Z.8/P.23	LXVI-E	F.4(B.13)	Wood/Charcoal Piece
596	650	Z.10/P.36	LXXXIX	-	Wood/Charcoal Fragments
561	637	Z.6/P.7	LXIX-A	F.3(B.12)	Charcoal Piece
(627) 675	850	Z.7/P.15	LXIX	-	Wood Piece
690	880	Z.8/P.23	LXIX	F.4(B.13)	Wood Piece
(665) 700	790	Z.6/P.5-6	LXVIII-D	-	2 Charcoal Fragments
(675) 750	780	Z.6/P.5-6	LXIX-A	-	Wood Piece
790	890	Z.3/P.33	LXIX	-	Wood Piece
(730) 790	825	Z.6/P.6	LXXI	F.3(B.12)	Wood Fragments
-		Z.2	Surface	-	Wood Piece

**( ) Date without calibration

***AMS-Applied to technique
Accelerator Mass Spectrometry

pyramid, and three samples were from remains of post wood forming the internal structure within the original construction fill of the pyramid. Although they may have been made at different times, all of them were buried during the single construction stage of the FSP. The results show a wide range extending from 215 B.C. to A.D. 405.

The first three early dates (dates in parentheses indicate the interval with 68% probability) are Sample 1: 215 B.C. (320–110 B.C.), Sample 2: 168 B.C. (366–10 B.C.), Sample 3: 110 B.C. (331–9 B.C.). These may indicate earlier dates because of intrusion of earlier material or reuse. The first one has a counterpart (Sample 7) from the same posthole, and the two results provide unacceptable ages relative to each other. The next eight samples seem to indicate dates nearer to that of the construction of the FSP: A.D. 69 (11 B.C.–A.D. 116) for the baton found in Burial 13 (Sample 4); A.D. 72 (40 B.C.–A.D. 193) for carbon in Burial 4 (Sample 5); A.D. 119 (A.D. 66–216) for a cuneiform bone from an individual in Burial 190 (Sample 6); A.D. 175–225 (130–255) for a wood sample in a post pit, counterpart of Sample 1 (Sample 7); A.D. 215 (119–250) for another cuneiform from an individual in Burial 190 (Sample 8); A.D. 250 (175–345) for charcoal fragments in Burial 14 (Sample 9); A.D. 342 (245–410) for shell beads in Burial 190 (Sample 10); and A.D. 405 (264–442) for a wood sample in a posthole (Sample 11).

Sample 4 is from a complete wooden artifact that may have been an old object of symbolic importance or an object made with old material. Samples 6 and 8, the bones, should indicate the time of burial, since the death of the victim would theoretically correspond to the time of preparation of the grave. Sample 10 may also indicate the time of burial directly, since a large number of shell beads in unique forms appear to have been produced exclusively as offerings at the time of the pyramid construction. However, C14 dating with shell might be less precise because of the type of material.

Possible differences between the C14 dates and the construction date of the FSP cannot be quantified in a simple way because uncertainty involved in testing different kinds of materials may differentially affect the dating of the construction and burials. Therefore, I tentatively propose that the mean, A.D. 210, is reasonable for the mean date of the period in which the construction was in process. If the possibilities of reuse and lapse between the time of death and that of the construction are considered, a slightly later date seems more likely. The dates given for the bone samples support this date. In

more general terms, I conclude that the construction of the pyramid and the associated burials took place in the first half of the third century—in which five of the six latest dates among eleven samples fall with 68% probability. The ceramics obtained in different layers in the fill of the FSP also indicate that the pyramid and the associated burial complex correspond to the Miccaotli–Early Tlamimilolpa phases, suggested as between A.D. 150 and 300 (Millon 1973; Rattray 1981). It was not possible, however, to infer the duration of the construction itself from C14 analyses, since there was no correlation between the stratigraphic sequence in the monument construction fill and the C14 dates.

The dates given by twenty-five of the twenty-six samples from the looters' layers[6] in the tunnel extend from A.D. 15 to 743 (table 13.2). They were selected from a large collection of charcoal and unworked wood fragments found in the tunnel. Almost all of them were more or less burned, so they may have been used by looters for light inside the dark tunnel. If so, the plot of the last twenty-five samples in figure 13.2 should indicate the lapse of time during which the tunnel was open, since they were from the looters' layers in the tunnel that became completely closed in ancient times. It should be remembered, however, that the pyramid contained many wood posts as internal structure, and we know that at least seventeen of them were disturbed by the looters' tunnel, so that fragments may have fallen into the looters' layers. If these were among the samples dated, they logically would date to the construction of the monument or earlier. Some of the samples, in fact, seem to indicate dates of the construction of the FSP. If we consider all ten samples (12–21) dating with 68% probability to the third century or earlier as those belonging to the original fill, fifteen samples (22–36) dating later than the third century seem to refer to the time of looting, since humans would have been the main introducers of burned wood. However, if Samples 19–21 are considered as post-FSP material, it is also possible, though less likely, that the looting began as early as the late third century.

The last fifteen samples in table 13.2 cover a lapse from A.D. 391 (253–435) to 743 (669–790). This implies that the activities in the looters' tunnel may have begun late in the fourth century, if not earlier, or at the latest during the fifth century and that the tunnel may have been abandoned in the eighth century (see fig. 13.1). Thus, the pyramid was probably looted when at least some sectors of the city were functioning, and the tunnel was possibly closed to humans, or abandoned, in the eighth century. In other words, if the current assignment of absolute dates to the ceramic chronology is accurate, the looting did not begin with the collapse of the city; rather, it was an episode of the functioning city's history and ceased in the eighth century when the thorough destruction of the metropolis is thought to have taken place.

Matching the stratigraphy of the tunnel with the results of C14 analysis did not define clear chronological relationships among layers, zones, and looted burials. The stratigraphic relationship of several superimposed floors found in the tunnel does not seem to reflect different periods of looting in chronological order, since there is no correlation between the given dates and the stratigraphic depth of layers from which the samples were taken. Nor was there any correlation between the horizontal distances of the sample locations from the entrance and the dates. This does not support the idea of any time lapse between excavation near the entrance and at the end. The results instead support the possibility that the entire excavation of the tunnel may have been carried out during a rather short period, although irregularity of the dating could also be caused by other variables. The samples from the looted burials also suggest that the looting of the two burials was more or less contemporaneous. However, the long lapse indicated by the results of fifteen samples covering four centuries or more suggests at least two looting episodes during this period. The most recent date (eighth century) does not necessarily indicate that the tunnel was sealed at that time, but seems to mean that the intrusion of the burned wood, and probably looting activity, ceased at that time.

Ceramics found inside the looters' tunnel do not appear to be very helpful in dating the tunnel precisely. Datable ceramics may not have been introduced into the tunnel in conjunction with looting. Therefore, it is not surprising that we did not find any sherds postdating the Early Tlamimilolpa phase corresponding to the FSP—except (according to Cowgill's ceramic examination) two possible Coyotlatelco sherds and a few Aztec or colonial sherds found near the entrance of the looters' tunnel. These may simply be posterior intrusions, or perhaps the tunnel remained open until that period. At any rate, the proposition that the intensive looting began in the fourth century and ceased in the eighth century is consistent with the ceramic data.

DISCUSSION

There was a long-standing tradition in Mesoamerica of monuments being renewed repeatedly in relation to calendrical cycles, reigns of kings, victory in war, conquests, and other religious or sociopolitical occasions. These constructive works were usually accompanied by acts of destruction, which may or may not have had specific ritual meanings. Archaeological data sometimes show considerable deliberateness in the display of specific ritual meanings, but they also may reflect sociopolitical aims that go beyond the actors' ritual intentions. Some destruction was tied to political goals, such as conquest or revenge, regardless of the particular gods profaned and specific ritual meanings attached to the temples that were destroyed. Contextual "reading" of archaeological records on the acts of violence may occasionally refer to types and causes of the destruction.

As shown in figure 13.1, the acts of destruction at the FSP can be grouped temporally into four sets in relation to three major construction stages: pre-FSP, FSP, and the Adosada. In the pre-FSP stage, there were at least two architectural stages. Although there are no detailed data about architectural features, iconography, and precise chronology, it is significant that the location seems to have been associated with masonry construction (perhaps monumental) and sacrificial ritual before the construction of the FSP.

The second stage, the erection of the FSP, evidently involved the almost total destruction of the earlier structure or structures. The Ciudadela complex enclosing the FSP vicinity seems to have been constructed shortly before the FSP. The removal of the earlier building may have been part of an exceptionally large-scale renovation program. The erection of the pyramid with its associated sacrificial burial complex should have been one of the most important events in Teotihuacan history because it was carried out at the center of the sacred city. I have previously suggested that this was part of a long-term state program in which a specific world view related to calendar systems was given material form in the city layout, monumental buildings, sculpture, and commemorative burials (Sugiyama 1993). Human sacrifice appears to have contributed to animation of the monument and to an invocation of certain supernatural forces. It was probably an important element in the dramatization of a myth describing the creation of a new era (López et al. 1991; Sugiyama 1995). Although these commemorative public works at the Ciudadela may represent a substantial morphological change from the earlier structures for the celebration of a new "world" in time and space, there may also have been a cultural continuity attached to the spot.

The later, first partial modification of the staircase of the FSP does not suggest a shift in the original plan of the pyramid, since the staircase was then reconstructed by covering the surface of the repaired walls with stucco, as they had been originally. At least, there was no intent to change the iconography of the pyramid, as shell motifs drawn on the repaired side walls of the staircase fit well into the original cosmological program of the pyramid. The modification may instead have been motivated by a plan to add another burial below the staircase. If so, the breakage and repair of the staircase may have been for burying someone who died after the completion of the pyramid, someone significantly different from those buried during its construction, as the location and grave form suggest. The analogy with tombs found below the staircase of Teotihuacan-style structures in Kaminaljuyú (Kidder et al. 1946) seems to support the interpretation that people of high social rank were buried below staircases of prominent buildings. If the modification of the stairway was not for burying an elite individual, it may have been caused by another looting episode directed at a burial interred during the pyramid construction. These propositions should be tested by careful excavation in the future.

The third construction stage is represented by the Adosada. The covering of the west façade of the pyramid by the Adosada, which bore murals with new types of motifs, has been pointed out as an indication of a ritual change and political shift from despotic to collective rulership (Cowgill n.d.; Millon 1988, 1992; Pasztory 1992). This argument appears to have been based mainly on a pronounced shift in architecture and artistic expression in the city at the approximate time of the Adosada construction. This proposition should be tested with detailed information from the Ciudadela, as discussed below.

It is probable that at the time of the Adosada construction, other acts of profanation took place, as previously mentioned. Although these desecrating actions cannot precisely be dated by archaeological data, the construction of the Adosada, the demolition and burning of the old temple, the looting of the burial to the west outside the pyramid, perhaps the looting of two burials inside the pyramid by the looters' tunnel, and the defacement of the supernatural forces represented on the façades all seem to make sense as events of the same desecration program or process. C14 analysis of the samples obtained in the Adosada also provides data supporting this assertion. Two carbon samples taken from the construction fill near the upper level of the Adosada—the place where the previously mentioned fragments of burned clay from the temple were found—yield calibrated dates of A.D. 134 (65–250) and 385 (265–414), while another from the same construction fill at the lowest platform of the Adosada (Pit 4) indicates A.D. 343 (238–421). This may mean that the first was from the wood of the original fill of the FSP and that the others were from wood introduced for the Adosada construction. The two fourth-century dates are consistent with the argument that the Adosada was approximately contemporaneous with the beginning of the looters' tunnel, which also dates to the fourth century. If so, demolition of the temple itself also makes sense as part of this termination program.

If the temple was indeed demolished as part of a termination program, what are the implications of this finding? That some sculptures on the other three sides may have been defaced intentionally and painted intermittently with stucco and red paint suggests ritual destruction. In Mesoamerican cultural tradition, monuments were often animated through dedication rituals, caches, and human sacrifices, and then finally terminated ritually. Freidel and Schele (1989:237–241) discuss defacement of mask façades of Structure 5C-2nd at Cerros, Belize—perhaps analogous to the case of the FSP at Teotihuacan—as evidence for termination ritual. The façades were deliberately and systematically defaced and were carefully covered with the construction fill of a new building. Different kinds of dedication programs also took place with this new phase of construction, as if actions of destruction and creation were conceptually connected. The case of the Adosada program in Teotihuacan is also somewhat analogous to the mutilation of Olmec monuments that Grove (1981) interpreted as repositories of supernatural powers. The mutilation at the FSP might have been intended to eliminate the danger to society of uncontrolled supernatural powers of the feathered serpent, or it may have signified the end of a meaningful cycle that had begun with the erection of the FSP. If the interpretation of the pyramid as a dedication to the creation of a new era is correct (Coe 1981:167–68; López et al. 1991; Millon 1981:230–33), the termination of a period, represented by a deity or deified ruler, would be more likely in terms of ritual significance.

However, in the case of the FSP, the acts of destruction were far more extreme. This is reminiscent of the way in which, during Postclassic times in the Mexican Highlands, the act of burning temples was depicted in ethnohistorical documents and codices as a symbol of conquest (e.g., *Códice Mendocino* 1979). That the FSP was almost certainly demolished with intense firing, probably at the same time as the obscuring of its front by the Adosada, also seems to indicate a strong opposition to the preceding symbolic manifestation, if not a consequence of actual political confrontation. In addition, the large pit west of the staircase was looted just before the Adosada was constructed. The pyramid itself was probably desecrated at the same time by the looters' tunnel that disturbed two multiple burials near the center of the pyramid. In fact, this looting must have destroyed at least one part of the façade of sculptured stones at the tunnel entrance near the southeast corner of the pyramid, and we know that the tunnel was open at least until the eighth century without the repair of the broken part. Although the initial dismantling of the stone blocks cannot be dated precisely, it could have begun at this early time. Based on these data, we may assert that the covering of the principal façade did not simply reflect modification or change of the existing religious forms, but rather was part of the excessively destructive activities at the monument that terminated the original ritual meanings, probably for political ends, during the florescence of the city.

Archaeological records hardly provide comprehensive explanations of who carried out these acts of destruction and looting, and why. However, the data about how the destruction was carried out seem to give some clues. The looting of the inner burials by means of the tunnel was committed because the looters evidently knew that the burials were there. The fact that the looting began only one or two centuries at most after the construction of the pyramid is consistent with this. However, they probably did not know precisely where the burials were. Except for one in front of the staircase, they did not loot any of the easily accessed, exterior burials whose offerings were just below the floors outside the pyramid. They hit two burials near the center in the pyramid, but they failed to reach the outermost graves and the central burial with extremely rich offerings that we found intact. Moreover, the tunnel branches toward the north, west, and south that were made after the looting of the two burials indicate that the looters looked for more burials without success. All these data suggest that the looters were not acquainted with the precise locations of the burials. This does not necessarily mean that the looters were outsiders, but it may imply a significant difference between the people who constructed the FSP and executed the mass sacrifice and those who committed the desecration.

An alternative, though less likely, explanation derives from the possibility that the first looting was aimed specifically at the two burials that were actually reached (Burials 12 and 13). First, the looters' tunnel runs from the southeast corner to the center diagonally instead of by the shortest way, starting from the middle point of the south, north, or east façade. This gives the impression that the looters may have known that there were multiple burials of sacrificed warriors on the axis lines of the pyramid and may have intentionally avoided hitting them. Second, the looters' tunnel heading to the northwest deviated slightly to the south, so that the looters did not get to the central burial (no. 14) but instead directly reached the two burial pits. If the looters did not know exactly where the burials were, they were lucky to reach them so precisely (map 13.1). They might even have avoided hitting the central one, which contained the bodies of sacrificed priest/warriors, if they had in mind looting others—especially Burial 13, which Cowgill (1992:106) and Millon (1992:396) think may have contained the body of a ruler. This alternative explanation depends on whether Burial 13 actually contained the body of a ruler. However, the two looted burials were too stripped to allow for a comprehensive reconstruction of the original contents, and as a result these conjectures cannot be confirmed.

At any rate, the repeated looting episodes at one of the central places of the city also suggest that the looting was not likely to have been just sporadic and individualistic actions for procurement of objects, as the word *looting* suggests in a modern sense. It seems to have been a part of institutionally organized "legal" actions, combined with other official dedication and termination programs. In fact, as described below, the Ciudadela was apparently functioning with the Adosada as a meaningful sacred space during the Xolalpan and Metepec phases, when the looting activities took place on an occasional basis. Further, the looters not only took offerings, they also disturbed skeletons and took bones of buried people out of the tunnel. These data suggest that the acts of destruction had, in ritual form, particular sociopolitical significance.

My proposition of an excessive termination program may be supported by the fact that there is no archaeological evidence of a new structure replacing the FSP when the Adosada covered the west façade of the monument. This would not have been unusual if the Adosada was just an added structure for the FSP, and if the FSP remained continuously in use as the principal pyramid after the Adosada construction. However, we now have evidence indicating that the FSP was excessively destroyed, desecrated, and looted as the Adosada was added to it. Then, we might expect that a new construction with a new temple would have been built at that time over this desecrated pyramid. However, stratigraphic data around the pyramid demonstrate that the Adosada was standing, meaningfully by itself, in front of the ritually destroyed FSP.

Although the FSP was ritually terminated, residential areas adjoining it seem to have continued in use. Architectural data and ceramic analysis indicate that a fairly complete modification program was carried out at the North and South Palaces (1-D and E: N1E1, Millon et al. 1973) during the Early Tlamimilolpa phase (third century A.D.: Cowgill 1983:328–29, 336; Millon 1992:364, 370), probably several decades after the completion of the FSP. The grid layout, the orientation, the types of materials used, and other architectural features in the modified complex basically followed those of the earlier one. There are even data that suggest later enlargement of the "palace" units and possible increase of the population in the Ciudadela as this modification was carried out (Cabrera et al. 1982a). The termination program represented by the Adosada was likely executed just after, if not at the same time as, this modification program of the residences, probably in the fourth century.

During the following Xolalpan and Metepec phases (A.D. 400–750; Millon 1992:402), there was no major rebuilding or significant alteration of the residential complex (Cowgill 1983:328–29). A small amount of modification made in these later periods shows continuity in previous space management and architectural style, suggesting that people later occupying the palace compounds were cultural descendants of the earlier residents. Millon (1988:113), Cowgill (1983:337), and others consider a period from Late Tlamimilolpa to Xolalpan (A.D. 350–600) as the time when the Teotihuacan state was most established and influential throughout Mesoamerica. How are we to reconcile the continuous use of the palaces as a politico-religious center with the symbolic destruction of the principal monument in the Ciudadela?

Millon has suggested that in relation to this modification, the ruling group later moved their residence outside the Ciudadela, returning there only on state occasions for ceremonial and ritual activities (Cowgill 1983:337).

Alternatively, Cowgill (1983:337) has proposed that political management activities of the government may have shifted away from the Ciudadela to the "Street of the Dead Complex" and that the nominal head of state continued to reside in the Ciudadela palaces for his ritual activities. The destruction in question might have been caused by these postulated changes in administrative forms within the continuing government, but the data described previously suggest more strongly that the ritual termination program of the pyramid was indicative of political discord or even replacement of rulership among sectors competing for political hegemony, and that the Ciudadela was then devalued, though not abandoned. The FSP may afterward have become a symbol of the termination and one of the principal symbolic objects for the legitimacy of a replacement priesthood and rulership during the following periods. In fact, militaristic aspects can be widely recognized in iconography, both in Teotihuacan and outside, after the termination program at the Ciudadela in the fourth century (see Millon 1988:146–49). The changing ritual meanings and political function of the Ciudadela are also suggested by a radical decrease of Xolalpan and Metepec sherds in the collections of the Teotihuacan Mapping Project from the surface of the Ciudadela (table 13.1). It has been argued that the small percentages of sherds in this later period indicate that the Ciudadela was kept in good repair, with no major rebuilding and no significant alterations for about 350 years (e.g., Cowgill 1983:327–28). However, this may indicate instead fewer activities with less political importance for the Ciudadela during this later period of the city.

A somewhat analogous case, evidently in a different sociopolitical situation, can be seen at the principal pyramid of Tlatelolco.[7] An archaeologist would have considered Tlatelolco as a sector of Mexica society if written records had not been left. According to the chronicles (e.g., Durán 1967:2:264–65), the pyramid was destroyed and looted after the defeat by the Tenochca Mexica in 1473 during the reign of Axayacatl. The statue of Huitzilopochtli was removed from the temple, and the pyramid became a "privy and dung heap" for the Mexicas until Motecuhzoma II permitted rebuilding of the temple (Durán 1967:2:264, 420). In other words, the major pyramid at another sacred precinct adjacent to Tenochtitlán and within a living city was destroyed intentionally during the period of strong expansion of the Aztec kingdom. Umberger (1987b) believes that this was the time when the victory in the war was reflected metaphorically in symbolic settings at the Aztec Templo Mayor that reaffirmed the political legitimacy of the Mexicas. This type of political conflict among various sectors of a polity, together with manipulation of symbolic monuments and the looting of ritual objects by a new or ascendant leading group, might have happened in the Teotihuacan state, which is supposed to have had a multi-ethnic population at that time.

We cannot easily assert where the ruling groups resided in the later period. My study (Sugiyama 1993) of the city layout and architecture shows that the monumental buildings were concentrated in the northern part of the city between the Moon Pyramid and the Río San Juan along the Avenue of the Dead, with the Sun Pyramid at the center. Cowgill (personal communication 1993) points out that there is generally a higher proportion of Metepec ceramics in surface collections in most parts of the ceremonial core, except for the Ciudadela, than in other parts of the city. This finding may indicate that the functioning political centers were likely located north of the Río San Juan along the Avenue of the Dead. However, precise reconstruction of intrasite spatial relations among competing sectors requires detailed examination of much broader data from the rest of the city. The termination at the FSP simply suggests the existence of political conflict executed in ritual fashion in the fourth century.

The changing meanings and functions of symbols attached to the terminated monument evidently continued as a legacy for later rulership, after the collapse of the state's bureaucratic apparatus. Teotihuacan remained a meaningful religious center and the "official" place to search for (that is, loot) the legacy of rulership, especially for Mexicas who needed legitimization of their reign in the late Postclassic period (e.g., Carrasco 1981; López 1989; Umberger 1987a). This essay suggests that these types of changing function and ritual meanings of the FSP may have begun as early as the fourth century during the middle of the city's history.

The last stage of the extensive destruction has not been clearly defined in terms of an absolute date, as discussed above. This strongly limits the discussion of the sociopolitical implications of the termination programs. The nearer in time the Adosada profanation programs were to the final abandonment of the city, the more should the two events—the Adosada termination program and the final collapse of the Ciudadela—be viewed as facets of the same sociopolitical process. It is clear that even if the collapse of the city occurred earlier than Millon and others think, the palaces at the Ciudadela lasted at least a century longer, and probably more, than the FSP itself did. This seems to me evidence that the original ritual meanings were short-lived and related to sociopolitical conditions. More chronological information of different types, accurate stratigraphic records, and refinement of the Teotihuacan ceramic chronology are needed to clarify the questions raised in this essay.

ACKNOWLEDGMENTS

This chapter integrates data of the C14 analysis of the samples that I collected in PAT80–82 and PTQ88–89. I am thankful to the coordinators of the project, Rubén Cabrera C. and George Cowgill, for permission to use them here. A brief version of this essay was read at the 58th Annual Meeting of the Society for American Archaeology in St. Louis, Missouri, in April 1993. The final version was completed in 1995. I am grateful to George Cowgill, Emily Umberger, Barbara Stark, Debra Nagao, and Ian Robertson for their valuable comments and editorial suggestions on this paper. Although the essay benefited from their comments, I take full responsibility for the interpretations. I also thank Shirley Mock, who invited me to join in this volume and made helpful suggestions.

NOTES

1. The extensive excavation at the Ciudadela in the early 1980s was carried out by the Proyecto Arqueológico Teotihuacán 1980–1982 (cited hereafter as PAT80–82), directed by Rubén Cabrera (Cabrera et al. 1982a 1982b, 1991) of the Instituto Nacional de Antropología e Historia of Mexico (INAH). I supervised the excavation of the FSP in 1982 (Cabrera and Sugiyama 1982) and again in 1983–1984 (Sugiyama 1985, 1989, 1991). After the discovery of three burials on the south side of the pyramid, Cabrera, George Cowgill, and I formed a new project, the Proyecto Templo de Quetzalcoatl 1988–1989 (cited hereafter as PTQ88–89), to explore the monument intensively. The project was funded by the National Geographic Society, the National Endowment for the Humanities, the Arizona State University Foundation, and other resources, and permission was generously granted by the Consejo de Arqueología of INAH for both field seasons in 1988 and 1989.

2. The symbolism of the sacrificial burials at the FSP was evidently encoded in a complicated presentation of

different kinds of materials. Analyses and interpretations of burial patterns and symbolic offerings are included in Sugiyama 1995.

3. George Cowgill (personal communication 1993) argues that test excavations by the Teotihuacan Mapping Project along the Avenue of the Dead repeatedly show that the last construction stages were built during the Metepec ceramic phase (A.D. 650–750, according to Millon 1992:402).

4. Archaeomagnetic dating provides two alternative periods. The dates mentioned in the text are later periods indicated by the three samples. Earlier ones, which Wolfman thinks do not correspond to the time of actual buring, are A.D. 285–330, 295–325, and 285–310, respectively.

5. The list does not include the results of C14 analyses of five samples obtained by the excavations of Cabrera and Cid on the east side of the FSP.

6. One sample (no. 37) found on the surface of the floor of the looters' tunnel dates to modern times. This unburned wood fragment seems to have fallen from the modern layer near the present pyramid surface into the looters' tunnel through a large, deep, empty posthole, below which the sample was collected.

7. Emily Umberger (1996:256) kindly reminded me of the case of the desecration at the Tlatelolco pyramid. Interestingly in contrast to the case of the FSP at Teotihuacan, only "natural accumulations" that Umberger interprets as evidence of abandonment after this civil war were found archaeologically at the pyramid.

REFERENCES CITED

Bernal, Ignacio
1965   "Teotihuacán: Nuevas fechas de radiocarbono y su posible significado." *Anales de Antropología* 2:27–35.

Cabrera C., Ruben, Ignacio Rodríguez G., and Noel Morelos G., coordinators
1982a   *Memoria del Proyecto Arqueológico Teotihuacán 80–82, Volumen 1.* Colección científica 132. Mexico City: Instituto Nacional de Antropología e Historia.
1982b   *Teotihuacán 80–82: Primeros resultados.* Mexico City: Instituto Nacional de Antropología e Historia.
1991   *Teotihuacán 1980–1982: Nuevas interpretaciones.* Mexico City: Instituto Nacional de Antropología e Historia.

Cabrera C., Ruben, and Saburo Sugiyama
1982   "La reexploración y restauración del Templo Viejo de Quetzalcóatl." In *Memoria del Proyecto Arqueológico Teotihuacán 80–82,* coordinated by Ruben Cabrera C., Ignacio Rodríguez G., and Noel Morelos G., 163–83. Mexico City: Instituto Nacional de Antropología e Historia.

Cabrera C., Ruben, Saburo Sugiyama, and Gorge L. Cowgill
1991   "The Templo de Quetzalcoatl Project at Teotihuacán: A Preliminary Report." *Ancient Mesoamerica* 2:77–92.

Carrasco, Davíd
1981   *Quetzalcoatl and the Irony of Empire: Myths and Prophecies in the Aztec Tradition.* Chicago: University of Chicago Press.

Códice Mendocino
1979   Facsimile edition by Francisco del Paso y Troncoso. Mexico City: Editorial Cosmos.

Coe, Michael D.
1981   "Religion and the Rise of Mesoamerican States." In *The Transition to Statehood in the New World,* edited by Grant D. Jones and Robert R. Kautz, 157–171. Cambridge, England: Cambridge University Press.

Cowgill, George L.
1983   "Rulership and the Ciudadela: Political Inferences from Teotihuacán Architecture." In *Civilization in the Ancient Americas: Essays in Honor of Gordon R. Willey,* edited by Richard M. Leventhal and Alan L. Kolata, 313–43. Albuquerque: University of New Mexico Press and Peabody Museum of Harvard University.
1992   "Toward a Political History of Teotihuacán." In *Ideology and Pre-Columbian Civilizations,* edited by Arthur A. Demarest and Geoffrey W. Conrad, 87–114. Santa Fe, N.M.: School of American Research Press.
n.d.   "Symbolic and Material Aspects of Teotihuacán War." In *Socioeconomic Perspectives on Ancient Teotihuacán,* edited by James Sheehy. Boulder: University Press of Colorado. In press.

Cowgill, George L., and Mercedes O. Cabrera C.
1991   "Excavaciones en el Frente B y otros materiales del análisis de la cerámica." *Arqueología* 6:41–52.

Durán, Diego
1967   *Historia de las Indias de Nueva España e islas de la tierra firme, Tomo 2.* Mexico City: Editorial Porrua.

Freidel, David A., and Linda Schele
1989   "Dead Kings and Living Temples: Dedication

and Termination Rituals among the Ancient Maya." In *Word and Image in Maya Culture: Explorations in Language, Writing, and Representation,* edited by William F. Hanks and Don S. Rice, 233–43. Salt Lake City: University of Utah Press.

Grove, David

1981 "Olmec Monuments: Mutilation as a Clue to Meaning." In *The Olmec and Their Neighbors,* edited by Elizabeth P. Benson, 49–68. Washington, D.C.: Dumbarton Oaks.

Jarquín P., Ana M., and Enrique Martínez V.

1982 "Las excavaciones en el Conjunto 1D." In *Memoria del Proyecto Arqueológico Teotihuacán 80–82, Vol. 1,* coordinated by Rubén Cabrera C., Ignacio Rodríguez G., and Noel Morelos G., 89–126. Mexico City: Instituto Nacional de Antropología e Historia.

Kidder, Alfred V., Jesse D. Jennings, and Edwin M. Shook

1946 *Excavations at Kaminaljuyu, Guatemala.* Carnegie Institution of Washington Publication 561. Washington, D.C.: Carnegie Institution of Washington.

López A., Alfred, Leonardo López L., and Saburo Sugiyama

1991 "The Temple of Quetzalcoatl at Teotihuacán: Its Possible Ideological Significance." *Ancient Mesoamerica* 2:93–105.

López L., Leonardo

1989 *La recuperación mexica del pasado teotihuacano.* Mexico City: Instituto Nacional de Antropología e Historia.

Marquina, Ignacio

1979 [1922] "Arquitectura y Escultura, Primera parte: Arquitectura." In *La Población del Valle de Teotihuacán,* edited by Manuel Gamio, 5 vols., 2:99–164. Mexico City: Instituto Nacional Indigenista. Original edition in 3 vols., 1922. Mexico City: Secretaría de Agricultura y Fomento, Dirección de Antropología.

Millon, René

1973 *Urbanization at Teotihuacán, Mexico, Vol. 1: The Teotihuacán Map, Part 1: Text.* Austin: University of Texas Press.

1981 "Teotihuacán: City, State, and Civilization." In *Supplement to the Handbook of Middle American Indians, Vol. 1: Archaeology,* edited by Victoria Bricker and Jeremy A. Sabloff, 198–243. Austin: University of Texas Press.

1988 "The Last Years of Teotihuacán Dominance." In *The Collapse of Ancient States and Civilizations,* edited by Norman Yoffee and George L. Cowgill, 102–64. Tucson: University of Arizona Press.

1992 "Teotihuacán Studies: From 1950 to 1990 and Beyond." In *Art, Ideology, and the City of Teotihuacán,* edited by Janet C. Berlo, 339–429. Washington, D.C.: Dumbarton Oaks.

Millon, René, R. Bruce Drewitt, and George L. Cowgill

1973 *Urbanization at Teotihuacán, Mexico, Vol. 1: The Teotihuacán Map, Part 2: Maps.* Austin: University of Texas Press.

Pasztory, Esther

1992 "Abstraction and the Rise of a Utopian State at Teotihuacán." In *Art, Ideology, and the City of Teotihuacán,* edited by Janet C. Berlo, 281–316. Washington, D.C.: Dumbarton Oaks.

Rattray, Evelyn C.

1981 "The Teotihuacán Ceramic Chronology: Early Tzacualli to Metepec Phases." MS on file with George Cowgill.

1991 "Radiocarbon Dates for Teotihuacán." *Arqueología* 6:3–15.

Sugiyama, Saburo

1988 "Nuevos datos arqueológicos sobre el Templo de Quetzalcóatl en la Ciudadela de Teotihuacán y algunas consideraciones hipotéticas." In *XLV Congreso Internacional de Americanistas: Arqueología de las Américas,* compiled by Elizabeth Reichel D., 405–429. Bogotá: Banco Popular, Fondo de Promoción de la Cultura.

1989 "Burials Dedicated to the Old Temple of Quetzalcoatl at Teotihuacán, Mexico." *American Antiquity* 54(1):85–106.

1991 "Descubrimientos de entierros y ofrendas dedicadas al Templo Viejo de Quetzalcóatl." In *Teotihuacán 1980–1982: Nuevas interpretaciones,* coordinated by Ruben Cabrera C., Ignacio Rodriguez G., and Noel Morelos G., 275–326. Mexico City: Instituto Nacional de Antropología e Historia.

1993 "Worldview Materialized in Teotihuacán, Mexico." *Latin American Antiquity* 4(2):103–29.

1995 "Mass-Human Sacrifices and Symbolism of the Feathered Serpent Pyramid in Teotihuacán, Mexico." Ph.D. diss., Arizona State University.

Umberger, Emily

1987a "Antiques, Revivals, and References to the Past in Aztec Art." *Res: Anthropology and Aesthetics* 13:63–105.

1987b "Events Commemorated by Date Plaques at the Templo Mayor: Further Thoughts on the Solar Metaphor." In *The Aztec Templo Mayor,* edited by Elizabeth H. Boone, 411–50. Washington, D.C.: Dumbarton Oaks.

1996   "Appendix 3: Material Remains in the Central Provinces, Assembled by Emily Umberger." In *Aztec Imperial Strategies*, edited by Frances F. Berdan, Richard E. Blanton, Mary G. Hodge, Michael E. Smith, and Emily Umberger, 247–64. Washington, D.C.: Dumbarton Oaks.

Wolfman, Daniel

1990   "Mesoamerican Chronology and Archaeomagnetic Dating 1–1200." In *Archaeomagnetic Dating*, edited by Jeffrey L. Eighmy and Robert S. Sternberg, 261–391. Austin: University of Texas Press.

CHAPTER FOURTEEN

The Writing on the Wall

Political Representation and Sacred Geography at Monte Alban

Marilyn A. Masson
State University of New York (SUNY)
Albany, New York

Heather Orr
Western State College of Colorado
Gunnison, Colorado

ASPECTS OF PARALLEL INTERREGIONAL INSTITUTIONS of Mesoamerican state shamanism are reflected in monuments of dedication at Monte Alban. Zapotec dedication ceremonies involved the public display of rulers in shamanic *nahual* transformation (that is, in the form of animal spirit companions) as part of the commemoration of significant events of war or of a calendrical nature. Additional dedication events incorporated monuments that portray captive-taking and human sacrifice. These sacrificial monuments were used in a cyclical manner to create sacred geography. The cyclical reuse of such monuments, primarily danzantes slabs, reinforced expressions of the power of the Monte Alban state and its links to the past.

The association of carved monuments with building dedication is generally observed throughout the archaeology of Mesoamerica, though interpretations of the meaning of this association depend on historical information. Recent research in Maya historical texts provides valuable descriptions of rituals of dedication and their meaning. Rituals associated with building dedication at Monte Alban can be reconstructed through the use of analogies with Zapotec ethnographic and ethnohistoric records and through comparisons to the Maya area. Such comparisons help illuminate the nature and intended meaning of building dedication rituals at Monte Alban.

A major problem in interpreting the dedication of carved monuments is their mobility and changing contexts in the archaeological record. As objects of accumulated sanctity and power, carved monuments were often reused and moved from their original location, as observed in the burial and "rededication" of monuments described in this chapter. Results of analyses by Urcid (1992) suggest that the carved monuments along the frontal façade of the South Platform at Monte Alban, the location of the majority of historical monuments from this site, are represented in secondary or even tertiary contexts.

The use of carved monuments in building dedication must thus be considered from both primary and secondary contextual positions. Monuments dedicated initially in primary contexts appear to have commemorated historical events. Carved monoliths were later used in secondary dedication contexts for the purpose of empowering and sanctifying architectural works in the creation of sacred geography. Making such a distinction does not imply that historical programs were not regarded as sacred, for they almost certainly were. Nor were secondary uses ahistorical. In secondary contexts, however, the iconographic and epigraphic content of the monument does not represent events that directly refer to the latest deposition of the monuments.

Fig. 14.1. *Nahual* transformation in warfare and capture at Monte Alban: (a) feline-clad ruler seated on a throne (Stela 1); (b) captive taken in feline form (Stela 2); and (c) an additional captive in the form of another animal (Stela 3). Other associated captives with these stelae recovered from the South Platform were portrayed in human form. (Redrawn from Caso 1928:fig. 58)

NAHUALISM AT MONTE ALBAN

The beliefs in animal transformation, tiered worlds, and the ability to pass among these worlds during trance states of magical flight or while sleeping represent fundamental traits of New World shamanism found throughout the Americas (Chang 1989; Furst 1976). Shamanism may have entered the New World with the peoples who crossed over the Bering Strait, resulting in the development of structural parallels among many Native American religions. Evidence for the early existence of this practice may be found in figurines of Early Formative villages in Mesoamerica, as Clark (1991) suggests for Paso de la Amada at 1600 B.C. Furst (1968) identified evidence of shamanic jaguar transformation in Olmec were-jaguar iconography by analogy to South American and Mesoamerican beliefs and shamanic experiences. The state-level practice of this template of New World cosmology has been documented among the pre-Columbian Maya (Freidel, Schele, and Parker 1993) and Olmec (Reilly 1994), and by analogy is present in various forms in religious programs throughout Mesoamerica.

The best documented dedication assemblage at Monte Alban was found at the South Platform, where carved monoliths, cache-filled boxes, and heirloom vessels were recovered from the structure's corners (Acosta 1959).

Acts of warfare, sacrifice, and calendrical commemoration have been previously recognized on monuments found at the base of the South Platform (Caso 1928; Marcus 1976, 1980). Several characters on the South Platform stelae are portrayed in animal form (fig. 4.1), which suggests that rituals of *nahual* transformation represented a significant ingredient of such dedication events. Public performance of nahualism is prevalent in the pre-Columbian art and ethnohistoric records of the Zapotec and other Mesoamerican cultures (Chang 1989; Foster 1944; Furst 1976; Reilly 1989). The actors depicted on these South Platform monuments were engaged in acts of warfare while transformed into their *nahual,* a consistent theme in Mesoamerican political art.

An alternative explanation proposes that these representations are of individuals wearing the costumes of their warrior orders (Spencer 1982:239–45). Although compatible with the psychological and spiritual advantage of transforming into one's *nahual* for battle, this interpretation is hard to verify due to the individualistic nature of Zapotec art. No extensive scenes are shown of warriors clad alike that might imply the existence of orders.

Nahual transformation—the interpretation adhered to in this examination—formed an integral part of dedication ceremonies that commemorated the passage of calendric time and architectural construction. The capacity to transform into one's animal supernatural demonstrated the spiritual powers of Monte Alban leaders and warriors, as did the capacity to capture and conquer the *nahual* of one's opponent. Public display of such shamanic prowess was probably critical in legitimizing claims of rulers of Monte Alban and elsewhere in Zapotec-speaking Oaxaca. The role of effective shamanic practice in legitimizing political position is now evident for rulers throughout the Maya historic record (Freidel, Schele, and Parker 1993). The propagandistic nature of Mesoamerican religious art is prevalent and consistent in Aztec, Maya, and Zapotec programs (Demarest 1992; Marcus 1993).

The representation of Zapotec political leaders in their animal companion forms thus tended to emphasize their capacity to interact with the supernatural realm. While many pre-Columbian Mesoamerican cultures appear to have shared a belief in the existence of animal soul companions, public displays of animal transformation are more common in Monte Alban Zapotec programs of politico-religious art than at Teotihuacan or in Classic Maya art. The depiction of rulers in animal (primarily feline) form (Caso and Bernal 1952) represents a particularly Zapotec strategy.

WARFARE MONUMENTS AND
FELINE TRANSFORMATION AT MONTE ALBAN

Ritual animal transformation appears to be the dominant theme in Zapotec carved monuments that commemorate historical events in dedication. South Platform stelae at Monte Alban show a ruler (fig. 4.1a) and a bound captive (fig. 4.1b) in feline form (Stelae 1 and 2 respectively [Caso 1928]). On Stela 3 an additional captive is shown as an opossum-like animal (fig. 4.1c). It is clear that animal transformation in the stelae of this program takes place in the context of warfare (Marcus 1976). The capture of human war captives (Stelae 5–8) as well as apparent *nahuales* of captives (Stelae 2 and 3) further testifies to the military accomplishment of the captor. This individual has been identified as a probable ruler (fig. 4.1a), with a day name of 13F, by Javier Urcid (1992:310), who believes that these monuments were moved to the South Platform from their original context.

Nahualism becomes significant in the context of building dedication in two ways. First, it demonstrated the ritual prowess of the ruler. This shamanistic expres-

Fig. 14.2. Monte Alban Stela 11, from North Platform, showing a figure in feline costume/transformation gesturing with a fish in hand. This monument is not clearly associated with warfare but portrays the individual in feline form. (Redrawn from Caso 1928:fig. 58)

sion of power is traced back to Olmec times (Coe 1962; Reilly 1989). Second, the portrayal of rulers in animal transformation probably signified that they were acting in the supernatural realm and were able to exert influence in this realm on behalf of the living.

FELINE TRANSFORMATION IN
CONTEXTS OTHER THAN WARFARE

Elsewhere at Monte Alban, feline-clad rulers are clearly shown in events that may not be related to warfare. Specifically, Stela 11 (fig. 14.2) from the North Platform (Caso 1928:fig. 58), the Lapida de Bazan (Caso 1938), and the stone from Mound II (Caso 1965:fig. 17) all show feline-clad actors performing rituals such as scattering (Mound II stone) or conjuring (Stela 11). Until verbs can be identified in the texts found on these monuments, the specific acts will remain unknown, but it is likely that these rituals were performed on dates marking significant calendrical passages, as found throughout the Maya area.

Feline transformation is also displayed on monuments outside of Monte Alban, often in funerary context. Examples in funerary context are noted at Dainzu (Bernal 1968) and in the upright-walking felines on the Reyes Etla doorjambs (now in the Museo Regional de Oaxaca,

Fig. 14.3.   Ceramic effigy illustrating a figure moving in feline transformation. (Drawn from Boos 1966:fig. 272)

Fig. 14.4.   Stela from Cerro del Rey, Oaxaca coast. This stela vividly illustrates the concept of a feline double soul and transformation. (Redrawn from Jorrin 1974:fig. 4)

Oaxaca City). Tomb friezes at the same museum that are thought to come from the floor of the Valley of Oaxaca show prowling felines with name glyphs. Anthropomorphic felines frequently portrayed in Zapotec effigy ceramics also depict humans in their animal soul form (Boos 1966; Caso and Bernal 1952). Figure 14.3 shows one such ceramic effigy (from Boos 1966:fig. 272), in which a human wearing a feline skin is poised on all fours, clearly in transformation. These effigies are most often recovered from funerary context (Caso and Bernal 1952). The funerary contexts suggest that dedication events were not the only occasion for the depiction of powerful individuals in feline transformations. It may be significant that contexts for the display of transformed humans are generally funerary outside of the regional capital of Monte Alban, although this pattern may be temporal rather than spatial. Many of the funerary monuments from the valley floor are poorly dated, making this determination problematic. However, the absence of large-scale public scenes of transformed rulers outside of Monte Alban is a probable testimony to a prerogative of representation that was confined to this central site at the height of its power.

Feline representation is also found on monuments from the Oaxaca coast, where stelae from the sites of Cerro del Rey (fig. 14.4) and Rio Grande blatantly depict men in feline transformation (Jorrin 1974:figs. 4 and 5). These coastal monuments were publicly displayed and may have been part of a dedication ceremony.

THE FELINE AS AN EMBODIMENT OF PLACE

It has been proposed that Formative Period feline ceramic motifs have associations with the earth, fissures within it, or the earth's surface (Marcus 1989:172–73). At the height of the Monte Alban state, felines may have served as powerful symbols of territory and lineage ownership of property. Ethnohistoric records refer to Monte Alban as "the hill of the jaguar" (or "hill of twenty jaguars" [Cruz 1946; Marcus 1980:58]). Perhaps significant as a dedicatory affirmation of this relationship is the interment of the giant feline urn reported in the plaza of Monte Alban (Caso and Bernal 1952). Patron deities may also have existed for Maya cities (Schele and Miller 1986). For example, a giant jaguar spirit looms over Ah Cacaw on Lintel 3 of Tikal, specifically in the context of a dedication ceremony (Schele and Freidel 1990:211; Schele and Miller 1986:287).

ETHNOGRAPHIC ACCOUNTS OF NAHUALISM OR TONALISM IN OAXACA

Ethnographic accounts of nahualism are documented throughout Oaxaca. At least one confession of a belief in an animal companion is noted in Burgoa's account (1934 [1674]:356). Alcina Franch (1970–1971) documents four cases in seventeenth-century records from the Archivo General de Indias de Sevilla, in which individuals transformed themselves into natural forces or animals. According to Alcina Franch (1970–1971:26) this power was possessed only by certain individuals, who were not taught it but rather inherited it by birth. The belief in *tonales* (animal companions) is reported in ethnographic works at Yalalag by De la Fuente (1949) and at Ixtepeji by Kearney (1972:51–53). In piecing together references to beliefs in *nahuales* at Mitla, Parsons suggested that transformation was formerly associated with the office of shaman among the prehispanic Zapotec (Parsons 1936:225–27). In Juchitan it is believed that the "ancient ones" *(binigulaaza)* are capable of transforming themselves into animals, according to Hernestrosa (1977:12–13). Transformed *binigulaaza* in this case are referred to as *dobles* or *guenda* (Hernestrosa 1977:13). In addition to the term *guenda*, Cruz (1935:119) notes that the words *quella* and *guela* also refer to *nahual*. Kaplan (1956:364) reported, among villages in the Mixteca Costa, the belief in *sana nduii* ("this animal which you own," referred to in Spanish as *tono*). Belief in *nahuales* is also reported among the Chontal by Carrasco (1960:107–8) and among the Mixe by Walter Miller (1956:138) and Beals (1945). Thomas (n.d.) has documented extensive references to animal companion spirits in Zoque lore. In his folklore and literary surveys, Thomas has tracked the transformation of indigenous pre-Columbian beliefs in *nahuales* to expressions influenced by beliefs in witchcraft brought by Europeans.

A key theme emerges from studying the ethnographic accounts. While all individuals may have an animal soul companion, often assigned at birth (Cruz 1935:119–20; Gay 1982:67–68), the ability to transform into this animal is possessed only by certain individuals, often mystics. The monopoly of such powers probably also existed in the past, when Zapotec rulers or priests operated as mediators with the supernatural world. Current Zapotec beliefs about animal companions hold that these entities are capable of wandering about at night while their human counterparts sleep (Cruz 1935; Parsons 1936). In such guises, these spirits are capable of acts of revenge on slumbering mortals. Rulers may have cultivated fear or awe of their omniscient prowling among supporting populations. These instances of self-portraiture in feline form may thus be interpreted as construed strategies of social identity. Joyce and Winter (1996) have suggested some ways in which actor-based strategies of self-legitimization may be used to explain Zapotec representation in political dynamics.

ETHNOGRAPHIC AND PRE-COLUMBIAN EVIDENCE FOR NAHUALISM OUTSIDE OF OAXACA

Transformed individuals depicted on Monte Alban monoliths and ceramic art are often shown as large cats, opossums, and bats. Pre-Columbian Maya rulers are also depicted in animal costumes, such as the jaguar helmet being presented to Shield Jaguar at Yaxchilan Lintel 26 (Schele 1991:107; Schele and Freidel 1990:267; Schele and Miller 1986; Tate 1991) and the boots and claws worn on Dos Pilas and Aguateca monuments (Schele and Miller 1986). Maya rulers could transform into a variety of supernatural personages, not just animal soul companions (Looper 1991). In contrast to the Zapotec, the Classic period Maya rarely showed rulers in complete transformation, perhaps as a result of a preference for individual portraiture.

This contrast raises some interesting issues about Highland/Lowland differences in political strategy. Political art among Highland cultures, such as the Zapotec and Teotihuacanos, appears to have been less oriented toward the feats of individuals (Pasztory 1978). Monuments depicting important historical individuals at Monte Alban, probably the rulers, more frequently show them in feline than in human form. Such depiction in feline form facilitates the de-emphasis of the identity of the individual actor in favor of the powerful *nahual* companion shared by many Zapotec leaders.

These general observations about the existence of prehispanic nahualism, despite its variability, provide time depth to the ethnographic research of Foster (1944), who documented the prevalence of this pattern throughout living populations in Mesoamerica. Later ethnographic studies of the belief in animal soul companions *(chanuletik)* have further documented this phenomenon at the modern Maya community of Zinacantan (Vogt 1969:372) and throughout many language groups of Mesoamerica (Spero 1988).

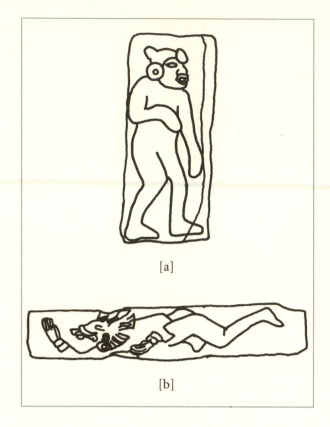

Fig. 14.5.   Monte Alban danzantes from recycled contexts in Building M (a) and South Platform (b). (Redrawn from Urcid 1991)

Linguistic data also supplement the evidence for iconographic and ethnographic beliefs in nahualism. Epi-Olmec texts translated by Justeson and Kaufman (1993) have revealed a proto-Mixezoquean term for spirit companion, *jama.* The Classic period Maya glyph *wai* is translated as a verb meaning "to sleep, to dream, to transform" or as a noun meaning "companion spirit" (Grube 1989; Houston and Stuart 1989). Studies of the context of the *wai* glyph indicate that the ability of kings to transform into spirit companions was an essential component of their right to rule (Freidel and Schele 1988; Freidel, Schele, and Parker 1993). Mediating with the supernatural was also a significant aspect of the role of Zapotec political leaders in a range of performances (Marcus 1989:154,193), and the ability to transform into one's companion spirit may be added to the list.

Captive sacrifice is another aspect of shamanistic strategy at Monte Alban, which is not always linked to the depiction of rulers in *nahual* transformation. However, the association of sacrifice with dedication makes similar political statements about the supernatural qualities of rulership and sacred geography. The danzantes slabs of Building L at Monte Alban represent one of the most impressive expressions of captive sacrifice and dedication in Mesoamerica (Coe 1962:95; Marcus 1976:126–27, 1978, 1980; Scott 1978). In the danzantes program, the captive portrait stones are positioned as stair treads, analogous to Maya captive staircases in which victims are symbolically trodden underfoot (Flannery and Marcus 1990:59; Marcus 1976:131, 1980). The carved depiction of a sacrificial victim named 1 Earthquake at San Jose Mogote may also have been placed in a position in which he was trodden upon (Marcus 1976). Captive staircases in the Maya area are documented at the sites of Palenque, Bonampak, Copan, and Yaxchilan (Freidel, Schele, and Parker 1993:350–72). Additional danzantes are present in recycled contexts at the Mound M complex (fig. 14.5a) and the South Platform (fig. 14.5b). Recycled danzantes monuments appear to have fulfilled a role similar to that of the ones placed in Building L.

Bloodletting (autosacrifice) and animal or human sacrifice are widespread in Mesoamerican ritual traditions (Cabrera, Sugiyama, and Cowgill 1991; Schele and Miller 1986; Sugiyama 1989), including those of the Zapotec, according to ethnohistoric documents (Cordova 1942; Flannery and Marcus 1976; Marcus 1976; Seler 1904:278; Spores 1965; Zeitlin 1984:68). Captive sacrifice and bloodletting in these contexts are associated with the opening of portals of communication to ancestors and supernatural beings. The act of sacrifice is an inextricable ingredient in dedication. In shamanic ritual, the act of dedication manifests sacred space in this world (Eliade 1959:45, 1963:32) or draws holiness into a building (Freidel, Schele, and Parker 1993).

The positioning of certain danzantes at Monte Alban suggests that they are specifically associated with portal passages (fig. 14.5b). Studies of danzante anatomical postures have identified individuals referred to as "swimmers or flyers" (Scott 1978), as illustrated by one recycled monument located on the South Platform (fig. 14.5b). Eliade (1964:293) reported that Eskimo shamans make motions as if they are diving when they are about to enter a trance, and that entrance into subterranean areas is conceived of as "diving and returning to the surface of the ocean." A flying position is commonly portrayed by ancestors and supernatural beings in Zapotec art. Friezes depicting ancestors at Lambityeco (Rabin 1970:figs. 3 and 5a) and the Mixtec/Zapotec Yahui/Xicani supernatural character observed at Zaachila (Gallegos 1978; Urcid 1992) and Noriega (Caso 1965) show supernatural beings in the flying position. "Flyers" emerge from cloud scrolls in the Monte Alban North Platform lintel published by Batres (1902) and a slab reported from Cerro de la Campana at Huitzo-Suchilquitongo (Miller 1992). Magical flight is the prerogative of shamans in Siberia and North America, and among the Eskimo, according to Eliade (1964:289, 477–79).

In some cultures, it is only through death that non-shamans can achieve the disincarnate condition of souls, which Eliade believed is expressed in magical flight (1964:479). Eliade further characterized shamanistic magical flight as a victorious passage from life to death and back again (1964:481). In the case of the danzantes, this passage appears to have been a one-way trip. At Building L, sacrificed danzantes slabs in primary context served to empower and activate architectural complexes in this specific and sanctified corner of the Monte Alban main plaza. Evidence suggests that recycling and rededication of danzantes and other monuments at Monte Alban was common.

PRIMARY AND SECONDARY DEDICATION AT MONTE ALBAN

Danzantes are heavily recycled in secondary contexts at Monte Alban. In some instances, this recycling is patterned and symmetrical, as in the System M complex. In this complex, danzantes slabs were used in cornerstones for the Building M temple, and they are located in the stairs and patio risers in the interior of the complex. They also make up a portion of the basal array of recycled monoliths along the front and sides of the South Platform. As cornerstones or components of basal architectural arrays, danzantes slabs were almost certainly used in the context of building dedication. Their antiquity no doubt contributed to their value as objects of power, and their meaning as sacrificial victims would easily have melded into the metaphors of dedication anew.

The outer basal façade of the South Platform was faced with an array of broken and complete danzantes slabs as well as a range of other types of carved monoliths, including the previously discussed captive stelae showing *nahual* transformation, which appear related to the feline-clad ruler 13F (Urcid 1992). Together, the assemblage exhibits little logic in composition, and Urcid (1992) believes the front of the building was probably plastered over. Not united by a historical theme, these stones are recycled from a variety of original contexts (Urcid 1992). This jumbled array demonstrates a behavioral complex of reuse of monuments in later dedication ceremonies at the site. The stelae located in the South Platform were thus placed there primarily because of their sacred status as objects of cumulative historical power, and they were probably considered to possess great *pee*. (*Pee* is the Zapotec term for animatism, the life force believed to be embodied in organic and inorganic objects [Cruz 1935:117; Flannery and Marcus 1976:76; Marcus 1983:345; Marcus and Flannery 1978:57].)

Although probably concealed from view, the iconographic themes of redeposited monuments in the South Platform may be symbolically related to the function of this area of Monte Alban. The dedicated and rededicated carved monuments in the southern buildings (South Platform, Building L, and System M) of Monte Alban have themes that are primarily related to sacrifice and warfare. In contrast, the carved monuments recovered from the North Platform lack the warfare theme and possess low frequencies of danzantes compared to the south end of the plaza (North Platform danzantes, N=7, according to Scott [1978:2:figs. E1–E7]). The north area of Monte Alban appears to have been the focus of most of the mortuary activity at the site, as previous investigators have observed (Acosta 1965; Caso 1938; Robertson 1983:135; Urcid 1991).

The mobility of carved monuments contributes to the difficulty of interpreting their role in dedication contexts. As objects of historic value and power, they were reused and moved from their original context in the archaeological record. For example, the Lapida de Bazan was recovered from a fill layer in Mound X at Monte Alban, where it was probably cached in a dedication ceremony similar to that of Stela 31 of Temple 33-2nd at Tikal (Schele and Freidel 1990:197). In practice, it is probable that a range of events were responsible for the prevalent reuse of Monte Alban monoliths in ongoing architectural dedications and creation of sacred geography at this site. These varied occasions, however, appeared to call for a piece of antiquity, and stones from the past may have helped to sanction shamanic claims to power, described in this chapter in the context of building dedication.

Public exhibition of shamanic practice through *nahual* transformation is significant in the context of building dedication at Monte Alban. The depiction of rulers in feline transformation demonstrates military and shamanic prowess in warfare on monuments at the South Platform and other structures at the site, such as Mound II and Mound X. Feline transformation in warfare is associated with taking human and *nahual* captives. Warfare has long been noted as a prominent theme of Monte Alban public art, beginning with the Building L danzantes and Mound J monuments (Marcus 1976). These themes of conquest and sacrifice appear to be associated with the dedication of buildings and the intent of rulers to exert their claims to control the supernatural world. Once created, carved monoliths became powerful cache objects, which were reused in dedication perhaps after the destruction or termination of their original context. The cycling of monuments through dedication and rededication may have fit logically into a worldview that emphasized a cyclical view of time embodied in the sacred round calendar. Although Zapotec dedication rituals are functionally and contextually analogous to those of other regions in Mesoamerica, their expression at Monte Alban shows a uniquely Oaxacan emphasis on feline transformation associated with more common interregional themes of warfare and captive sacrifice.

References Cited

Acosta, Jorge R.
1959   "Exploraciones arqueologicas en Monte Alban: XVIIIa temporada (1958)." *Revista mexicana de estudios antropologicos* 15:7–50.
1965   "Preclassic and Classic Architecture of Oaxaca." In *Handbook of Middle American Indians, Vol. 3: Archaeology of Southern Mesoamerica, Part 2,* edited by Robert Wauchope and Gordon R. Willey, 814–36. Austin: University of Texas Press.

Alcina Franch, Jose
1970–1971 "Nahuales y nahualismo en Oaxaca, siglo XVII." *Ahuano del Instituto de Antropologia e Historia, Universidad Central de Venezuela, Caracas* 7–8:23–30.

Batres, Leopoldo
1902   *Explorations of Mount Alban.* Mexico City: Inspeccion y Conservacion de Monumentos Arqueologicos de la Republica Mexicana and Gante St. Press.

Beals, Ralph L.
1945   *Ethnology of the Western Mixe.* University of California Publications in American Archaeology and Ethnology 42(1). Berkeley: University of California Press.

Bernal, Ignacio
1968   "The Ball Players of Dainzu." *Archaeology* 21(4):246–51.

Boos, Frank H.
1966   *The Ceramic Sculpture of Ancient Oaxaca.* New York: A. S. Barnes.

Burgoa, Francisco de
1934 [1674] *Geografica Descripcion.* Publicaciones del Archivo General de la Nacion 25–26. Mexico City: Talleres Graficos de la Nacion.

Cabrera Castro, Ruben, Saburo Sugiyama, and George L. Cowgill
1991   "The Templo de Quetzalcoatl Project at Teotihuacan." *Ancient Mesoamerica* 2:77–92.

Carrasco, Pedro
1960   "Pagan Rituals and Beliefs among the Chontal Indians of Oaxaca, Mexico." *Anthropological Record* 20:3.

Caso, Alfonso
1928   *Las Estelas Zapotecas.* Mexico City: Secretaria de Educacion Publica, Talleres Graficos de la Nacion.
1938   *Exploraciones en Oaxaca, quinta y sexta temporadas, 1936–1937.* Instituto Panamericano de Geografia e Historia Publicacion 34. Mexico City: Instituto Panamericano de Geografia e Historia.
1965   "Zapotec Writing and Calendar." In *Handbook of Middle American Indians, Vol. 3,* edited by Robert Wauchope and Gordon R. Willey, 931–47. Austin: University of Texas Press.

Caso, Alfonso, and Ignacio Bernal
1952   *Urnas de Oaxaca.* Mexico City: Instituto Nacional de Anthropologia e Historia.

Chang, K. C.
1989   "The Circumpacific Substratum of Ancient Chinese Civilization." MS adapted from work in preparation for inclusion in *Continuity and Rupture: Ancient China and the Rise of Civilizations.*

Clark, John E.

1991 "The Beginnings of Mesoamerica: Apologia for the Soconusco Early Formative." In *The Formation of Complex Society in Southeastern Mesoamerica,* edited by William R. Fowler, Jr., 13–26. Boca Raton, Fla.: CRC Press.

Coe, Michael D.

1962 *Mexico.* New York: Frederick A. Praeger.

Cordova, Fray Juan de

1942 [1578] *Vocabulario en Lengua Zapoteca.* Mexico City: Pedro Charte y Antonio Ricardo.

Cruz, Wilfredo

1935 *El Tonalmatl Zapoteco: Ensayo Sobre Su Interpretacion Linguistica.* Imprenta del Gobierno del Estado Oaxaca de Juarez.

1946 *Oaxaca recondita: Razas, idiomas, costumbres, leyendas y tradiciones del estado de Oaxaca.* Mexico City.

De la Fuente, Julio

1949 *Yalalag: Una villa zapoteca serrana.* Serie Cientifica Museo Nacional de Antropologia 1.Mexico City.

Demarest, Arthur A.

1992 "Ideology in Ancient Maya Cultural Evolution: The Dynamics of Galactic Politics." In *Ideology and Pre-Columbian Civilizations,* edited by Arthur A. Demarest and Geoffrey W. Conrad, 135–58. Santa Fe, N.M.: School of American Research Press.

Eliade, Mircea

1959 *The Sacred and the Profane: The Nature of Religion.* New York: Harcourt, Brace, and World.

1963 *Myth and Reality.* New York: Harper and Row.

1964 *Shamanism: Archaic Techniques of Ecstasy.* Translated by Willard R. Trask. Bollingen Series 76. Princeton, N.J.: Princeton University Press.

Flannery, Kent V., and Joyce Marcus

1976 "Formative Oaxaca and the Zapotec Cosmos." *American Scientist* 64(4):374–83.

1990 "Borron y Cuenta Nueva: Setting Oaxaca's Archaeological Record Straight." In *Debating Oaxaca Archaeology,* edited by Joyce Marcus, 17–69. Anthropological Papers No. 84. Ann Arbor: Museum of Anthropology, University of Michigan.

Foster, George W.

1944 "Nagualism in Mexico and Guatemala." *Acta Americana* 2:85–103.

Freidel, David A., and Linda Schele

1988 "Kingship and the Late Preclassic Lowlands: The Instruments and Places of Power." *American Anthropologist* 90(3):547–67.

Freidel, David, Linda Schele, and Joy Parker

1993 *The Maya Cosmos: 3000 Years on the Shaman's Path.* New York: William Morrow.

Furst, Peter D.

1968 "The Olmec Were-Jaguar Motif in the Light of Ethnographic Reality." In *Dumbarton Oaks Conference on the Olmec,* edited by Elizabeth P. Benson, 143–178. Washington, D.C.: Dumbarton Oaks Research Library and Collection.

1976 "Shamanistic Survivals in Mesoamerican Religion." In *Actas del XLI Congreso Internacional de Americanistas 3,* 149–57. Mexico City.

Gallegos Ruiz, Roberto

1978 *El Senor 9 Flor en Zaachila.* Mexico City: Universidad Autonoma de Mexico.

Gay, Jose Antonio

1982 *Historia de Oaxaca.* Mexico City: Biblioteca de Autores y de Asuntos Oaxaquenos.

Grube, Nikolai

1989 "A Glyph for *Way* (Sorcery, Nahual Transformation)." MS (notes for epigraphers) on file with Kinko's Copies Maya Files, Austin, Texas.

Hernestrosa, Andres

1977 *Los hombres que disperso la danza.* Mexico City: Editorial Porrua.

Houston, Stephen, and David Stuart

1989 *The "Way" Glyph: Evidence for "Co-essences" among the Classic Maya.* Research Reports on Ancient Maya Writing 30. Washington, D.C: Center for Maya Research.

Jorrin, Maria

1974 "Stone Monuments." In *The Oaxaca Coast Project Reports: Part 1,* by Donald Brockington, Maria Jorrin, and J. R. Long, 23–81. Vanderbilt University Publications in Anthropology 8. Nashville, Tenn.: Vanderbilt University.

Joyce, Arthur A., and Marcus Winter

1996 "Ideology, Power, and Urban Society in Pre-Hispanic Oaxaca." *Current Anthropology* 37(1):33–47.

Justeson, John S., and Terrence Kaufman

1993 "A Decipherment of Epi-Olmec Hieroglyphic Writing." *Science* 259:1703–11.

Kaplan, Lucille N.

1956 "Tonal and Nagual in Coastal Oaxaca, Mexico." *Journal of American Folklore* 69(264):363–68.

Kearney, Michael
1972   *The Winds of Ixtepeji: World View and Society in a Zapotec Town.* New York: Holt, Rinehart, and Winston.

Looper, Matthew G.
1991   "The Dances of the Classic Maya Deities Chak and Hun Nal Ye." M.A. thesis, University of Texas at Austin.

Marcus, Joyce
1976   "The Iconography of Militarism at Monte Alban and Neighboring Sites in the Valley of Oaxaca." In *The Origins of Religious Art and Iconography in Preclassic Mesoamerica,* edited by Henry B. Nicholson, 123–39. Los Angeles: University of California at Los Angeles Latin American Center.
1978   "Archaeology and Religion: A Comparison of the Zapotec and the Maya." *World Archaeology* 10(2):172–91.
1980   "Zapotec Writing." *Scientific American* 242(2):50–79.
1983   "Topic 97: Zapotec Religion." In *The Cloud People: Divergent Evolution of the Zapotec and Mixtec Civilizations,* edited by Kent V. Flannery and Joyce Marcus, 345–51. New York: Academic Press.
1989   "Zapotec Chiefdoms and the Nature of Formative Religions." In *Regional Perspectives on the Olmec,* edited by Robert J. Sharer and David C. Grove, 148–97. New York: Academic Press.
1993   *Mesoamerican Writing.* Princeton, N.J.: Princeton University Press.

Marcus, Joyce, and Kent V. Flannery
1978   "Ethnoscience of the Sixteenth Century Valley Zapotec." In *The Nature and Status of Ethnobotany,* edited by Richard I. Ford, 52–79. Museum of Anthropology, University of Michigan, Anthropological Papers 67. Ann Arbor: University of Michigan.

Miller, Arthur
1992   "The Carved Stela in Tomb 5, Suchilquitongo, Oaxaca, Mexico." *Ancient Mesoamerica* 2:215–24.

Miller, Walter S.
1956   *Cuentos Mixes.* Mexico City: Instituto Nacional Indigenista.

Parsons, Elsie Clews
1936   *Mitla, Town of Souls.* Chicago: University of Chicago Press.

Pasztory, Esther, ed.
1978   *Middle Classic Mesoamerica: A.D. 400–700.* New York: Columbia University Press.

Rabin, Emily
1970   *The Lambityeco Friezes: Notes on Their Content, with an appendix on C14 dates.* Boletin Estudios Oaxaquenos 33.

Reilly, Kent
1989   "The Shaman in Transformation Pose: A Study of the Theme of Rulership in Olmec Art." *The Record* 48(2):5–21.
1994   "Visions to Another World: Art, Shamanism, and Rulership in Middle Formative Mesoamerica." Ph.D. diss., University of Texas at Austin.

Robertson, Donald
1983   "Topic 40. Functional Analysis of Architecture at Monte Alban." In *The Cloud People: Divergent Evolution of the Zapotec and Mixtec Civilizations,* edited by Kent V. Flannery and Joyce Marcus, 131–36. New York: Academic Press.

Schele, Linda
1991   "Workbook for the XV Maya Hieroglyphic Workshop at Texas, March 9–10, 1991." Austin: Department of Art, University of Texas.

Schele, Linda, and David A. Freidel
1990   *The Forest of Kings: The Untold Story of the Ancient Maya.* New York: William Morrow.

Schele, Linda, and Mary Ellen Miller
1986   *The Blood of Kings: Dynasty and Ritual in Maya Art.* Fort Worth: Kimbell Art Museum.

Scott, John F.
1978   *The Danzantes of Monte Alban, Volumes 1 and 2.* Studies in Precolumbian Art and Archaeology 19. Washington, D.C.: Dumbarton Oaks.

Seler, Eduard
1904   "The Mexican Chronology, with special reference to the Zapotec Calendar." *Bureau of American Ethnology Bulletin* 28:13–55.

Spencer, Charles S.
1982   *The Cuicatlan Canada and Monte Alban: A Study of Primary State Formation.* New York: Academic Press.

Spero, Joanne
1987   "Lightning Men and Water Serpents: A Comparison of Maya and Mixe-Zoquean Beliefs." M.A. thesis, University of Texas at Austin.

Spores, Ronald M.
1965   "The Zapotec and Mixtec at Spanish Contact." In *Handbook of Middle American Indians, Volume 3,* edited by Robert Wauchope and Gordon Willey, 962–90.

Sugiyama, Saburo
1989   "Burials Dedicated to the Old Temple of Quetzalcoatl at Teotihuacan, Mexico." *American Antiquity* 54(1):85–106.

Tate, Carolyn

1991 "Yaxchilan: The Design of a Maya Ceremonial City." Austin: University of Texas Press.

Thomas, Norman

n.d. Notes on file, Department of Anthropology, Texas A&M University, College Station.

Tozzer, Alfred M.

1941 *Fray Diego de Landa, Relación de las cosas de Yucatán.* Translated and edited by Alfred M. Tozzer. Papers of the Peabody Museum of American Archaeology and Ethnology, Harvard University, 18. Cambridge, Mass.: Peabody Museum, Harvard University.

Urcid, Javier

1991 "Stelae NP-9 and PH-1 of Monte Alban, Oaxaca." MS on file at Dumbarton Oaks, Washington, D.C.

1992 "Zapotec Hieroglyphic Writing." Ph.D. diss., Yale University.

Vogt, Evon Z.

1969 *Zinacantan: A Maya Community in the Highlands of Chiapas.* Cambridge, Mass.: Belknap Press of Harvard University Press.

Zeitlin, Judith

1984 "Colonialism and the Political Transformation of Isthmus Zapotec Society." In *Five Centuries of Law and Politics in Central Mexico,* edited by Ronald Spores and R. Hassig, 65–86. Vanderbilt University Publications in Anthropology 30. Nashville, Tenn.: Vanderbilt University.

Fig. 15.1.   Excavation of Offering 11 in 1978. (Courtesy of Instituto Nacional de Antropología e Historia)

CHAPTER FIFTEEN

Recreating the Cosmos
Seventeen Aztec Dedication Caches

Leonardo López Luján
Museo del Templo Mayor, Mexico City

DURING FIVE SEASONS OF FIELDWORK (1978–1997), the Templo Mayor Project of the National Institute of Anthropology and History (INAH) recovered one of the most prominent ritual scenarios of the Mesoamerican world: the Sacred Precinct of Mexico-Tenochtitlán. Among the most significant discoveries during the past fourteen years are the remains of fifteen buildings, more than eight thousand objects, and a considerable agglomeration of sculptures, reliefs, and mural paintings (Matos 1987, 1988). In addition, our explorations have recovered a surprising number of buried offerings—134 in all (fig. 15.1).

One of the most significant results of the project was the discovery and recording of the complex disposition of the archaeological materials in the offerings. During the excavations we observed that each and every object was carefully placed, following strict principles of spatial composition.

Five years ago I began to study the offerings under the assumption that the arrangement of materials obeyed a code that, once deciphered, would contribute to an understanding of Mexica ideology (López Luján 1989, 1994; López Luján and Polaco 1991). In an analogy to verbal language, each component of the offering functioned as a sign or symbol that transmitted information when combined with others. Unfortunately, for more than two hundred years studies of Mexica offerings have been limited to the analysis of their contents, thus obscuring contextual relationships. For this reason, although today we are aware of the significance of many of the buried materials, we still do not understand the meaning of the whole complex. To continue the linguistic analogy, we understand the letters and even the words, but not the syntax of the phrase.

This study is based on the assumption that the systematic correlation of archaeological materials with architectural, historical, and ethnographic information will help not only to decipher the code of the offerings but also to identify the ritual ceremonies during which the offerings were made. I carried out a variety of descriptive as well as complex statistical analyses in order to detect possible patterns. The sample studied included more than 9,000 objects from 118 offerings, excavated by 4 different archaeological projects (López Luján 1994).

With the help of simple statistical techniques, it was possible to detect two classes of archaeological syntax: an "internal" one, corresponding to the distribution of the objects within each receptacle, and an "external" class, relating to the organization of the offerings with respect to architectural structures (López Luján 1994:chap. 6). With regard to the internal syntax, the organization of the objects observed one or more principles of a predetermined spatial arrangement: (1) the distribution of the objects followed imaginary axes on a horizontal plane

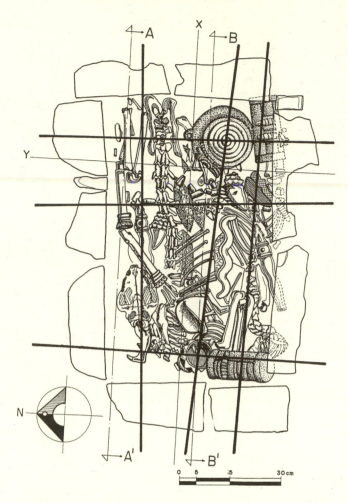

Fig. 15.2.   Distribution of objects following imaginary axes: Temple B, Offering H, Level 1.

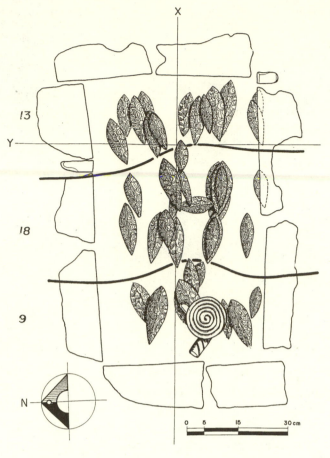

Fig. 15.3.   Groups of 13, 18, and 9 flint knives from Temple B, Offering H, Level 3.

(fig. 15.2); (2) objects with the same morphofunctional characteristics tended to cluster horizontally in groups, with the number of components related to Nahua concepts of the cosmos (fig. 15.3); (3) the objects overlapped vertically in levels or superpositions. Each level contained the same type of objects, following taxonomic criteria based on indigenous "cosmovision" (fig. 15.4).

As for the external syntax, groups of offerings were clearly visible with respect to the general layout of the Templo Mayor. Their locations were dictated by the following principles: (1) the differential importance of the structures in which they were found; (2) the imaginary axes that dictated the distribution of architectural space in each building (fig. 15.5); and (3) the religious significance of the buildings, as well as their vertical and horizontal sections.

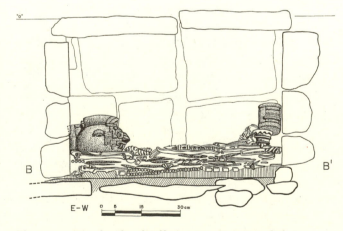

Fig. 15.4.   Five levels of Offering H: ceramics, skeletons of mammals, flint knives, shells/greenstone sculptures, and marine sand.

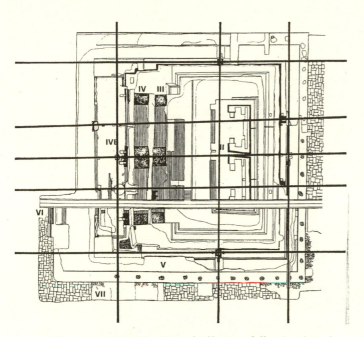

Fig. 15.5. Distribution of offerings following imaginary axes.

Other patterns could be detected only through the use of more complicated techniques. Thus, the second stage of analysis involved the classification of the 118 offerings using more complex statistical techniques (López Luján 1994:chap. 7). One of these was numerical taxonomy. This classification provided the basis for the analysis of the religious significance of the offerings and the reconstruction of the associated ritual ceremonies. In this chapter I will analyze two groups obtained by use of the computer, both of which relate to the ceremonies associated with the construction and inauguration of the Templo Mayor.

According to sixteenth-century Nahua concepts, the Templo Mayor was built in the center of the universe, exactly in the place where high, middle, and low articulated with the four directions of the universe. According to an indigenous myth, the foundation site was revealed to the migrants by the presence of a savine that had taken root on two large rocks (Alvarado Tezozómoc 1949:62–63; Durán 1984:2:44–48). Each of these rocks covered a pair of caves from which two springs flowed, one with blue water, the other with red. Later, both of these colors and the insistent duality of sacred geography would lend a distinctive note to the temple of Huitzilipochtli and Tlaloc.

This duality is reflected in the inauguration offerings of the Templo Mayor and seems to allude to "time-des-

tiny" forces of the Mesoamerican cosmovision that ran in a helicoidal pattern through the interior of the cosmic trees: descending, warm, and masculine, on the one hand, and ascending, cold, and feminine on the other (López Austin 1980:58–75, 1990:178).

Various authors agree that the form of the Templo Mayor reflected the spatial configuration of the universe (López Luján 1990:chap. 5; Matos 1988:133; Zantwijk 1981:71–73). Each time that it was enlarged, the architects were careful to repeat the previous structure and in this way to re-create the cosmos. However, similarity of form was not the only requirement to be met in order for the new addition to become a sacred space. It was also indispensable to carry out rituals, during the construction as well as at the dedication. These rituals repeated the primordial creation of the world in order to assure the vitality and permanence of the temple. The offerings described below are precisely the remains of rituals of this type, which reenact the cosmogonic acts of the gods.

The first group of offerings to be analyzed was interred during the construction of the third enlargement of the Templo Mayor (approximately A.D. 1427–1440). While the

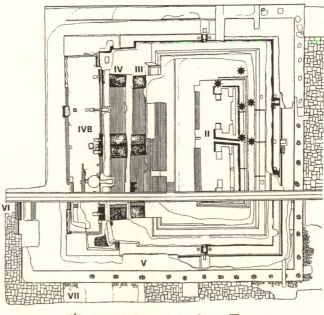

✱ 6 Offerings of the Stage III

Fig. 15.6. Spatial distribution of the first group of offerings.

Fig. 15.7. Globular jar and bowl, from Offering 43. (Courtesy of INAH)

construction was still in process, a ritual was conducted, during which six offerings were buried in the fill of the northern part of the building, in the half dedicated to Tlaloc (fig. 15.6). These offerings formed part of a ceremony to ensure rain and fertility, which would grant its distinctive character to the new temple.

The six offerings are relatively poor. Each includes one bowl and a globular jar containing three or four beads of greenstone (fig. 15.7). Bowls and jars were made from an orange monochrome ceramic, splashed with a blue pigment of organic origin.

The correlation of the globular jars with the cult of the Rain God is unquestionable. The primary link involves their presumed function as containers for liquids and their blue color. A second connection is the northern position of these artifacts with respect to the Templo Mayor. In various sixteenth-century documents the image of the Temple of Tlaloc is crowned with parapets in the form of water vessels (*Códice Ramírez* 1944:pl. 19; Durán 1984:2:pl. 30). The globular jars also recur in the representations associated with the month of *Etzalcualiztli,* the principal festival dedicated to Tlaloc (*Codex Magliabechiano* 1983:fol. 34r; *Códice Vaticano Latino 3738* 1964–1967:pl. 60). Thanks to Sahagún, we know that blue-painted receptacles called "cloud jars" were used during this festival (*Códice Florentino*

1979:book 2, fols. 37v–46r; *Códice Matritense del Real Palacio* 1906:fols. 76r–83v).

The jars also appear in association with Tlaloc in Mexica myths. For example, the supposed function of these receptacles is mentioned in the *Historia de los mexicanos por sus pinturas* (1965:26):

> Of that god of water they say that he has a chamber with four rooms, and in the middle of a great patio, there are four great tubs of water …. And this god of water, to make it rain, created many small assistants, who were in the rooms of that house, and they had pots in which they took the water from those tubs and some clubs in the other hand, and when the god of rain orders them to go and water some ground, they take their pots and their clubs and scatter the water that they send, and when it thunders, it is when they break the pots with the clubs, and when there is lightning, it is from what they have inside, or part of the pot. (my translation)

At the same time, the greenstone beads were one of the symbols par excellence of fertility. The aquatic significance of greenstone probably comes from its color, its shine, and its texture. Sahagún mentions the indigenous belief that greenstone had the double property of attracting as well as exuding humidity (*Florentine Codex* 1950–1969:11:222–23). In this century, Seler (1960:2:852) and Krickeberg (1975:152) have correctly surmised that beads of this material deposited inside ceramic receptacles could symbolize drops of water.

The full significance of the six offerings cannot be determined by a simple enumeration of their parts: Further contextual information is required. The key to their interpretation is found in the position of the jars, bowls, and beads. The archaeological record shows that the jars were regularly and intentionally buried lying down. The bowls were always found in a horizontal position, exactly below the opening of the jars (fig. 15.8). In other words, in each case we registered the presence of (1) a jar decorated with blue pigment, (2) containing greenstone beads, (3) lying on its side, and (4) with its opening associated with a bowl.

Based on this description, it is reasonable to propose that these offerings represent the jars of the *tlaloque* in a position that simulates the pouring of precious water on the surface of the earth. Perhaps all these objects formed part of a propitiatory act that endowed the building with the qualities appropriate to the world of Tlaloc: a chamber from which the rains were generated, to ensure the fertility of the earth.

This suggestion is supported by further evidence, which I will enumerate briefly.

First, a Mexica stone box now in the British Museum, London, bears on one side the image of Tlaloc holding a jar decorated with a large greenstone bead (Box 13 in the catalogue of Gutiérrez Solana 1983:62–65). Maize cobs and streams of water ending in beads and shells emerge from this jar. Furthermore, we found a similar representation in Chamber 3 beneath Stage IVb of the Great Temple. It is painted on the ceramic lid of a Cholula-style polychrome jar (fig. 15.9).

The second piece of evidence is found in a mural painting covering the north side of the doorframe of Building A at Cacaxtla, Tlaxcala, dated to A.D. 750. There, a personage dressed in a jaguar skin and a blue pectoral holds with his right arm a jar decorated with a Tlaloc mask from which flow streams and drops of water.

Finally, in both the *Códice de Dresde* (1988:36c, 39b, 43b and 74) and the *Códice Madrid* (1985:9, 13 and 30), Chaac and the Old Red Goddess of Weaving appear, pouring water out of pitchers over the surface of the earth (fig. 15.10a-b). It is significant that almost all these scenes occur in sections dedicated to peasant almanacs and the glorification of the rainy season (Thompson 1988:214–216, 242, 245, 252).

The second group to be discussed here is made up of eleven offerings. All were interred during the ceremony to dedicate and consecrate Stage IVb of the Templo Mayor (approximately A.D. 1469–1481). Their distribution follows the principal architectural axes of the platform and maintains strict bilateral symmetry (fig. 15.11). This group is characterized by richness of offerings and by its dual significance.

The objects in the interior of each box of the offerings form Six vertical levels, which represent scale reproductions of the three levels of the indigenous cosmos: the deepest level, with aquatic characteristics; the intermediate, signifying earth; and the highest, presided over by the gods of fire and water. Among the objects representing the highest level we find symbols denoting opposition, the insignias of Xipe Totec, and the skulls of decapitated humans (fig. 15.12).

Initially, a homogeneous layer of marine sand was placed at the bottom of each box. Next, a second layer made up of small shells was laid down, followed immediately by a third composed of corals and larger shells.

Fig. 15.8. Archaeological context of Offering 26. (Courtesy of INAH)

Fig. 15.9. Tlaloc pouring water: Element 256, Chamber 3, Great Temple.

[a]

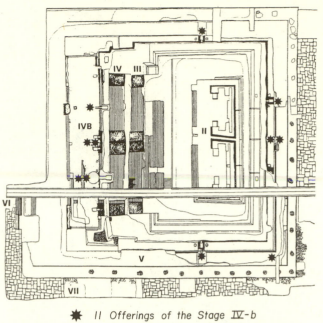

* || Offerings of the Stage IV-b

Fig. 15.11.   Spatial distribution of second group of offerings.

[b]

Fig. 15.10.   Chaac pouring water: (a) *Códice Madrid*:13; (b) *Códice Madrid*:30.

Fig. 15.12.   Archaeological context of Offering 61. (Courtesy of INAH)

The fourth layer was made up exclusively of remains of fish and reptiles. However, only the external parts of these animals were deposited: the heads and skins of crocodiles, serpents, and fish; the rostral cartilages of sawfish; and turtle shells. The original impression given by this level would have been that of a "dermic layer," which physically and visually separated the aquatic, deepest level from those above. In my judgment, this intermediate level could be associated with Cipactli, original monster, feminine and aquatic, symbol of the earth. It is sufficient to recall here that the iconographic representation of Cipactli was in the form of a crocodile, a sawfish, or a serpent.

The fifth level was the richest of all, composed of images of the gods, miniatures representing divine paraphernalia, autosacrificial implements, and the skulls of decapitated humans. Outstanding among these objects are sculptures of Xiuhtecuhtli and the Tlaloc jars. The images of the God of Fire and the God of Rain were always found at the head of the deposit, as though presiding over the offering. Five objects related to divine paraphernalia occurred consistently: a scepter in the form of a deer head, symbol of the sun, fire, and drought; a scepter in the form of a serpent, associated with currents of water and with fertilizing rays; an *ollin* glyph, symbol par excellence of the unity of opposites (water-fire); a *chicahuaztli* and a plaque with a cleavage in both extremities, attributes of Xipe Totec (fig. 15.13). Also, there were numerous human skulls (fifty in all) with the first cervical vertebrae. These skulls were situated in the corners and the principal axes of the building.

The sixth and last level was detected just on top of the layer of stone slabs that covered the boxes of hewn stone. It contained ceramic incense burners that had been ritually destroyed.

From my point of view, an important key to the significance of this group of offerings is found in the presence of the skulls of decapitated individuals. Various scholars have pointed out that the rite of decapitation always took place in ceremonies of a dual character, such as the ball game, the ritual of planting and harvesting, the sacrifice of war prisoners to renew the *tzompantli*, and the consecration of temples (see Moser 1973). In relation to this last type of ceremony, there have been abundant discoveries of crania with their first cervical vertebrae in the corners of numerous religious structures, spanning the Middle Preclassic to the Late Postclassic, from the Maya area to the Tarascan Highlands

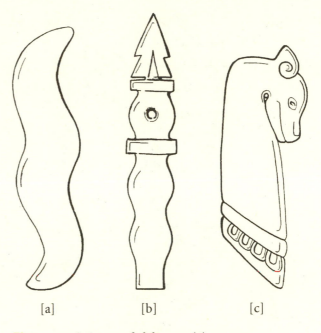

Fig. 15.13.   Scepters of alabaster: (a) serpent; (b) Chicahuaztli; (c) deer head.

(Ruz 1968:160, 198–99). At the time of Contact, the indigenous population believed that the burial of heads provided the energy necessary for the functioning of the temples and the expulsion of negative forces (fig. 15.14a).

The sixteenth-century Nahua peasants conducted rites to consecrate their houses. They decapitated a bird and smeared its blood on the corners of the structure. Then they carried a lighted branch to each of the four posts and poured *pulque* on it. The ceremony was called *calmamalihua*, referring to the helicoidal movement of the *malinalli* in which the warm forces, represented by fire, were interlaced with the cold, symbolized by *pulque* (López Austin 1990:317).

More than a few traces of this practice remain today. The Huastecs, Nahuas, Tzotziles, and Tzeltales reproduce the structure of the universe each time they build a house. Before the final placement of the wooden posts, the heads of sheep, hens, or turkeys are buried in the foundation, synonymous with the ancient human heads. Somewhat later, during the dedication ritual, offerings are made that have complementary significance: *pulque* and fire, pine needles and red geraniums, or chicken broth and *aguardiente* (López Luján 1994:chap. 8).

Returning to Tenochtitlán, the burial of decapitated heads in the offerings of the Templo Mayor was fortunately drawn and described in sixteenth-century docu-

[a]

[b]

[c]

ments (Barlow 1949:126–128; *Codex en Cruz* 1981:ii, years 1483 and 1487; *Códice Azcatitlan* 1949:xxi–xxii; Quiñones Keber 1984:101–2; fig. 15.14b–c). Just as various chroniclers reported, the Mexica offered heads in honor of the inauguration and consecration of the additions to their main temple. For example, Alva Ixtlilxóchitl (1975:2:157) mentions that during the dedication festival of the Templo Mayor that took place in *Tlacaxipehualiztli* of 1487, numerous prisoners of war were taken to the sacrificial stone (fig. 15.15), "all of whom were sacrificed before this statue of the demon, and the heads were placed in some niches that were intentionally made in the walls of the Templo Mayor" (my translation).

It is important to note that just as the colonial documents of the Tradition of Chronicle X reported, *all* the inauguration ceremonies of the Templo Mayor were celebrated at the same time of the year—during the twenty-day period of *Xipe Totec.* This twenty-day period coincided with the spring equinox, the point of equilibrium between day and night. According to Kurath and Martí (1964:68–70, 76–77), at that time the rituals represented the conflict between heaven and earth, light and darkness, drought and rain. From this perspective, it seems logical that the consecration festival of this temple of dual composition, dedicated to a solar deity and an aquatic one, should take place during a period of twenty days associated with the concept of equilibrium among opposites. A recent discovery by Aveni and colleagues (1988:294) also agrees with this idea. While calculating the orientation of the Templo Mayor, they found that the sun rose exactly between the sanctuaries of Huitzilopochtli and Tlaloc on March 4 of each year—that is, the first day of the twenty-day period of *Tlacaxipehualiztli.*

Also to be noted is the political character of the dedications during *Tlacaxipehualiztli,* as revealed in the documents of the Tradition of Chronicle X. The following features are common to all the inaugurations mentioned:

Fig. 15.14. Burial of human heads in temples: (a) head of Mocatzin, Temple of Chiquiuhtepec (*Historia Tolteca-Chichimeca*:fol. 41r); (b) heads of warriors with forked heron feathers, Ahuítzotl's dedication of the Great Temple of Tenochtitlan (*Códice Azcatitlan*:XXI); (c) head of Xipe Tótec, Great Temple in 1506 (*Códice Azcatitlan*:XXII).

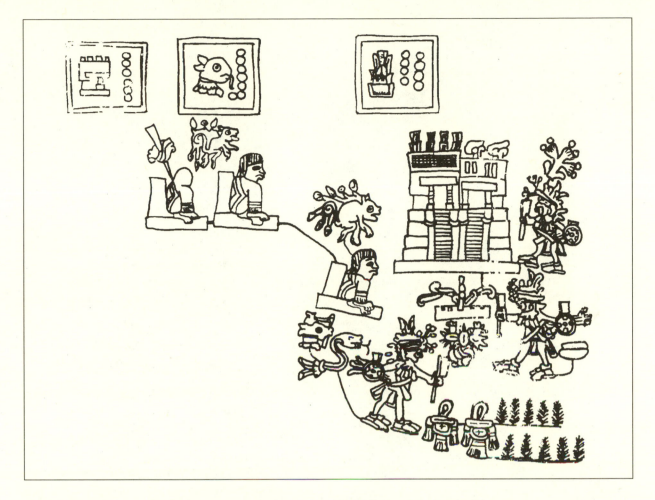

Fig. 15.15. Inauguration of the Great Temple in 1487. (*Códice Telleriano-Remensis*:xix)

1. As the addition to the temple was on the verge of completion, a conquest expedition was launched against an independent realm in order to obtain prisoners to be sacrificed during the consecration of the Templo Mayor.

2. Following the victorious return of the Mexica warriors, the twenty-day period of *Tlacaxipehualiztli* was awaited.

3. The governors of the allied realms, as well as those hostile to the Triple Alliance, were invited to the inauguration.

4. During the festivities, compatriots of the enemy lords were sacrificed.

5. The heads of the victims were interred in the corners of the Templo Mayor, and goods were distributed among the participants as a symbol of their subordination to the Mexica *tlatoani*.

A careful reading of these documents reveals one transcendent point: the Templo Mayor grew in accordance with the increase in size of the empire. Thus, the frequent architectural additions glorified the voracious expansionist politics of the Mexica.

REFERENCES CITED

Alva Ixtlilxóchitl, F. de
1975   *Obras históricas.* Mexico City: Universidad Nacional Autónoma de México.

Alvarado Tezozómoc, H.

1949 *Crónica mexicáyotl.* Mexico City: Universidad Nacional Autónoma de México/Instituto Nacional de Antropología e Historia.

Aveni, A. F., E. E. Calnek, and H. Hartung

1988 "Myth, Environment, and the Orientation of the Templo Mayor of Tenochtitlán." *American Antiquity* 53(2):287–309.

Barlow, R. H.

1949 "El Códice Azcatitlan." *Journal de la Société des Américanistes* 38:101–35.

Codex en Cruz

1981 Salt Lake City: University of Utah Press.

Codex Magliabechiano

1983 Berkeley: University of California Press.

Códice Azcatitlan

1949 *Journal de la Société des Américanistes* 38:i–xxix.

Códice de Dresde

1988 Mexico City: Fondo de Cultura Económica.

Códice Florentino

1979 Mexico City: Archivo General de la Nación.

Códice Madrid

1985 In *Los códices mayas,* 79–140. Tuxtla Gutiérrez: Universidad Autónoma de Chiapas.

Códice Matritense del Real Palacio

1906 Madrid: Fototipia de Hauser y Menet.

Códice Ramírez

1944 Mexico City: Leyenda.

Códice Telleriano-Remensis

1964–1967 In *Antigüedades de México, Vol. 1,* 151–337. Mexico City: Secretaría de Hacienda y Crédito Público.

Códice Vaticano Latino 3738

1964–1967 In *Antigüedades de México, Vol. 3,* 7–314. Mexico City: Secretaría de Hacienda y Crédito Público.

Durán, D.

1984 *Historia de las Indias de Nueva España e Islas de la Tierra Firme.* 2 vols. Mexico City: Porrúa.

Florentine Codex: General History of the Things of New Sapain, Fray Bernardino de Sahagún

1950–1969 Santa Fe, N.M.: School of American Research and University of Utah.

Gutiérrez Solana, N.

1983 *Objetos ceremoniales en piedra de la cultura mexica.* Mexico City: Universidad Nacional Autónoma de México.

Historia de los mexicanos por sus pinturas

1965 In *Teogonía e historia de los mexicanos: Tres opúsculos del siglo XVI,* edited by A. M. Garibay K., 21–90. Mexico City: Porrúa.

Historia Tolteca-Chichimeca

1976 Mexico City: Centro de Investigaciones Superiores del Instituto Nacional de Antropología e Historia.

Krickeberg, W.

1975 *Las antiguas culturas mexicanas.* Mexico City: Fondo de Cultura Económica.

Kurath, G., and S. Martí

1964 *Dance of Anahuac: The Choreography and Music of Precortesian Dances.* Chicago: Aldine.

López Austin, A.

1980 *Cuerpo humano e ideología: Las concepciones de los aniguos nahuas.* Mexico City: Universidad Nacional Autónoma de México.

1990 *Los mitos del tlacuache: Caminos de la mitología mesoamericana.* Mexico City: Alianza Editorial Mexicana.

López Luján, L.

1989 *La recuperación mexica del pasado teotihuacano.* Mexico City: Instituto Nacional de Antropología e Historia.

1994 *The Offerings of the Templo Mayor of Tenochtitlán.* Niwot: University of Colorado Press.

López Luján, L., and O. J. Polaco

1991 "La fauna de la ofrenda H del Templo Mayor." In *La fauna en el Templo Mayor,* edited by O. J. Polaco, 149–69. Mexico City: Instituto Nacional de Antropología e Historia.

Matos, E.

1987 "The Templo Mayor of Tenochtitlán: History and Interpretation." In *The Great Temple of Tenochtitlán, Center and Periphery in the Aztec World,* 16–60. Berkeley: University of California Press.

1988 *The Great Temple of the Aztecs: Treasures of Tenochtitlán.* London: Thames and Hudson.

Moser, C.

1973 *Human Decapitation in Ancient Mesoamerica.* Washington, D.C.: Dumbarton Oaks.

Quiñones Keber, E.

1984 "Art as History: The Illustrated Chronicle of the Codex Telleriano-Remensis as a Historical Source." In *The Native Sources and the History of the Valley of Mexico,* edited by J. de Durand-Forest, 95–116. BAR International Series 204. Oxford: BAR.

Ruz Lhuillier, A.

1968 *Costumbres funerarias de los antiguos mayas.* Mexico City: Universidad Nacional Autónoma de México.

Seler, E.
1960   *Gesammelte Abhandlungen zur Amerikanischen Sprach- und Altertumskunde.* 5 vols. Graz: Akademische Druck und Verlangstalt.

Thompson, J. E. S.
1988   *Un comentario al Códice de Dresde: Libro de jeroglifos mayas.* Mexico City: Fondo de Cultura Económica.

Zantwijk, R. van.
1981   "The Great Temple of Tenochtitlán: Model of Aztec Cosmovision." In *Mesoamerican Sites and World-views,* edited by E. P. Benson, 71–86. Washington, D.C.: Dumbarton Oaks.

Sacred Work
Dedication and Termination in Mesoamerica

David Freidel
Southern Methodist University

Taken together, the contributors to this book are generally in agreement on some principal points:

    1. The way that Mesoamerican people conceive of their world, and have conceived of it for thousands of years of civilized life, has direct bearing on the work they do in it.

    2. Effective analysis of the world as made by Mesoamericans, artifactual and material, requires useful models of their intentions in making it, based on their world views and cosmologies.

    3. Mesoamerican cosmologies combine matter and spirit, such that work with material is usually also work with spirit and vice versa.

    4. "Sacred" and "practical" are aspects of work aimed at common goals of social, cultural, and physical reproduction.

A corollary of these premises is that, broadly, what we term "dedication rituals" are acts of ensouling or engendering built places and made things; what we call "termination rituals" are acts of killing, sacrificing, capturing, or exorcising spiritual force from such places or things.

Theory, Contexts, and Cosmology

These ideas paraphrase some of the cogent theoretical observations of the ethnographers, Evon Z. Vogt, Brian Stross, R. Jon McGee, and John Monaghan, in Part One of this book. They are by no means unanimously accepted tenets in Mesoamerican scholarship. On the contrary, many experts denounce them in lively and vocal debate: We are blessed with many interesting debates in Mesoamerican research. They constitute a direct affront to the notion that, as outside observers, we should measure and evaluate what Mesoamericans do and have done with their material world by universal standards of what people do and have done everywhere in similar circumstances. Moreover, critics point out that, as outsiders and scientists, we look at aspects of the material world that certainly affected Mesoamericans but which they did not identify or understand as we do: market economics, plant genetics, soil chemistry, and climate dynamics, for example. Some leaders in Mesoamerican archaeology—Gordon Willey and Kent Flannery stand out—have for years tried to guide us to some middle ground here. But no doubt heated debate will go on, and these essays will add fuel to them. This book will make a difference in the long term, however, because its chapters impressively apply the tenets outlined at the outset to a wide array of empirical cases. It is not naive empiricism to insist that if ideas make sense of evidence, they are worth serious consideration.

Vogt's contribution confirms the validity and the complexity of the conceptual framework of this book in dedication and termination rituals. His brilliant research and teaching program in Chiapas provides long-term ethnographic documentation that the cultural premises of contemporary Zinacanteco Maya ritual practice are an enduring expression of ancient Maya traditions. Continuity between contemporary indigenous cultures and the pre-Columbian cultures is the basis of the direct historical approach to interpretation of the past in Mesoamerica. Generations of archaeologists have accepted the validity of this idea. And while it is helpful in dealing with prosaic matters, such as what perishable houses of the past might have looked like, it is crucial to gaining access to the beliefs informing ritual behavior.

The chapters by Monaghan, McGee, and Stross further explore and detail the ritual practices of contemporary Mesoamericans in ways that should stimulate archaeologists to look at their data from the vantage point of coherent cosmologies. Monaghan rejects the term *ritual,* for if the sacred is potentially or actually an aspect of all important work, then to distinguish ritual is to obscure the pervasive spirituality of Mesoamerican life and the efficacy of explaining behavior through cosmology. While I embrace this principle, my own regular encounter with the material aspects of Mesoamerican culture leads me not only to accept the idea of ritual behavior, but also to defend it as useful. The Yucatec Maya people whom I know live within a cosmologically informed daily existence, but they still distinguish ritual events as times of sacred work, and they make places and things in concert with those events. The rituals are vitally connected to their daily lives; the sacred things and prepared places have metaphorical and analogical correspondence with everyday things and places. Indeed, Mesoamerican rituals use artifacts that are common to daily life in addition to special ones. Nevertheless, ritual actions bring the material and the spiritual into conjunction in potentially dangerous or beneficial ways that require deliberation but do not necessarily make sense as ordinary work.

For example, I once proposed that the Temple of the Grinding Stones (Structure 3C5) at Chichen Itza was part of an elite residence complex because of the associated remains. But in light of the kind of analysis reported in this book, I can see that it was not a place of food preparation, despite the presence of the four small and two large metates and grinders found on the floor. The context of these ordinary tools was extraordinary and cannot be used to identify the function of the buildings as domestic. In retrospect, the tools were found within a typical termination ritual deposit, including an abundance of smashed and complete pots, arrowheads, obsidian bloodletters, and human remains laid in white marl with the beam-and-mortar roof brought down on the whole. Grinding stones happen to be a prosaic artifact type that the Maya used in some termination contexts. And the deposit on the floor of this temple can only be usefully understood as the result of ritual activity.

DEDICATION AND TERMINATION IN THE MAYA AREA

The essays on Maya civilization display a wide range of ritual behaviors covered by the terms *dedication* and *termination.* Still looking at definitions, are there actually Mesoamerican concepts that parallel these terms and ideas? Monaghan again usefully challenges the idea of dedication as perhaps a gloss that obscures rather than illuminates ethnographically observed practice in his experience. The alternative concepts he brings to bear are relevant to the Maya context—but there is indeed something akin to dedication, and to termination, in ancient Maya thought. The act of consecration of a space, an explicit and direct analogue to dedication, is a named and fundamental one in the Classic texts, as discovered by Barbara MacLeod. The chapters in the Maya section of this book go a long way toward confirming that dedication rituals have epigraphic, iconographic, and archaeological reality in the record of the past. Termination, as declared by the Maya, is more in keeping with the general notion of killing the place as a living thing, but desecration includes such epigraphic descriptions as "burning" and "chopping." There is much room between consecration and desecration for another category yet to be usefully identified epigraphically in ancient Mayan: reverential termination, as described archaeologically by Debra Selsor Walker in her essay. The ancient Maya buried important dead in the anticipation of resurrection; how did they textually discuss the burial of venerated places?

David M. Pendergast's observations challenge such attempts to construct normative categories of ancient Maya activity on the basis of the archaeology of any one place or time period. His points are well taken, and we need analyses that detail local practices as the foundation for any effective comparison across regions. When compared, however, major Maya patterns do transcend local conventions, as he indicates in his discussion of the importance of building and plaza centerlines in dedication deposits. Part of the challenge facing archaeologists is recognizing patterns in evidence in the first place, and recording them carefully even when we are not sure what they mean. This is particularly true of termination deposits, but it also holds for preparatory and dedicatory events. One of the valuable contributions of this book is to provide an array of local contexts to compare in light of framework concepts.

Sandra Noble Bardsley offers a new interpretation of Maya dedications in elite residence complexes at Copan. Her work shows the vital roles epigraphy and iconography can now play in elucidating Maya ritual behavior in archaeological contexts. No doubt it is true that subsidiary nobles in Classic period royal capitals also dedicated places and monuments. Indeed, as James F. Garber and colleagues document and underscore in their contribution to this book, ordinary Maya also dedicated their homes as sacred places in communities far from such capitals. Their identification of a parallel between Blackman Eddy Cache 8 and the Highland K'iche'wakibal is an impressive example of direct historical analogy.

In the context of enduring basic ideas, the Maya no doubt modified their dedication practices as they charted political and social history. If Bardsley is right, we should find evidence for the increasing replication of royal ritual practices by subsidiary elite at other contemporary Maya capitals as they mature. But, in general, rituals in the center represented complex Maya communities, as Walker shows at Cerros in the Early Classic ceramics linking residences with the reverential termination deposit at the summit of the highest pyramid in the settlement. The same holds for Blue Creek, if Thomas H. Guderjan is on the right track in his interpretation of the massive jade deposit there as a prelude to cessation of the center as a political power.

Termination rituals as I originally thought of them at Cerros involved abandonment, but I must now regard them also in light of internal revolt and inter-realm warfare. I have proposed that Cerros may have been defeated and its temples destroyed in the wake of war. Shirley Boteler Mock at Colha confronts graphic violence in the termination of an elite group of people, possibly the leaders of the community and their families. In our contribution about Yaxuna, Charles K. Suhler, Rafael Cobos Palma, and I are grappling with such evidence for politically potent terminations. Whether one is looking at an internal overthrow or conquest from without in termi-

nation rituals of that kind is going to be matter for archaeologists to thrash out with fine-grained arguments over contextual patterns in the field. One clue that David Johnstone, ceramicist for the Selz Foundation Yaxuna Project, proposes is the idea of "signature ceramics." He hypothesizes that conquerors from outside sometimes, if not always, used some of their own pottery in Maya termination deposits. Suhler and I have found that this idea makes good sense of the termination of major buildings at Chichen Itza as the result of defeat by Mayapan.

Contexts and Cases in Highland Mesoamerica

Saburo Sugiyama is dealing with the complex possibilities of interpreting termination rituals at Teotihuacan in Part Three of this book. He makes a very convincing case for the desecratory nature of the termination of the Feathered Serpent Pyramid early in the Classic history of the city. Subsequently, there is unequivocal evidence for the sacking of the urban core of Teotihuacan as a consequence of internal revolt, outside conquest, or perhaps a combination of the two. These remarkable and exciting developments in research at Teotihuacan have outlined a social history of much more realistic dimensions than heretofore possible, more in line with the tumultuous and militarily energetic late prehistoric and Contact period states of Highland Mexico.

Evidence for the sacrifice of elite captives in the wake of war occurs not only in the archaeology of Maya country and in Teotihuacan, but also at Monte Alban in Oaxaca—as long proposed for the famous Danzantes by Joyce Marcus (1976). In their chapter, Marilyn Masson and Heather Orr extend the argument for the Danzantes and other reliefs of that center into roles as animal spirit companion portraits and as part of the dynamics of "ensouling" dedication of buildings. They persuasively argue that the Zapotec shared fundamental cosmological beliefs with other Mesoamericans concerning the capacities of soul force to materially transform from human to animal, and to abide in monuments placed in buildings. The very deliberate and often atrocious manner in which powerful captives were sacrificed, as at Colha and Teotihuacan, is more understandable when one considers that the soul force inhabiting the earthly frame had to be effectively contained, channeled, or dispersed so as not to seriously harm the captors.

The "wounding" of Feathered Serpent elements at Teotihuacan and the careful reuse of Danzante reliefs at Monte Alban affirm the tenet that material objects in the past, like the contemporary Lacandon god pots described by McGee, held soul force that had to be dealt with appropriately even in disposal. The desecration of Classic Maya carved monuments through breakage, burning, abrasion, dumping, and other means is a vital source of information for future understanding of political struggle in that area. I now think that "gaps" in textual history at such sites as Tikal resulted less from lapses in public writing and royal sculpture than from the selective destruction of texts and images by enemies of those who had written them.

This book ends on the side of dedication with the contribution by Leonardo López Luján. His meticulous research and that of the entire INAH project in the Templo Mayor complex is a clear affirmation of the basic ideas proposed thematically in preceding chapters. The combination of extraordinarily elaborate contexts and detailed ritual interpretation based firmly in ethnohistory is compelling and inspiring in this presentation. There can be little doubt that Aztec religion and philosophy, while original in its details, drew deeply upon ancient and broadly shared cosmological principles in Mesoamerica. Moreover, the Templo Mayor research affirms the centrality of cosmology and ritual to Mesoamerican definitions of government. Analyses of broad regional economic, military, and social institutions in Mesoamerica are valuable and laudable goals of archaeology, but the essence of civilization is government manifest in central institutions and public places.

HISTORY AND ARCHAEOLOGY:
A MAYA CASE OF COMPOUND CONTEXTS

As a Maya archaeologist, I am particularly interested in the complex stratigraphic interplay of dedication and termination rituals where they occur together, and I will close with a consideration of these contexts. Simply put, these are "compound contexts" where both termination and dedication are signaled. The compound contexts I have studied in Maya country seem to convey important political succession statements—successions that were probably controversial and contested (and therefore especially informative). In my original comments on the conference session that led to this book, I mentioned the

famous Stela 31 at Tikal as an example of a reverentially recycled monument in Maya country analogous to the recycled Danzante reliefs at Monte Alban referred to by Masson and Orr. Now I think that monument was desecrated in a particularly significant way. When Linda Schele and I wrote about Tikal in *A Forest of Kings,* we understood desecratory termination of stelae and posited reverential "healing" of broken stelae (and I still think we were correct in identifying the "healing" of Stela 26 as described in one of our vignettes).

What I did not understand, before William Coe's monumental *Tikal Report 14,* were the stratigraphic connections between the spectacular desecration of the magnificent front temple of the North Acropolis, Structure 5D-33-2nd; the burning, mutilation, and burial of Stela 31; the reverential entombment of an obviously royal person in the trenched-out centerline; and the initiation of construction on a new pyramid over this whole pattern. In Coe's words, "it may well be that the killing (so to speak) of St. 31 symbolized severance of a long forceful foreign connection reaching as far as Teotihuacan. Expiration of those ties was foreordained by Bu. 23's occupant."

In Coe's view, the occupant of Burial 23 who repudiated the early dynasty and its foreign ties was the twenty-sixth successor and the immediate predecessor of Ruler A, a famous Late Classic king. Ruler A (Has-Ka'an-K'awil in Classical Yucatecan) came to the throne in A.D. 682. Coe goes on to reason that Ruler A later reconciled himself with Mexican symbolism at Tikal—"backsliding," as he puts it. What Coe could not have known when he wrote the summary to his monograph is that Ruler A's father was a champion of the city, and presumably of the dynasty, who vigorously fought its enemies all his life. The enemies of Tikal, led by Calakmul and abetted by Caracol, did defeat the realm in the later sixth century. If anyone wanted to desecrate the North Acropolis and its imperial kings, those enemies did.

So how can we explain a combination of desecration and reverential entombment there in the mid-seventh century? I suggest that the several kings buried along the front of the North Acropolis, in conjunction with the desecration of the centerlines of the pyramids, were individuals placed on the throne of Tikal by Calakmul and subservient to that enemy kingdom. Those kings, beginning with the twenty-second successor, Animal-Skull, and continuing through the twenty-fifth successor, were sufficiently of the right family pedigree to be acknowledged as successors, but they were quislings. Their burials—especially Burial 23, as Coe notes—had the effect of repudiating the defeated ancestral dynasts while asserting the occupants' positions as the heirs to the ancient throne. In my view, when Ruler A's father retook Tikal for the old dynasty, he desecrated the tomb of the last of these quisling kings (Burial 8 in Structure 5D-34), but left the complex abomination of patterns of 5D-33-2nd sealed under the later pyramid then in progress but unfinished. Subsequently his son Ruler A defeated Calakmul, captured its king, finished the pyramid 5D-33-1st, and rededicated temples of the North Acropolis with a series of cached offerings inside them. In this way, Ruler A worked to "heal" the desecration of his enemies. He had the great satisfaction of sacrificing the king of Calakmul and members of his court on the occasion of rededicating the North Acropolis and the Great Plaza of Tikal.

The exceptional complexity of archaeological interpretation now possible for Classic Maya civilization may be distinctive in Mesoamerica, but the problem of compound contexts is a general one there. Sugiyama's discussion of the Feathered Serpent Pyramid at Teotihuacan suggests a complicated and compound series of reverential and desecratory acts. The struggle for succession in Mesoamerican governments might well be expected to display such a series of contradictory dynamics, a stratigraphic history quite revealing of a political one.

Which returns me to the tenets I outlined at the beginning. To understand architectural stratigraphy in Mesoamerica, we need adequate approximations of how Mesoamericans thought about the material world they were building and burying through their sacred work. It is not enough to simply suppose that government buildings and places became dirty and worn and therefore had to be refurbished. It is not enough to suppose that rulers wished to aggrandize themselves through public works that overwhelmed, literally and figuratively, those of their predecessors. The language of power and of production in Mesoamerica was a sacred one, entailing blessing and cursing, consecration and desecration. The process of creating the public stratigraphic record was a conscious and self-reflecting one, registering the history of intentions—one that we can indeed interpret as social history. And it is also true of the more humble places and remains of ordinary people that their stratigraphic deposits were accumulative sacred work, known over generations. As Patricia McAnany has noted in the Maya case, kin-groups created ancestors of their revered dead by burying them in their midst, and in the middle of compound termination-dedication activities within their built places. This book is a promising and impressive presentation of what should become a central methodological and theoretical subject in Mesoamerican archaeology.

Index